THE SOVIET UNION AND BLACK AFRICA

THE SOVIET UNION AND BLACK AFRICA

Christopher Stevens

© Christopher A. Stevens 1976

First published 1976 by
THE MACMILLAN PRESS LTD
London and Basingstoke
Associated companies in New York
Dublin Melbourne Johannesburg and Madras

SBN 333 18052 6

Printed in Great Britain by
COX & WYMAN LTD
London, Fakenham and Reading

To my Mother and Father

Contents

List of Tables

Acknowledgments

This book began life as a doctoral thesis written at the University of London, where for three years I was a student at the London School of Economics and the Institute of Commonwealth Studies. My research took me some 14,000 miles through the portals of universities, ministries and archives in eleven countries on two continents. Clearly these few notes cannot hope to express my appreciation to all those men of letters and men of affairs who gave me information and advice, or to all my colleagues in Britain and Africa who encouraged me. I am deeply grateful to them all; only other researchers can understand the debt that I owe them.

Some of my counsellors simply must be referred to by name. Above all comes my wife for her intellectual as well as her domestic support: only after my efforts had passed her critical eye were they deemed fit for inspection by others. More often than not these 'others' were my two supervisors Professor L. B. Schapiro and S. K. Panter-Brick, who guided me throughout my three years' work and bore with fortitude all the burdens that I heaped on them; I am much indebted to them. Thanks are also due to Professor F. S. Northedge and Dr Peter Lyon for their many kindnesses and advice. Professors Peter Wiles and Tony Killick gave me the benefit of their specialist knowledge and saved me from many errors in the economic sections of the thesis. I am also beholden to the staff of the Institute of Commonwealth Studies library and to Pat Tankard at the British Library of Political and Economic Science for their help in locating published material. Of my colleagues, I must tender especial thanks to Ann Bone for her characteristically generous support throughout. Nora Gottlieb and Dr B. Johnson laboured hard and long to teach me Russian and to them I am most grateful.

I was particularly fortunate in obtaining financial support for my research. The first year's work was supported by the S.S.R.C. A generous scholarship from the Leverhulme Trust enabled me to travel extensively in Africa. Junior Fellowships at the London School of Economics Centre for International Studies and the University of London Institute of Commonwealth Studies allowed me to write up my fieldwork, while a travel scholarship from the University of Wales permitted a final foray in Paris and Brussels.

My research and my doctorate were both completed before I took up my present post. The views expressed in this book do not reflect in any way those of the Overseas Development Institute or the government of Botswana. Needless to add, any errors or omissions in the book are my responsibility.

Gaborone, Botswana
June 1975

List of Abbreviations

A.A.P.S.O.	Afro-Asian Peoples' Solidarity Organisation
A.S.P.	Afro-Shirazi Party
C.F.A.	Communauté Française Africaine
C.G.C.E.	Comptoir Guinéen du Commerce Extérieur
C.G.C.I.	Comptoir Guinéen du Commerce Intérieur
C.G.T.	Confédération Générale du Travail
C.M.E.A. (Comecon)	Council of Mutual Economic Aid
C.P.E.	centrally planned economy
C.P.P.	Convention People's Party
C.P.S.U.	Communist Party of the Soviet Union
G.N.T.C.	Ghana National Trading Corporation
I.B.E.C.	International Bank for Economic Co-operation
I.I.S.S.	International Institute for Strategic Studies
K.A.D.U.	Kenya African Democratic Union
K.A.N.U.	Kenya African National Union
K.P.U.	Kenya People's Union
N.C.N.C.	National Council of Nigeria and the Cameroons (later National Council of Nigerian Citizens)
N.L.C.	National Liberation Council
N.P.C.	Northern People's Congress
N.R.C.	National Redemption Council
P.C.F.	Parti Communiste Français
P.R.C.	People's Republic of China
R.D.A.	Rassemblement Démocratique Africain
S.I.P.R.I.	Stockholm International Peace Research Institute
S.O.M.I.E.X.	Société Malienne d'Importation et d'Exportation

1 Introduction

This book covers the period from 1953 to 1972. At the start of this period there were virtually no contacts between the Soviet Union and Black Africa; by the end there were many. In the early fifties many observers saw a red under every nationalist bed, and in the early sixties talk of a Soviet or Chinese takeover of Africa was commonplace; in the early seventies there is little such speculation as the Soviet presence in Africa has become an accepted part of the international scene. Why? Why did the Soviet Union wish to make friends in Africa, and why did Africa forge links with Russia? How? How did the U.S.S.R. show its friendship and how did Africa achieve the goals that encouraged its *rapprochement* with the Soviet Union. These are the questions to which this work addresses itself. It seeks to illuminate a number of problems that intercourse between the superpowers and Africa during the 1960s present to the student of international relations, political science and economics. The observer of the international political scene must explain why, for possibly the first time in history, the great powers apparently preferred to woo their weaker neighbours rather than dominate them. The political scientist has to show how the Africans developed administrative structures with which to pursue their new-found foreign policy as well as how domestic and foreign politics interacted with one another. The economist must consider the value and implications of resource flows between Africa and the developed world.

These are major tasks and this book does not pretend to offer more than a shaft of light that may clarify a number of the issues involved in these questions. It attempts to do so by setting a detailed investigation of relations between the U.S.S.R. and seven African countries within the broader context of superpower policies towards the Third World as a whole. The Soviet Union has been chosen both because the interest it took in the continent is particularly surprising in view of its earlier indifference, and because the distinctiveness of its political practices simplifies the task of charting the growth of its influence. The seven African states given special attention have been chosen because they illustrate different aspects of the Soviet connection, and together they cover the main geographic and linguistic divisions of the continent south of the Sahara. Guinea was the first Black African country to receive serious Soviet attention, and together with Mali provides an opportunity to assess the effects of the French colonial background on subsequent relations with the U.S.S.R. The three West African countries, Ghana, Guinea and Mali, were for a number of years identified by the Soviet Union as a group apart from other Black African states, and experienced to a fuller extent than most the advantages and limitations of the Soviet connection. The fourth West African state singled out, Nigeria, has never been as close to the U.S.S.R. as its near neighbours, but its very reticence in the face of Soviet advances forms an important focus for attention. The same applies to Kenya, which gives us an example of Soviet involvement in the parliamentary process. Somalia and Tanzania introduce the strategic element in Soviet calculations, and the latter also illustrates successful competition from the Chinese.

There is no precisely defined rationale to justify choosing these seven countries and excluding others: Congo (Brazzaville) also has a French background and has had strong ties with the U.S.S.R.; Senegal, like Nigeria, has been ambivalent towards Soviet wooing; yet both Congo (Brazzaville) and Senegal are considered only in passing. Similarly, although the Sahara is frequently taken as a line dividing the continent into two parts, there is no compelling reason for excluding all the countries of North Africa from special consideration, particularly since these countries were important influences on the development of Soviet perceptions of Black Africa. Only superficial attention is given to the role of China as a factor in the growth of Soviet relations with Africa. It is taken as axiomatic that the Chinese were an extremely important influence on this relationship, but in only a few places is their role described in detail. Finally, the book is largely concerned with bilateral, interstate relations. Activities within the United Nations and other international organisations do not, therefore, receive major attention; neither do the U.S.S.R.'s links with liberation movements.

The defence for the arbitrary way in which these limits have been defined is simply that the scope of this work is appropriate to the current level of scholarship within the subject. A start has already been made on constructing a diplomatic history of Soviet and Chinese relations with Africa. Working largely from Soviet and Chinese documents, the scholars who have tackled this problem have begun to rationalise the confusing welter of official statements, press reports and contradictory statistics into a recognisable pattern.[1] However, it is already clear that the term 'Black Africa' conceals a multiplicity of widely differing states, and that no true picture of Soviet–African relations will emerge until case studies of all the more important countries have been concluded. In between the continental histories and the individual case studies there is the need for a work that analyses in some detail the contacts between a small, carefully selected group of African states and the Soviet Union, and, by isolating a number of apparent trends, gives depth to the existing histories while providing a perspective for the future case studies. By working primarily from Soviet material, the histories have inevitably had to gloss over Soviet experiences within Africa and their effect on subsequent policy, and so underestimate the extent to which the Africans could influence Russia.

There are three primary and interrelated themes running through this book. The first is a concern to record facts. This is not a product of an Actonian view of history, but simply a belief that on a topic such as this it is very easy to be carried away by bold but untested, or untestable hypotheses. When possible, motives and strategies are inferred from events that can be isolated. However, no attempt is made to propound a Grand Theory of Afro-Soviet Relations; rather, a cluster of theories are put forward to illuminate limited aspects of the connection.

The second theme is that a central position should be given to the economic aspects of the relationship. This does not imply any Marxist determinism, but is a corollary of the concern for facts; economic ties are the most tangible and pervasive aspect of the Afro-Soviet relationship, and so the book seeks to begin from a core that is measurable (or at least partially measurable) and then to move out to aspects of the connection that are more imponderable.

Thirdly, the book assumes that the aphorism 'Foreign policy is the pursuit of domestic policy by other means' incorporates a good measure of truth as far as the African reaction to Soviet advances is concerned. Some African politicians responded to these advances largely because they felt that by so doing they were strengthening their position at home. Similarly, other African leaders were lukewarm or hostile because they feared that contacts with the U.S.S.R. would undermine their domestic position. Foreign policy *qua* an activity with semi-independent, or even independent short-term goals was not a major aspect of Africa's relationship with the Soviet Union. The arena in which it was most apparent was the United Nations, but, of course, this arena receives only passing attention. The suggested close relationship between foreign and domestic politics should not be taken to imply that close ties developed between the Soviet Union and some African states as a consequence of a carefully designed strategy on either part. On the contrary, the important role of chance is frequently apparent in the pages that follow. Rather, what happened is that as they reacted to the situation in which they found themselves, some African politicians came to believe that the U.S.S.R. could provide a solution to some of their problems. Raymond Aron suggests as one possible classification of the goals of foreign policy the triumvirate of power, security and glory. All three were sought by Africans from the relationship with the U.S.S.R. Technical assistance and trade held promise of increased power; Soviet military assistance was sought to improve security, while the support of the socialist bloc of votes at the U.N. and Soviet hospitality to visiting delegations produced an aura of heightened self-esteem. What the Soviet Union expected from the relationship is less clear, but a number of suggestions are put forward in the pages that follow.

THE PERSPECTIVE OF HISTORY

The history of Afro-Soviet relations does not provide any very full perspective, largely because of its brevity. What history does show is the position of Africa within the context of the Soviet Union's growing awareness of the Third World, and it also clarifies the chronology of those events that may be taken as landmarks of the Afro-Soviet *rapprochement*.

During the nineteenth century Russia was too involved with expansion eastwards to consider Africa, although the Russian Orthodox Church for long cherished a union with the Ethiopian Church and made a few contacts in that direction. After the Bolshevik revolution there were no substantial, direct links between the U.S.S.R. and Africa until the later 1950s. In the early 1930s, George Padmore, a West Indian who was later to play a prominent role in the Gold Coast's passage to independence, was installed in Moscow as a Comintern official and editor of the *Negro Worker*. However, this newspaper dealt only with the position of Blacks in general and, in any case, Padmore soon became disenchanted with Stalinist Communism and in his book *Pan-Africanism or Communism?* he opted for the former. A Communist party was formed in South Africa as early as 1921 but it was composed largely of whites. Moreover, the very fact that it was the only one on the continent and that even it lost all contact with the Communist Party in the Soviet Union for more than three years in the 1920s only emphasised Africa's isolation.

Until the late 1950s the Soviet Union delegated responsibility in Africa to the Communist parties in the colonialist states. The British Communist Party organised a fairly active League Against Imperialism during the interwar period, but it was unable to attract Africans as members because those in Britain were largely students from wealthy backgrounds. The French Communist Party (P.C.F.), with its industrial wing, the C.G.T., was much more active in promoting revolutionary consciousness among francophone Africans. Before the Second World War there were a number of left-wing organisations in France in which blacks met Communists. Although only a few Africans came to France, these organisations reached a wider audience through their publications, which as early as 1930 were being seized by the police in the larger population centres in French West Africa. More important were the *'groupes sociales'* formed during the Popular Front days, and based on the schools, the civil service, African urban organisations and even the armed forces. These introduced Africans to French Communists who had taken jobs in the administration. By their personal behaviour, treating Africans as colleagues rather than inferiors, and by their appealing doctrines, the Communists won the respect of many African activists. During the war, they formed study groups for young African intellectuals in the major French West African towns. These were not organs of the Communist Party and they discussed anti-colonialism rather than socialism, but they were directly linked with the P.C.F., and the writers they studied were mainly Russian and French Communists.[2] A number of individuals who were later to become notable figures in the independence movements attended these groups.* The P.C.F. did not support the immediate creation of an African Communist party. This was partly because it rightly saw that the necessary raw materials were simply not present. However, it was also partly because it saw the metropolitan and colonial struggles as integrally related: it argued that the trusts which exploited Africa must be attacked at their roots, and that premature independence for Africa would lead to its succumbing to imperialism from the U.K. or the U.S.A., which would be worse than French imperialism because the British and American Communist parties were weaker than the P.C.F.[3] At first this viewpoint did not adversely affect their relations with Africans.. After the Second World War there was a period of close collaboration between the Communist and African deputies in the French national assembly, where the P.C.F. was a member of the government. Raymond Barbé, who was in charge of the overseas affairs of the P.C.F., spoke at the conference convened in Bamako in October 1946 at which the Rassemblement Démocratique Africain (R.D.A.), the first important French African nationalist movement, was formed.[4] The president of the R.D.A., Félix Houphouet-Boigny of the Ivory Coast, saw the alliance in purely tactical terms but its general secretary, Gabriel d'Arboussier, was more sympathetic to the aims of the P.C.F. *per se*, and the R.D.A. acquired an organisation which, in form if not in function, bore similarities to that of a Communist party: a cell system, democratic centralism, and so on.[5]

The two viewpoints within the R.D.A., that which favoured a tactical alliance, and that which favoured a strategic alliance with the Communists, co-existed happily so long as the P.C.F. was a member of the French government. When, after 1947, it was no longer a member, strains developed. After leaving the Ramadier government in May 1947, the French Communists were criticised by their Cominform colleagues for 'opportunism, legalitarianism and parliamentary illusions' and they changed tack to a more militant programme of industrial strikes in which they fully intended their African allies to take part. When the C.G.T. organised its general strike in October 1947, its African branches were also called out. R.D.A. deputies continued to find the alliance with

* They included Sékou Touré, Modibo Keita, Idrissa Diarra, and Diallo Saifoulayé.

the P.C.F. valuable, but the price of this alliance was now 'the implacable and uncomprehending hostility of the parties which remained in the government, and therefore controlled the colonial administration.'[6] The alliance came under pressure from Africans who felt that this hostility outweighed any advantages it gained, but d'Arboussier managed to persuade the majority of his colleagues that a break with the Communists would be a bad mistake.[7] By 1950, however, Houphouet was convinced that the Communists' main aim was to create martyrs in Africa and so have a club with which to beat the government in Paris. The role of a pawn in a domestic French power struggle did not appeal to him. D'Arboussier was edged out of the general secretaryship and on 1 December 1950 the R.D.A. announced that it would vote in favour of the government on a motion of confidence.[8]

Collaboration between the C.G.T. and African trade unionists lasted a little longer. The C.G.T. was particularly strong in francophone Africa both because it was first in the field, with roots dating back to the time of the Popular Front, and because the colonial authorities too conspicuously supported its main rival, the socialist Force Ouvrière.[9] However, metropolitan and colonial interests began gradually to diverge. The first big break was the secession from the C.G.T. of the railwaymen in Senegal and Soudan in 1948, following their five-month action in favour of the C.G.T. general strike which did not directly concern them at all. Then in 1952 an autonomous trade union was formed in Ivory Coast, while in 1955 the Senegalese and Mauretanian C.G.T.s disaffiliated and took the name of C.G.T.A., the 'A' standing for Africa.[10] Nevertheless, Africa's most influential *cégétiste*, Sékou Touré still remained loyal. He had founded the first trade union in Guinea in 1945, and in the following year he became secretary-general of the co-ordinating committee of the C.G.T. of French West Africa and Togoland. He attended the March 1946 C.G.T. congress in Paris and there met leading French Communists. Afterwards it is believed that he continued on to Prague, for study.[11] However, in 1955 the Communists tried to form a pan-African trade union conference through their international organisation the World Federation of Trade Unions (W.F.T.U.). The plan was resisted by Sékou Touré, who resented the 'artificial divisions' being created in Africa; on 15 February 1956 he, and others, were expelled from the C.G.T. He then began to organise the C.G.T.A. and won over about half the supporters of his erstwhile colleagues. In 1957 the orthodox African members of the C.G.T. reintegrated themselves into the mainstream of African trade unionism when they were permitted to disaffiliate from the French organisation and to merge with the C.G.T.A., forming a new organisation, U.G.T.A.N. The Communists were then represented in the new organisation, but their position was now distinctly subordinate to that of nationalists.

The dawn breaks in the East ...

The situation obtaining in the Africa of the 1950s was thus that there were few Communists and those that there were did not belong to Communist parties. While the U.S.S.R. shunned co-operation with bourgeois nationalists and insisted on the vanguard role of the Communist parties, there was thus little prospect of fruitful co-operation with Africa. After Stalin's death, however, the Soviet attitude towards the bourgeois-dominated nationalist movements, that had won independence in South Asia and were fighting for it elsewhere, underwent a transformation.

This transformation was first apparent in relation to the physically contiguous areas to the south of the Soviet Union. Following the acquisition of power by the Communists in China, India began to take military and diplomatic measures to secure the integrity of its northern borders. On the diplomatic front there was a sustained effort to normalise relations with China. These efforts began to bear fruit, particularly when India took an independent position on the Korean War. Within a year of the shift in China's policy, the Soviet Union also began to show signs of moderating its attitude towards non-Communist Asia. In 1952 there were a number of small incidents indicating some change in outlook.[12] The first important and formal sign came in August 1953 when Malenkov praised India's role in the Korean War during a speech to the Supreme Soviet.[13] Four months later the two countries signed a trade agreement. In 1954 India and China proclaimed the now famous Panch Shila, or five Principles of mutual non-interference. In June 1955 Nehru visited the Soviet Union and the following November and December, Khrushchev and Bulganin made an historic tour of Afghanistan, India and Burma. This tour by the Soviet leaders was immensely successful. It is now a matter of common knowledge that when, in the following year, Britain and France invaded Egypt and Russia invaded Hungary, it was the former conflict that absorbed Indian attention.

The Soviet Union began to generalise its interest and began to look at other new states. In 1954 Afghanistan became the first non-Communist country to receive Soviet aid. In the diplomatic field, the U.S.S.R.'s new approach was evidenced by the attention it began to give to the nascent Afro-Asian movement. The history of this important but rather ephemeral grouping started with the first major Afro-Asian conference convened at Bandung in Indonesia in 1955, at which representatives of twenty-three Asian and six African countries met together. Although the tangible results of the conference were not great it gave birth to the powerful myth of 'the Bandung spirit': a spirit of unity and commitment among the ex-colonial peoples who showed their determination resolutely to face the rest of the world. China was represented at the conference, and the Soviet Union sought to be represented on the basis of its

Central Asian Republic, but failed. Bandung was not a meeting of neutralists, for a number of participants like China and Pakistan were fully committed to one side or other of the Cold War. However, the Soviet Union followed up its new policy towards Asia with a reassessment of its view on neutralism. Stalin had seen a world clearly polarised between two camps: those who were not in the socialist fold could not but be in the capitalist camp. His successors took a more generous view of those who claimed to be charting a 'third way' between the two redoubts, and by 1956 a Soviet writer was claiming that the U.S.S.R. 'has repeatedly voiced its support of the movements for neutralism and non-participation in military blocs'.[14]

The next country after India to feel the breeze blowing through the Kremlin was Egypt. When, in January 1952, Neguib and Nasser seized power from King Farouk they were regarded with disfavour by the U.S.S.R. The *Large Soviet Encyclopaedia* sent to press in September 1952 referred to the *coup* as being organised by 'American–English imperialists', and to its main actors as 'a group of reactionary officers'. The *coup*, it argued, was not a breakthrough for the oppressed people but evidence of a sharpening of 'Anglo-American contradictions'.[15] The change in the published Soviet views of Egypt came in 1955, after the Bandung Conference.[16] The most concrete evidence that Moscow now regarded the Cairo regime in a more favourable light was, however, hardly mentioned in Soviet print; it was the Czech arms deal of 1955. Soviet interest in Egypt was stimulated largely by a desire to undermine the Baghdad Pact – part of a chain of alliances with which the West was attempting to encircle the U.S.S.R. – and followed immediately after the first signs that the cornerstone of the pact, the Turkish–Iraqi treaty, was being prepared. According to Uri Ra'anan the new policy was the culmination of a factional struggle within the Kremlin between Khruschev, who favoured a flexible outlook, and Molotov, who represented caution and orthodoxy.[17] Whether Ra'anan's inferences from a content analysis of Soviet publications are valid or not, in September 1955 it was made public that Egypt would receive military equipment from the U.S.S.R. via Czechoslovakia. From then until almost the present day, despite numerous ups and downs, there has been a clear secular trend towards the improvement and diversification of relations between the two countries.

Following the arms deal came a period in which Soviet favour was bestowed on a number of other Middle Eastern and Asian countries which were regarded as strategically significant. Between November 1955 and August 1956 Syria signed trade and aid agreements with the U.S.S.R., and began to receive Czech arms. In the second half of 1956 Indonesia signed trade and aid agreements with the Soviet Union, and the commodities subsequently 'traded' under the first of these pacts included Soviet military equipment. In assisting these countries the Soviet Union was moving with the tide of events. As in Egypt and Syria, Soviet contacts with Indonesia rapidly snowballed, for assistance from the Soviet bloc was seen by the nationalist leaders as a valuable asset to their domestic and international policies. When, in July 1958, the pro-Western regime of Nuri es-Said was overthrown in Iraq, the U.S.S.R. immediately welcomed its successors led by General Kassem. The new Soviet policy was rapidly achieving its desired strategic objectives, and on 22 July 1958 Khrushchev expressed his own surprise and satisfaction at the speed with which his goals were being reached. 'No one', he said, 'believed that the Baghdad Pact would so soon cease to exist.'[18]

... and spreads West

Egypt, the first Middle Eastern state to respond to the new approach was also an African country, and Africa's Mediterranean seaboard also had strategic significance for the Soviet Union. The new approach was not, however, immediately extended to North Africa. The constitutional monarchy of King Idris in Libya which came into existence in 1952 held little appeal for Moscow, and the British and American military bases at El Adem and Wheeler's Field held even less. The government of Habib Bourguiba which brought independence to Tunisia in 1956 but gave France military bases was similarly regarded as solidly pro-West, as was the regime of King Mohammed V in Morocco. The third Maghreb territory, Algeria, could have been expected to excite more interest from the U.S.S.R. given the violent nature of its independence struggle. However, Moscow was still viewing French Africa through the spectacles of the P.C.F., which was still loth to regard national independence *per se* as a favourable objective. The Soviet Union did not immediately recognise the Provisional Government of Algeria (G.P.R.A.) when it was formed on 20 September 1958; the Chinese, by contrast, had no such qualms and on the day of its formation, a Chinese diplomat met G.P.R.A. ministers in Cairo, and recognition followed quickly.[19]

While its links with the P.C.F. made Russia slower than China to realise the tactical significance of events in Algeria, they were more beneficial in initiating interest south of the Sahara. In 1956 the Sudan, which forms a bridge between Arab and Black Africa, gained independence, but its contacts with the Soviet Union were few. The Soviet Union did not respond enthusiastically to the independence in 1957 of the first new Black African state, Ghana, even though as the Gold Coast it had, together with Liberia and Ethiopia, been represented at Bandung. While the U.S.S.R. was perfectly cordial in its references to the new state neither side saw any great opportunities to be gained from close ties, and no Soviet ambassador was sent to Accra for over two years. The year following Ghana's independence, de Gaulle faced his African colonies with a choice: they should vote by referendum either to join a *communauté* in which they would have autonomy but France would retain control of economic affairs, or to be cast into the outer darkness of independence, by which de Gaulle meant a complete severance of ties between the metropole and the ex-colony. Only Guinea chose the latter, probably not realising the consequences. The French government pulled out of Guinea lock, stock and barrel, and exerted pressure on French companies to do the same. France's Western allies, unwilling to incur the General's ire, did not immediately attempt to fill the gap.

In Sékou Touré the Russians had an African leader they knew. In the recent past they had quarrelled with his trade union activities but this had since been patched up. Further, Guinea had none of the unappetising features that characterised Ghana in this period – strong tribal elements and close ties with the ex-colonial master.* They therefore responded quickly to the new opportunity for influence that presented itself. Three days after its independence, Soviet President Voroshilov described the new state's emergence as 'an important step on the path of the liberation of Africa from the colonialist yoke',[20] and the day after that the Guinean leader received a telegram from Khrushchev, which may have offered immediate economic and technical assistance, and diplomatic exchange. Sékou Touré, however, was more reserved, and he clearly had not given up hope of cordial relations with France. He announced that he would wait for French recognition before replying and explained that he would not disclose the contents of the telegram to avoid any appearance that he was playing a game of international 'blackmail'. However, no such French recognition was forthcoming as de Gaulle looked on with '*dédain massif*', and accordingly a Soviet delegation arrived in Conakry the following Monday, led by two Soviet diplomats from Egypt. In February 1959 a trade payments agreement that permitted Guinea a trade credit of up to $300,000 was agreed, and the following month Pavel Gerassimov, formerly counsellor at the Soviet Embassy in Cairo, was accredited as a temporary ambassador extraordinary and plenipotentiary. In late summer the Soviet Union promised $35 million of aid. In 1960 Daniel Solod, a successful career diplomat who had made his name shepherding Soviet–Egyptian relations between 1953 and 1956, arrived to take over as ambassador.

China also recognised the new state promptly, but without the Soviet Union's knowledge of Sékou Touré it hesitated to endorse his administration or policies until it became clear how the government would develop. Guinea was not cited at this time by Peking as an anti-colonial model for

* Robert Legvold, *Soviet Policy in West Africa*, pp. 61–2, suggests as a further reason for Soviet interest that Nasser's suppression of the Syrian Communist party at this time, following the creation of the United Arab Republic, may have prompted the U.S.S.R. to look elsewhere for new friends.

other African states to emulate, and when China did make a gesture by sending her ambassador in Morocco on a mission to Conakry, he took with him only a modest grant of 5000 tons of rice.*

The Congo – a landmark

In the same year that the Soviet Union appointed its first high calibre diplomat to Black Africa, its attention was drawn to another new state experiencing troubled relations with its former mentor: the Congo. With hindsight, the Congo drama can be seen as a turning point in Soviet–African relations. Belgian activities in the independent Congo were just those that Communist philosophy had taught it to expect, but Soviet leaders discovered that they could not play the role that they might have hoped to play – the West was too strong, and wholehearted support from the Afro-Asian bloc was not forthcoming. Nevertheless, fruitful collaboration between the Soviet Union and many African countries did occur as part of the international response to the Congo crisis, and prepared the ground for the less bombastic and more practical activities of the U.S.S.R. in Africa since then.

Colonial rule in Africa was something of a mirage: vast tracts of land were apparently ruled by a handful of Europeans with ease and without the frequent use of force. The absence of force was, of course, not an additional, remarkable feature of this hegemony but the cause of it: colonial rule was effective because it was tacitly accepted by the population as a whole and because colonial objectives were limited and interfered minimally with the daily round. After the Second World War, this consent was withdrawn by many, and colonial objectives were widened. However, the rapid pace of decolonisation obscured the breakdown of colonial government, and at independence many Africans and many outside Africa still conceived a very rosy and mechanical view of government, believing that the mere possession of the institutions of government would bestow effective authority that could be used for any chosen ends. In African leaders this misconception often produced over-extension of the government's resources: in foreigners it instilled a belief that some other country might be able to step covertly in to the seat of the departing colonialists; this prospect was either met with an enthusiastic hope that the thinker could itself fill the chair, or more often with a pessimistic fear that the thinker's opponent would do so. It is within this framework of expectations that Soviet, Western and African actions both specifically in the Congo crisis and more generally should be viewed.

---

* Bruce D. Larkin, *China and Africa*, pp. 39–40. By contrast A. C. A. A. Ogunsanwo, *China's Policy in Africa*, and Legvold, *Soviet Policy in West Africa*, p. 163, see the gift of rice as a strong gesture of Chinese approval. In view of the probability that China was at the same time giving Algeria $10 million of military assistance, Larkin's view appears the more reasonable.

There was little contact between the Belgian Congo and Eastern Europe before 1960. The Czechoslovaks maintained a consulate in Léopoldville, but it was the only diplomatic contact between the two areas.[21] Of the leading Congolese nationalists, only Gizenga had visited Eastern Europe.[22] In the months preceding independence, the socialist countries collected all the information they could. They worked directly through their own people on the spot, and indirectly through the Belgian Communist Party. In the view of Thomas Kanza who played an eventful part in the dramas of independence, this was a grave mistake for the Belgian Communist Party contained many double agents and was, in any case, more Belgian than Communist.[23] The Communists approached Congolese whose nationalism could, they thought, be channelled into a general anti-Western direction, but it appears that their efforts were hindered by the parsimonious fashion in which they backed ideological with financial support.[24]

The first official contact between the U.S.S.R. and the new government of the Congo was provided by the low-level Soviet delegation sent to the independence celebrations. On 8 July 1960, after the army mutiny had begun, the leader of the delegation, M. R. Rachmatov, vice-president of the presidium of the supreme soviet of Tadjikistan, was received by Lumumba and Kasavubu and an accord was concluded for the establishment of diplomatic relations. Shortly afterwards, the delegation left the country, but not before having first-hand experience of the mutiny. Under the impression that Russian soldiers had been flown in to disarm them, some of the mutineers invaded the delegation's room and manhandled the Russians. No one was badly hurt, and another unfortunate incident at the airport, when Congolese soldiers at first refused to let the Soviet plane take off because they thought that it contained arms, was not as serious as it might easily have been.[25] Nevertheless, the Russians can hardly have been unaware after this of the true state of the Congolese army.

The Congo became independent on 30 June 1960; on 5 July the army mutinied; on 10 July the Belgians sent troops into the now independent state without the permission of the government, with the stated intention of safeguarding Belgian lives; the same day Kasavuba and Lumumba made their first appeal to the United Nations for assistance in reorganising the Congolese administrative and security services; and on 11 July Tshombe declared the region of Katanga an independent state. Thus within two weeks of independence, all the main events that provoked the ensuing tragedy had taken place.

The first Soviet reaction did not occur until 11 July when Khrushchev accused the Americans of interfering in Congolese affairs and continued, referring to the invasion, 'It does not only concern Belgium, but is in fact a concerted action of NATO, which includes West Germany.' He then added, 'Recourse to the Security Council of the U.N. will not serve any purpose other than to prove that this Council has become an instrument of the powers which wish to perpetuate colonialism.'[26] *Pravda* carried a page 4 article on the situation, and on the same day Khrushchev elaborated his proposition that the Belgian invasion was part of an overall NATO plan of aggression when he told a press conference:

> These measures against the Republic of the Congo affirm once more the aggressive reality of the military blocs of the imperialists, and their efforts to maintain the methods of the colonisers . . . It is not only Belgium that has sent troops to the Congo. It is NATO which has sent these troops to crush the people of the Congo by force of arms.[27]

Kasavubu and Lumumba were clearly more optimistic, for on the same day they requested U.N. military assistance. On 13 July they again asked for U.N. military support and intimated that if it were not forthcoming they would look elsewhere.[28] This was not the first indication that bilateral assistance would be acceptable: an appeal had already been made for American troops to the United States ambassador in Léopold-ville, who with two Belgian ministers had attended meetings of the Congolese council of ministers, and the U.S.A. was one of the alternative sources of assistance mentioned in the appeal of 13 July. However, for the first time possible non-Western sources of support were mentioned, for in addition to the U.S.A., Kasavubu and Lumumba said they would appeal to the 'Bandung powers'.[29]

There were now two aspects of the situation, the internal mutiny of troops and breakdown in administration, and the external aggression from Belgium. This dichotomy between internal and external was to remain, and differences of opinion between Lumumba and Hammarsk-jold over which element of the crisis the U.N. should concern itself with, was to prove the former's undoing. The first Congolese appeal to the U.N. had been for assistance with regard to the internal situation, but the telegram of 13 July made it clear that the government's aim was for the U.N. to raise a force from neutral states to put an end to the aggression. However, Hammarskjold, who had to take account of political realities in the security council, realised that he could not move so quickly: when the council met on 13 July it passed a resolution that pledged technical assistance to the new republic to overcome its domestic problems and requested Belgium to withdraw its troops, but forebore to condemn the Belgian act and offered no suggestion as to what might be done if Belgian troops were not withdrawn.[30]

Despite their apparent scepticism of the efficacy of the U.N., the Soviet leaders were vocal in support of the request from the Congolese for help to end the aggression. Internal disorder within the Congo was something that might or might not work to the advantage of the

U.S.S.R., but an opportunity to expose the perfidy of the West and perhaps win the confidence of the government in Léopoldville was a chance not to be missed. On the day that the security council met, Foreign Minister Gromyko delivered to Belgian, British and American diplomats in Moscow the text of a Soviet declaration which repeated the allegation of NATO complicity and accused the Americans of preparing to send the 24th Infantry Division from Germany to the Congo. It also referred to the activities of Belgian *agents-provocateurs* in creating the disorder, to an attempt to murder Lumumba, to British and Portuguese aggressive activities in territories neighbouring the Congo, and to the role of the colonialists in the secession of Katanga. It concluded :

> The Government of the U.S.S.R. considers that the grave situation created in the Congo threatens the peace and security of the people. The United Nations Organisation must take urgent measures to bring the aggression to an end, and to re-establish completely the sovereign rights of the independent Republic of the Congo.[31]

During the security council debate of 13 July, the U.S.S.R. submitted amendments that condemned the Belgian action, requested an immediate withdrawal, and authorised the secretary-general to give the Congolese government military assistance in the form of troops furnished by other African states.[32] The Soviet Union was the only member to submit amendments and they were all defeated.[33] In the course of the debate the Soviet Union also made its first attack on U.N. personnel when it criticised Ralph Bunche, Hammarskjold's representative in the Congo and an American, as an instrument of the U.S.A.[34]

The Congolese government was not completely satisfied with the U.N. resolution and on 14 July Lumumba and Kasavubu sent a telegram to Khrushchev in which they requested him

> to follow hour by hour the development of the situation in the Congo. It is possible that we will be led to seek the intervention of the Soviet Union if the Western camp does not put an end to the act of aggression against the sovereignty of the Republic of the Congo . . .[35]

In his reply of the following day, however, Khrushchev indicated that for the time being the U.S.S.R. was prepared to support the United Nations.[36] On 16 July Khrushchev sent another telegram to Lumumba making the first offer of Soviet bilateral assistance: 10,000 tons of emergency food supplies.[37] This was not, however, in conflict with U.N. assistance, and by 17 July eight countries had promised food supplies. By this time, the U.N. military airlift was under way, and the U.S.S.R., Britain and the U.S.A. provided the majority of air transport.[38]

So far, so good: Hammarskjold had managed to gain security council support for U.N. measures to restore stability and the U.S.S.R., despite its early bombast, was giving this operation its practical support. Unfortunately, the dichotomy between the internal and external elements of the crisis became critical. The U.N. force (ONUC) was charged with restoring order by pacifying the mutineers and re-establishing effective administration. However, Lumumba, with some justice, regarded the prime cause of the military disorder to be the Belgian intervention, and he began to suspect that the Belgians were planning to take over the country. He could not, therefore, afford to allow ONUC to disarm the Congolese soldiers, for if they did he would have no military to enforce his will, and consequently he began to feel the need for bilateral military assistance in case ONUC failed to neutralise the Belgians.

On 17 July Kasavubu and Lumumba issued an 'ultimatum' (the word is Thomas Kanza's) to Bunche in which they stated that if Belgian troops were not withdrawn before midnight on 19 July they would regretfully be obliged to solicit the intervention of the U.S.S.R. At this time the two leaders were touring the Congo trying to restore order and the telegram was sent from Stanleyville. Back in Léopoldville, the Senate refused to approve the ultimatum, but it was confirmed by a statement of the Council of Ministers on 19 July which read:

> In view of the refusal of the Belgian Government to *evacuate* its troops . . .
> In view of the powerlessness of the U.N.O. forces . . .
> The Council of Ministers has decided: to make an immediate appeal to the Soviet Union or all other countries of the Afro-Asian bloc to send their troops to the Congo. These troops will have the following missions:
> 1. to evacuate peacefully Belgian troops.
> 2. to contribute to the maintenance of order in the Congo, *conforming to the decisions of the Government of the Republic;*
> 3. to prevent all external aggressions . . .[39]

This request enraged the West. Although the communiqué of the Council of Ministers concluded with the optimistic statement that:

> The Military aid sought from the Governments of the Soviet Union or other countries of the Afro-Asian bloc has no political implications. The troops will withdraw from the Congo as soon as the Belgian troops have left and order has been re-established.

the West could not face with equanimity the prospect of the Red Army in the heart of Africa. On 18 July the Belgian government recalled its ambassador from Moscow, and the newspapers announced the presence of a mysterious Polish vessel carrying munitions headed for Matadi; Bunche placed the port under U.N. control.[40]

It was at this juncture that the security council met and passed its second resolution on the Congo. The Soviet representative put forward a strongly-worded resolution which did not win support. Instead, another compromise resolution was adopted which was nevertheless phrased in stronger terms that the first resolution passed by the council. It became clear during the debate that another element in the internal–external dichotomy was appearing, and concerned whether the Katanga secession was a domestic Congolese problem, or whether the fact that it was aided and abetted by Belgium made it an international dispute. Once again Lumumba was to find himself on the other side of the fence to Hammarskjold's mandate: Lumumba regarded Katanga as the result of external aggression and sought U.N. help to bring it to a close; the majority of the security council considered it to be a matter of internal Congolese politics and outside the U.N.'s jurisdiction. Nevertheless, Lumumba was at first pleased with the second resolution, showing as it appeared to do, a hardening of the U.N. attitude towards Belgium. He tried to explain away his appeal to the U.S.S.R., and on 22 July *en route* for New York he stated that 'Russian aid is no longer necessary.'[41] On 24 July he arrived in New York to attend the U.N., but he also wanted to take the opportunity to contact senior members of the American administration in Washington. However, before an itinerary in Washington was arranged, he held two unofficial meetings with the Soviet representative at the U.N., Vassili Kuznetsov. Within hours, the talks were reported on Radio Moscow as was a statement that Lumumba had accepted an invitation to visit the Soviet Union; the same evening the Congolese party was informed that President Eisenhower would be unable to meet Lumumba.[42]

During the visit to Washington, Lumumba's mood changed from the optimism he had expressed a few days earlier. He sought bilateral assistance from the Americans, but was told that all U.S. efforts would be directed through the U.N. Lumumba began to feel that ONUC was preventing him from taking decisive action. At the same time he learned that the U.N. action against Katanga had not prevented Belgian paratroopers killing members of the Congolese army at Kolwezi.[43] It seems that the possibility of bilateral Soviet assistance was discussed at the Kuznetsov meeting, and on 1 August *Pravda* carried a Soviet declaration which warned that if the aggression against the Congo did not cease the U.S.S.R. would have to take energetic measures to end it, and revealed that it was sending 100 lorries, a group of instructors and a medical mission.*

* A. Wauters, *Le Monde Communiste et le Crise du Congo belge*, p. 73. The information that assistance was discussed with Kuznetsov comes from T. Kanza, *Conflict in the Congo*, p. 273. C. Hoskyns, *The Congo Since Independence*, p. 158, is of the opinion that it was discussed at a later date by Lumumba and the Soviet ambassador to Canada. It is possible that both are correct.

Throughout August relations between Lumumba and the U.N. deteriorated, and the Congolese premier began to plan his own attack on Katanga and Kasai, another province which had seceded. For this he intended to use the Congolese army, but he needed additional military assistance. He followed up his discussions with Kuznetsov by negotiations with the Soviet ambassador in Léopoldville, Mikhail Yakovlev,[44] and on 15 August 1960 he addressed the following letter to the Soviet government:

The Government of the Republic of the Congo would be very grateful if you would indicate the aid in the following categories which your Government could send it *immediately*:

1. Troop and supply transport planes.
2. Troop transport lorries.
3. Sundry armaments of high quality.
4. Up-to-date military transmission equipment.
5. Food rations for troops in the field.

This urgent aid is needed immediately to enable the Government of the Republic of the Congo to assure the territorial integrity of the Republic which is being seriously threatened . . .[45]

Almost a month later, on 8 September, Gizenga sent a similar note on Lumumba's behalf to the Chinese.[46]

At some stage an accord was signed by Gizenga and Yakovlev on the supply of military assistance. In it the U.S.S.R. promised to put at the disposal of the Congolese government for a period of up to one year from the last quarter of 1960, thirty aircraft comprising ten IL–14s (transport version), five AN–12s, ten AN–2s and five KI–4 helicopters (transport version), with appropriate technical assistance, spare parts and fuel. They also promised food rations sufficient for 10,000 men for six months, and agreed to deliver thirty radio sets with spare parts. It was intended that some of the planes and helicopters be supplied by sea in crates and be assembled in the Congo.[47] On 2 September it was announced in Moscow that ten Ilyushin aircraft had been sent to Lumumba.[48] By then the Congolese army attack on Kasai and Katanga had already begun.

The only foreign troops involved in the operation appear to have been Soviet pilots. Nevertheless, according to Catherine Hoskyns, this attack caused a sudden hardening of opinion against Lumumba among senior officials in the U.N. secretariat, America and Britain, and Hammarskjold became convinced that Lumumba was providing the Russians with a toehold in Africa.[49] On 5 September Kasavubu dismissed Lumumba from his post. Lumumba responded by dismissing the president. The ONUC temporary head Andrew Cordier seems to have feared that Lumumba would use the Russian planes to fly in soldiers loyal to him, and he therefore ordered the closure of all major airfields to non-U.N. traffic. He then gave orders that the U.N. should take control of the radio station, which was controlled by Lumumba, and suspend broadcasting. Although the ban nominally affected both Lumumba and Kasavubu equally, the latter was able to cross the river Congo to Brazzaville and from there broadcast to the nation.[50] These actions caused a storm of anger from the Soviet Union and some African states, notably Guinea, Ghana and the U.A.R., but the anger was impotent.[51] On 14 September Mobutu, whose position in the army had, intentionally or unintentionally, been strengthened by Cordier's past actions,[52] announced that the army had taken power, at least until the end of the year; he also gave the Soviet embassy forty-eight hours to leave the country, because, he said, their presence could only provoke a civil war.[53] On the 17 September the Russian and Czech embassies were closed down.

From then onwards Soviet activities in the Congo were, as far as is known publicly, nominal. In the United Nations they fiercely attacked the secretary-general. This action did not win widespread African support, for the Africans were in general opposed to anything that might weaken the U.N. After the assassination of Lumumba, however, the attack was also joined by Guinea and Mali. Despite this bombast, Soviet assistance to the regime of Lumumba's heir, Gizenga, in Stanleyville, and to other revolts against Léopoldville appears to have been minimal. Gizenga received most assistance from the U.A.R., and only secondary support from Ghana, East Germany and the U.S.S.R.[54] After the installation of the Adoula government, the U.S.S.R. once again recognised a regime based in Léopoldville, but in 1963 relations between the two countries once again deteriorated. On 19 November 1963 two Russian diplomats were arrested on their return from Brazzaville and were accused of being in contact there with Christophe Gbenye and other rebels. On 21 November Adoula announced that documents seized from the diplomats substantiated the accusation, and he declared all the members of the Soviety embassy *persona non grata*.[55] Thereafter, relations remained at a very low level, with Mobutu suggesting in 1966 that the reason for the absence of diplomatic relations between the two countries was reserve on the Soviet part.[56] Nevertheless, the U.S.S.R. does not appear to have given any substantial support to rebel movements.[57]

The Soviet activities in the Congo are a landmark in the development of its relations with Africa. While they may have been rhetoric, the early references to the complicity of NATO in the Belgian invasion may have been indicative of the Soviet outlook in this period. If so, Soviet leaders badly misjudged the resolve of their antagonists to resist Soviet military incursions in Black Africa. The months following Congolese independence showed clearly the limits of Soviet power in Black Africa – limits imposed by the weakness of Soviet resolve compared to that of the West and the weakness of its African friends compared to those of the West. It also indicated the esteem in which African states held the U.N., but at the same time encouraged the U.S.S.R. in the tactical merit of its support for Sékou Touré.

Despite the disagreements which grew up as the Congo crisis developed, co-operation between the Soviet bloc and many of the new states became a notable feature of the United Nations scene. The period 1953–60, dating from the Soviet decision to contribute to EPTA, had witnessed increasing Soviet interest in the U.N. as a forum through which to 'achieve respectability among neutralist countries'.[58] 1960 was the great year of African independence. Seventeen new states, sixteen of them from Africa, entered the United Nations in that year, producing a 20 per cent increase in the membership of the organisation, and giving the Afro-Asian bloc almost 44 per cent of the total membership. The dominant member within the Afro-Asian bloc with twenty-four out of forty-four members was Africa. In this new situation the Communist bloc saw an opportunity to score propaganda points by supporting the general anti-colonial sentiments of the new members and attempting to direct them into specifically anti-Western channels. On 23 September 1960 it introduced into the general assembly a resolution calling for the liquidation of colonialism. This particular initiative fell wide of the mark: the resolution too clearly attacked the West, and Sékou Touré was moved to appeal publicly to the Communists not to use the ending of colonialism for Cold War propaganda because the issue was much too important for the Afro-Asians,[59] who then proceeded to introduce their own resolution. However, the exercise did bring the U.S.S.R. sizeable gains: it was the first time that the Soviet Union had taken an initiative on a major issue which had ultimately received the support of the whole assembly with the exception of the nine Western powers, who were forced into a position of ignominious abstention. During 1960 and 1961 most members of the Afro-Asian group publicly thanked the U.S.S.R. for its initiative. Thereafter, the Soviet bloc invariably supported the Afro-Asians on colonial issues, and in return was sometimes supported on Cold War questions.

The Black African countries fell into three main groups according to their voting for the U.S.A. or the U.S.S.R. David A. Kay has recorded voting on fifty 'selected East–West issues' which came before the fifteenth to twenty-second sessions of the general assembly.[60] The majority of ex-French states, like Ivory Coast, tended to vote with the U.S.A. and against U.S.S.R.; the 'radical' states, like Ghana, voted with the U.S.S.R. and against the U.S.A., while in the middle there were states like Nigeria which voted more often with the U.S.S.R. than with the U.S.A. but not so markedly as the 'radicals'. The matrix in Table 1.1 shows how often

Ivory Coast, Ghana and Nigeria voted with either of the superpowers on these fifty issues.

TABLE 1.1   U.N. voting on selected East–West issues,
fifteenth to twenty-second sessions of the general assembly

	U.S.A.	*U.S.S.R.*
Ghana	4	24
Nigeria	4	12
Ivory Coast	27	7

Note: The table does not take into account abstentions or absences, during voting by the three African states.
Source: David A. Kay, *New Nations in the United Nations 1960–1968* (New York and London, 1970).

A similar division was appearing in the Soviet Union's bilateral links with Africa. In 1960 Ghana's relations with the Soviet Union began to improve, and in the same year the new state of Mali made its first appearance on the world stage. When the Mali Federation, which had originally been planned as a union of Senegal, Soudan, Upper Volta and Dahomey, but which in fact only included the first two, finally broke up in August 1960, the U.S.S.R. found another ray of hope in the form of the Soudan, which took over the name of the defunct federation. The new state's early acts of foreign policy did much to raise it in Soviet estimation: it abrogated its treaties and agreements with France in October 1960, recognised the Algerian Provisional Government and the Gizenga regime in the Congo in February 1961, liquidated French bases in March, and was a most consistent ally of Guinea. In March 1961 the Soviet Union granted $44 million to Mali in credits and a trade agreement was negotiated leading to the immediate sale of five Ilyushin aircraft and several more Antonov 24s to Air Mali. On 2 June of the same year Tass announced that the one-year-old Republic of Somalia would receive R40 million in aid and a R7 million trade credit.

There were, however, other states, like Ivory Coast, Congo (Brazzaville), Gabon, and Madagascar, that did not welcome the Soviet Union's presence in Africa and in the main did not establish diplomatic relations. In between there was a third group: countries such as Nigeria, Senegal, and Tanganyika which established diplomatic relations with the U.S.S.R. but were not keen for contacts to develop. These categories were not rigid. A revolution in Congo (Brazzaville), for example, which overthrew the pro-French Abbé Fulbert Youlou in August 1963, moved the country into the same category as Ghana. However, this threefold division of Black African states was a feature of Soviet–African relations for the first half of the 1960s. The Soviet Union concentrated particularly on the first group of states, and Nkrumah, Touré and Keita were all awarded the Lenin Prize. However, Soviet analyses of social and economic conditions in Africa suggested to them that there were strong similarities between many of the Black African states; the main difference between them was the outlook of their leaders. In the hope that this outlook would change, the U.S.S.R. remained willing to develop cordial relations with most countries. In view of the ambivalent position of the third group of states it was with them that this willingness was most apparent, but diplomatic relations were even established with Ivory Coast for a short period between 1967 and 1969.[61]

These developments were mirrored by changes in the Soviet concept of Africa. Nationalism in Europe's colonies has always presented Soviet theorists with a problem because the nationalist movements have frequently been headed by members of the bourgeoisie. Official policy has fluctuated between support for the nationalists by virtue of their anti-imperialist stance, and opposition to them because of the conflict between their interests and those of the proletariat. After the Second World War the pendulum swung away from a united front towards savage exclusiveness, and no assistance was offered to the bourgeois nationalist states attaining independence in Asia.

After Stalin's death in 1953 a more flexible attitude slowly came into favour. The Soviet concept of the role of the bourgeoisie began to change. Divisions within the bourgeois ranks were stressed: in addition to the 'comprador bourgeoisie' who held interests similar to those of the colonialists, there was posited to be a 'national bourgeoisie' composed of those who wanted to further their own interests at the expense of the colonialists.[62] The view was heard that the U.S.S.R. should pay more attention to the objective results of national bourgeois actions than to the subjective ideas that motivated them.[63] It was possible that the bourgeoisie might do the right things for the wrong reasons.

These views were given an official stamp of approval in November 1960 by a declaration adopted by the Moscow conference of eighty-one Communist parties.[64] This declaration acknowledged the existence of a class of states that were 'national democracies'. The essential features of a national democracy were that it was ruled by the bourgeoisie and therefore often made reactionary moves such as suppressing Communists.[65] However, in its foreign policy it was anti-imperialist and anti-colonialist while in its domestic policy it was broadly democratic.

In 1962 a six-fold classification of new, non-Communist states was published:[66]

(1) states with fairly well-developed capitalist relations, e.g. India;
(2) states with less well-developed capitalist relations and a weaker

ruling bourgeoisie which has to collaborate with feudal elements, e.g. Somalia, Nigeria;

(3) states where the pro-imperialist bourgeoisie is still in power, e.g. Pakistan;

(4) Ghana, Guinea and Mali, which form a special group since capitalist relations are almost absent, no feudal class exists, and the proletariat is evolving;

(5) pro-imperialist ex-colonies in Africa which have many similarities with the states in group (4) but where the influence of imperialism is still very strong, e.g. Ivory Coast, Congo (K);

(6) states where capitalist relations and the bourgeoisie are very weak and where the feudalists are strong, e.g. Ethiopia.

Ghana, Guinea and Mali were thus placed in a category of their own. The main factor distinguishing these states from their neighbours in category (5) was stated to be the attitude of the political leadership. It was thus easy for the U.S.S.R. to believe that the only requirement for other African states to adopt similar policies to those of Ghana, Guinea and Mali was a change in their leaderships.

This emphasis on leadership was given concrete expression in the concept of 'revolutionary democrat' that was introduced in 1963. The term was used to describe leaders who, while not Marxist, saw themselves as allies of the socialist camp against imperialism.[67] Given the existence of revolutionary democratic leaders in some Black African states, and given the weakness of the reactionary forces, some Soviet theorists began to argue that the path to socialism could be traversed far more rapidly in Africa than hitherto thought possible. Although the proletariat was too weak to sustain a revolution, this did not matter: the revolution could be led from above and with the support of the world socialist system could withstand colonialist counter-measures until the proletariat had matured.[68] This idea seems to have gained a wide currency.[69] Khrushchev appears to have liked it and to have made it his own. Those states approaching this revolution from above were accorded a position in what was known as 'the non-capitalist path of development'.

The Soviet belief that their prospects in Africa were very encouraging, and that it was only necessary for leaders with the 'correct' outlook to achieve power for these prospects to reach fruition, was probably reinforced by events on the other side of the Atlantic. On 1 January 1959 the Batista regime in Cuba fell from power, and after an interval of some confusion Fidel Castro became the premier of the island. There is no evidence that the Soviet Union had any direct contact with Castro while he was a rebel in the Sierra Maestra, and official Soviet reaction to the new regime, while cordial, was cool and ambivalent.[70] The first formal contacts were not made until February 1960 when Anastas Mikoyan stopped off in Cuba after a visit to Central America. There followed a trade agreement which sought to reduce Cuba's dependence on the U.S.A. with the Soviet Union contracting to buy Cuban sugar, and so enabling Cuba to purchase Soviet oil. Following trade action against Cuba by the U.S.A., and in competition with assistance from China, the Soviet Union agreed in December 1960 to purchase 2.7 million tons of Cuban sugar at a guaranteed price in 1961.[71] In 1961 the U.S.A. imposed a complete commercial boycott on Cuba, and at the end of the year, Castro declared himself a Communist; the Soviet initiative appeared to have paid off handsomely.

For its success in Cuba the Soviet Union had had to rely on the personality of the nationalist leader. A similar situation obtained in the 'radical' states of Black Africa, but the U.S.S.R. soon discovered that some leading Black African radicals were not always stable in their radicalism. In 1961 the Soviet ambassador in Guinea miscalculated his position there and began to meddle in a left-wing teacher's strike, as a result of which he was forced to leave suddenly in December. This abrupt *hiatus* in its relation with the country that many in the West referred to as a Red enclave was a severe blow to Soviet prestige. The following year, Sékou Touré dealt an even more severe blow when during the Cuban missile crisis he refused permission for the Soviet Union's Cuba-bound jets to refuel at Conakry airport, which had been extended by the Russians precisely for this purpose.[72] The following year domestic trade liberalisation occurred, and there were suggestions that Guinea had experienced a counter-revolution.[73]

Competition from China

These setbacks were not accompanied by a fall in Russian interest in sub-Saharan Africa as a whole, largely as a result of competition from the Chinese. After its slow start, China developed a more active interest in the 'radical' states. When China gave aid it was often on better terms than those offered by the Soviet Union. Guinea was granted $26 million aid in 1960, and in 1961 Ghana and Mali received credits totalling $19½ million each. In each case Chinese loans were longer-term, with a more generous grace period than were those of the Soviet Union, and were interest free, while in Kenya Chinese aid included an outright grant. Contacts were even made with the 'moderate' states: in April 1961 the vice-minister of foreign trade, Lu Hsu-chang, led a delegation to Lagos to discuss the possibility of establishing diplomatic relations and improving economic and cultural relations. Approaches were also made to Senegal, Dahomey, Niger and Upper Volta, although without success.[74]

The main threat from the Chinese was not, however, to be found in the economic field, as the P.R.C. simply did not have the resources to compete with the Soviet Union: by the end of 1963 Soviet credits to Ghana, Guinea and Mali exceeded Chinese promises by $100 million, and between 1961 and 1963 the Chinese imported only one-third of the amount imported by the U.S.S.R. from these three countries.[75] In January 1961, faced with serious economic disarray, the P.R.C. ordered the redirection of its resources. The 1961 credits to Ghana and Mali included the proviso that they should not be drawn upon until July 1962.[76] The main threat from the Chinese lay in the fundamental difference between Soviet and Chinese conceptions of African development: the U.S.S.R. and Eastern Europe premised their approach on their global objectives of peaceful co-existence and economic development: the Chinese premised theirs on the need for anti-colonial revolution. Behind this difference lay a Chinese conviction that they understood the needs of developing nations better than did the U.S.S.R. The conflict between the Russians and Chinese in Africa was bitter and hard-fought not only because it was just one aspect of the whole Sino-Soviet dispute but also because the Russians had grounds to fear that Chinese success in fomenting internal disorder might provoke American activity such as the U.S.S.R. had already experienced in the Congo, and might scare off the more moderate states, some of which had real value to the U.S.S.R. as trading partners.

This ideological struggle between the two Communist viewpoints is most clearly seen in the context of the international Afro-Asian movement. Although no full, official Afro-Asian conference was held between 1955 and 1965, the spirit of Bandung was kept alive by its unofficial counterpart, the Afro-Asian Peoples' Solidarity Organisation (A.A.P.S.O.). This body was established at the Cairo Solidarity Conference of December 1957 following a number of efforts derived ultimately from the Communist-directed World Peace Council. Unlike the Bandung conference where the U.S.S.R. was unrepresented, the Cairo Solidarity Conference saw a large Soviet delegation headed by the Uzbeck vice-president of the Supreme Soviet of the U.S.S.R., and there were also delegates from Rumania, Czechoslovakia, and Yugoslavia. The conference saw itself as the apostle of Bandung and established the A.A.P.S.O. as a permanent organisation with a council, executive committee and secretariat. Both China and the Soviet Union were represented on its three governing organs.

Soviet interest in these bodies initially stemmed from a desire to express unity of interest with the Third World and to establish lines of contact with its leaders and future leaders, an essential prerequisite for any Soviet attempt to displace the West in the ex-colonies. However, as the Sino-Soviet dispute developed, meetings of A.A.P.S.O. and its numerous satellite groups – the Afro-Asian Women's Movements, the Afro-Asian Writers' Movement, the Afro-Asian Youth Movement – became more and more a battlefield on which were fought the heresies of the great schism. The role of China was essentially active, that of the Soviet Union passive: the Chinese wished to expose Russian revisionism and collaborationism, especially on issues such as Vietnam, while the Russians were just concerned to see that their rivals were outvoted. As time passed the verbal assaults grew worse. By the time of an executive committee meeting at Gaza in December 1961 the Chinese had moved from arguing with the Russian position within A.A.P.S.O. to declaring that the Russians were ineligible to belong to the organisation at all.[77] They continued with these tactics at both the third Afro-Asian People's Solidarity Conference convened at Moshi, Tanganyika in February 1962, and at the preparatory meeting held earlier in Cairo. Their arguments drew some support: President Nyerere, the host at Moshi, issued his well-known warning about a 'second scramble for Africa', arguing that both the rich capitalist states and the 'rich socialist countries' were using their wealth not to wipe out poverty but to gain might and prestige. While the Chinese failed to exclude Russia they did manage to obtain a ruling that representatives from Eastern Europe should not be admitted, even as observers. However, China's success was short-lived. Her position was fundamentally weak: having to be the active combatant and launch continual attacks on the Soviet Union she laid herself open to the charge of splitting the Afro-Asian ranks. At the sixth session of the A.A.P.S.O. council held in Algiers during March 1964 the Chinese onslaught became so vitriolic that it provoked an open rebuke from African delegates.[78]

The clearest indication that China had overplayed its hand came from its attempts to organise the second Afro-Asian conference: a second Bandung. The conference was initially proposed by Indonesia and China, and a preparatory meeting convened in Djarkarta in April 1964. The preparatory conference showed a clear rift between China, Indonesia and Pakistan on the one hand and India on the other, with India proposing membership for Russia and Malaysia; no solution was reached and it was finally decided to hold over a decision on this question until a later date. Algiers was chosen as the venue and a preparatory meeting took place in January 1965. The hosts obtained a postponement of the conference itself from March to May and then to 29 June 1965 as arrangements were incomplete. There was still no decision on Russian and Malaysian eligibility and the question was left to a foreign ministers' meeting planned for a few days before the main conference. In the early hours of 19 June the government of Ahmed Ben Bella in Algeria was overthrown by a military coup; the new government was a revolutionary council chaired by the minister of defence, Colonel Boumedienne, with the former foreign minister, Bouteflika, retaining his position. It was soon clear that the new government was in full control, and Bouteflika's continuance in office suggested that there would be no violent changes in foreign policy, although as Ben Bella had largely conducted Algeria's foreign policy himself there were some grounds for uncertainty. However, many participating governments speedily acted to have the conference postponed suggesting that they were glad to seize any credible excuse. China, actively concerned to see that the conference took place, immediately cast Ben Bella aside and gave full support to his usurper. This was a tactical error of the first order: military *coup* was anathema to the civilian leaders of sub-Saharan Africa, and the spectacle of China deserting an old ally for pragmatic self-interest was not endearing. Moreover, the sacrifice was in vain: after another postponement China withdrew, having failed to have the conference convened on acceptable terms, one of which was that the Soviet Union be not invited;[79] the second Bandung was then postponed indefinitely.

In the case of the Afro-Asian conference, the Soviet Union was, as it were, saved by a *coup*. It soon discovered, however, that *coups d'état* were by no means always favourable, as Nkrumah and Keita followed Ben Bella. By this time Khrushchev, who was closely connected with the Soviet 'offensive' in Africa had also been replaced, and Chinese competition had been overtaken by the Cultural Revolution. As Africa became more and more unstable, it became increasingly clear that the U.S.S.R.'s interests lay in developing cordial business-like relations with all states rather than striving for intimacy with a few, for the intimates of one regime were likely to become the enemies of its successor. In Ghana, for example, the Soviet Union developed close ties with Nkrumah and came to be associated with him. Largely because of this association the successor N.L.C. and People's Party governments were distinctly cool towards Moscow, and on friendly terms with the West. In January 1972, however, the pro-West government of Dr Busia was overthrown by another military *coup* and the new military government has been cool towards the West and sought to re-establish close ties with the East.

The instability of African regimes has shown the expected revolution from above led by 'revolutionary democratic' leaders to be rather fragile. The idea of the 'non-capitalist path' of development has not been scrapped as a reaction to these setbacks. What has happened instead is that the conditions for being placed on the 'path' have been hardened, while the pitfalls inherent in the 'path' have been emphasised.[80] This trend mirrors the tendency of the Soviet Union to prefer cordial relations with all to intimacy with a few. Whilst certain regimes are still singled out as progressive they no longer receive the attention that they used to do.

Since 1970 China has been re-emerging on the African scene and it is possible that this may provoke a further change in the Soviet outlook. Between 1970 and 1972 the Chinese government made promises of aid worth over £130 million to African states. At the same time, it launched a diplomatic offensive that proved generally successful, particularly after it had gained admission to the United Nations. Its success in mainland Tanzania has long been apparent, but it has also recently displaced the Russians in Zanzibar and has increased its activity in Somalia and Nigeria, both important foci of Soviet interest. Whether this competition from the Chinese will provoke heightened Soviet concern for the African continent is, however, not yet apparent.

2   Trade

On the day of its independence no African country had diplomatic relations with the U.S.S.R. and few had any substantial contact with the Russians. Today most African capitals have a Russian diplomatic mission and there is frequent movement of official delegations and private exchanges between the two continents. The reasons for this change have been complex and manifold, some subtle some brazen, but most persuasive of all the reasons has been the African desire for the economic benefits thought to flow from trade and aid connections with the U.S.S.R. The Soviet Union boasts that it will grant aid to all the countries of Black Africa and it is certainly prepared to trade with them all. The pace at which trade and aid and other ties have grown has depended, therefore, on whether the African state concerned considered that it would be in its interests to respond. Some countries, such as Guinea and the Congo called on the Eastern countries soon after independence for assistance of various kinds. Others, and here Ghana is notable, put the Soviet Union low on their list of priorities until economic needs became pressing. Yet others have resisted Soviet advances, sometimes but not always successfully.

When African governments approached the U.S.S.R. for economic reasons, they hoped for assistance on two fronts: help to strengthen their bargaining position *vis à vis* their main trading partners in the developed West, and economic and technical assistance to supplement Western aid. Despite some of the more extreme statements by the most enthusiastic supporters of commercial intercourse with the centrally planned economies (C.P.E.s), African governments did not consider these countries as alternative partners to the West, but as additional ones. And quite rightly, too; while the socialist countries have a great potential it will be a long time before they are able to substitute as trade partners and aid donors for the West, as the Russians themselves now realise.

The chief advantage of the Soviet Union and other C.P.E.s in the field of trade was that they were prepared to deal independently of the free market. By selling produce directly to them, Africans hoped that supplies to the free market could be reduced sufficiently to raise the price prevailing there. This strategy proved more complicated than anticipated and there were numerous problems. Nevertheless, the evidence available suggests that some African countries managed to benefit. The socialist countries have thus assisted African trade partners by improving their bargaining position with respect to their traditional exports. Contrary to some Soviet statements they have generally not assisted their partners to diversify their exports away from primary products, and when they have imported processed goods from Africa it has not always been on terms favourable to the exporter.

In order to establish a manufacturing capacity African states have tended to place great reliance on foreign aid. In the early years after independence no African politician worth his salt omitted to preface his remarks on development with the need for foreign aid, and all development plans included a section on foreign finance which formed as much as 60 per cent of the development budget in Mali and almost 100 per cent of that in Somalia. But in few cases were the Western countries prepared to provide all the finance that was planned for them, and when this was realised the Soviet promise to give aid to all was remembered. If historical precedents were required they were at hand in the U.A.R. and India for the first Black African states to take the plunge, who then became examples for others to follow. If examples of Soviet handiwork were required, the Aswan Dam on Africa's own soil was sufficient.

Interlaced with all this was an undoubted psychological attraction that the Soviet Union possessed for some. The U.S.S.R. had achieved economic development *and* had rejected the West, which was just what some Africans wished to do. Whether such motives were present or not, few would deny the technological achievements of the Soviet Union. A Kenyan reflected a common mood when he told the legislative council (*Debates*, 21 July 1962, col. 645) of his trip to Eastern Europe :

> The overall impression we received was that the countries we visited had achieved tremendous scientific and technical advance . . . we met the City Engineer of Moscow and we had discussions with him and he pointed out to us a building which was removed intact, in the course of town planning, over a distance of 20 yards to make room for a street . . . I pointed out a bigger building and asked him whether he could remove that building and he said, 'I cannot say whether we can or not now, but nothing is impossible.'

Nothing is impossible, indeed, and it was perhaps not impossible that with Soviet assistance in the fields of both aid and trade there could be rapid economic development in Africa.

Aid and trade are closely related phenomena and this is particularly so where the Soviet Union is concerned. Soviet aid normally takes the form of credits for the purchase of machinery and equipment and is often repaid in kind by shipments of the recipient's exports. The provision of aid may, therefore, produce a marked effect on trade. Indeed, one scholar who has attempted to calculate the real cost to the Soviet Union of its aid

TABLE 2.1　Development of the U.S.S.R.'s visible trade with the world by regions and groups 1955–71
Million U.S. dollars f.o.b. where 1 rouble = U.S.$1·111

	1955	1960	1965	1970	1971
Soviet imports from:					
Developed market economies	464	1,169	1,822	3,072	3,172
Developing countries	195	639	1,133	1,790	1,731
Centrally planned economies	2,400	3,821	5,078	6,868	7,573
Africa	31	176	243	537	585
Latin America	77	140	451	594	438
Middle East	25	41	66	134	192
Non-Communist Asia	58	253	391	508	453
TOTAL ALL STATES	3,061	5,628	8,058	11,730	12,474
Soviet exports to:					
Developed market economies	574	1,070	1,641	2,715	3,082
Developing countries	141	412	1,498	2,688	2,701
Centrally planned economies	2,710	4,082	5,035	7,396	8,021
Africa	13	100	329	579	607
Latin America	24	106	426	653	683
Middle East	32	66	104	422	469
Non-Communist Asia	21	107	372	238	242
TOTAL ALL STATES	3,426	5,562	8,174	12,799	13,805

	Percentage changes					
	1955–60		1960–5		1965–70	
	Imports from	Exports to	Imports from	Exports to	Imports from	Exports to
Developed market economies	152	86	57	53	67	64
Developing countries	227	192	77	263	58	79
Centrally planned economies	59	50	33	23	35	47
Africa	464	669	39	229	121	76
Latin America	80	341	222	302	32	54
Middle East	61	106	61	−58	103	305
Non-Communist Asia	338	409	47	248	30	−36
PERCENTAGE CHANGE IN TOTAL	85	62	43	47	46	57

Notes: Developed market economies = U.S.A., Canada, W. Europe, Australia, New Zealand, S. Africa and Japan.
Centrally planned economies = U.S.S.R. and other E. European countries, People's Republic of China, Mongolia, N. Korea, and N. Viet-Nam.
Developing countries = all other countries.
Africa includes Egypt and excludes South Africa.
Non-Communist Asia = Afghanistan, Burma, Ceylon, Hong Kong, India, Indonesia, Khmer Republic, Malaysia, Nepal, Pakistan, Singapore, Thailand.
Middle East = Cyprus, Iran, Iraq, Jordan, Kuwait, Lebanon, Saudi Arabia, Syria, Turkey, Yemen, People's Democratic Republic of Yemen.
Source: U.N. Statistical Office, *Monthly Bulletin of Statistics*, vol. xxvi, no. 6 (June 1972) Special Table C.

---

programme has estimated that in the period 1958–65 $6296 million worth of Soviet aid generated $3900 million worth of extra trade.* While such figures can be little more than 'guesstimates', and leave scope for value judgements, they are indicative of the closeness of the relationship. Some commentators have even seen aid as a kind of 'loss leader' designed to stimulate trade.[1] Nevertheless, for the purpose of analysis these two phenomena may usefully be taken separately, and it is logical to deal with trade first, both because it involves a larger number of African countries and because, historically, the establishment of trade relations has normally preceded the granting of aid.

THE GENERAL PATTERN

During the decade 1955–65 trade between the Communist countries and the developing countries (including Yugoslavia) formed a particularly dynamic sector of world trade increasing as it did from $1222 million in 1955 to $2778 million in 1960 and $6111 million in 1965; in other words it more than doubled every five years. Since then the rate of increase, as might be expected, has eased off but total trade had still risen to $8277 million by 1970. This increase has been particularly significant in relation to raw materials and agricultural products. Although the socialist countries purchased only a little over one-tenth of the agricultural exports of the developing countries in 1965, their purchases accounted for about one-third of the total rise in these exports between 1960 and 1965 if Cuba is included, or for over one-fifth of the increase if Cuba is excluded. Trade in the manufactured exports of the developing countries

* James Richard Carter, *The Net Cost of Soviet Foreign Aid* (Washington and London, 1969), p. 84. The figure of $3900 million is composed of $3700 million for aid deliveries and repayments, plus $174,700 million extra trade that would not otherwise have occurred.

TABLE 2.2a Soviet visible trade with major African countries 1955–71
(in million U.S.$ f.o.b. where 1 rouble = U.S.$1.111)

Country	1955 Soviet imports	1955 Soviet exports	1960 Soviet imports	1960 Soviet exports	1965 Soviet imports	1965 Soviet exports	1969 Soviet imports	1969 Soviet exports	1970 Soviet imports	1970 Soviet exports	1971 Soviet imports	1971 Soviet exports
Algeria	—	1	—	—	3	16	61	58	62	69	77	59
Libya	—	—	—	—	—	6	—	11	—	14	—	10
Morocco	2	1	4	4	11	9	18	37	20	36	21	31
Tunisia	—	—	1	1	3	7	3	4	3	3	7	4
Egypt	16	11	121	121	163	209	228	238	311	363	334	381
Cameroun	—	—	—	—	0	0	12	1	8	1	4	1
Congo (Brazzaville)	—	—	—	—	—	—	—	—	—	—	—	—
Dahomey	—	—	—	—	0	2	1	—	1	1	1	4
Ethiopia	11	—	—	1	2	8	4	2	1	1	1	1
Ghana	—	—	22	6	31	34	15	9	45	11	8	14
Guinea	—	—	2	6	3	10	3	9	3	12	6	34
Kenya	—	—	—	—	1	1	1	—	1	1	2	1
Mali	—	—	—	—	2	10	2	6	2	6	2	2
Nigeria	—	—	7	—	6	3	2	6	2	6	2	2
Senegal	—	—	—	—	1	3	24	17	22	12	46	18
Sierra Leone	—	—	—	—	1	0	—	1	1	1	—	1
Somalia	—	—	—	—	0	0	1	2	—	2	2	2
Sudan	—	—	6	6	12	8	13	15	50	36	2	7
Tanzania	—	—	—	—	2	0	3	1	1	1	52	22
Togo	—	—	—	—	1	1	1	1	1	1	2	1
Uganda	—	—	4	—	1	0	1	—	3	1	4	2
Zambia	—	—	—	—	—	—	—	—	3	1	—	4
Ivory Coast	2	—	6	—	—	—	6	—	2	—	12	1

Source: U.N. Statistical Office, Monthly Bulletin of Statistics, vol. xxv, 7 July 1971, Special Table B; vol. xxvi, 6 June 1972, Special Table C.

also increased and reached about one-fifth of the total imports of the socialist countries from the developing countries in 1965.[2]

The trade of the U.S.S.R. conforms roughly to the same pattern (see Table 2.1) and accounts for between one-third and one-half of the total trade of the socialist group in this period. Russia's trade with Africa has increased faster than its trade with any of the other major regional groups, and it is currently the greatest in absolute terms. However, of more significance than the regional distribution of trade is its concentration in a few major countries: in 1965 over one-third of the exports from Cuba, Egypt, Syria and Yugoslavia were sent to socialist countries while Afghanistan, Argentina, Burma, Cambodia, Ceylon, Ghana, Indonesia, Malaysia, Mali, Morocco, Pakistan, Sudan and Uganda shipped between one-tenth and one-third of their exports in that direction.[3] The figures for individual African states are given in Tables 2.2a and 22.2b.

TABLE 2.2b The visible trade of selected African countries with the U.S.S.R. as a proportion of their total trade in 1969 (in million U.S.$)

	(1) World trade		(2) Trade with U.S.S.R.		(2) *as a percentage of* (1)	
	Imports	*Exports*	*Imports*	*Exports*	*Imports*	*Exports*
Algeria	1,009	934	58	61	5·8	6·5
Morocco	561	485	37	18	6·6	3·7
Tunisia	265	166	4·5	3·5	1·7	2·1
Egypt	638	745	238	228	37·4	30·6
Ghana	347	301	9	16	2·6	5·3
Mali	39	17	5·5	2	14·1	11·8
Nigeria	696	905	17	24·5	2·4	2·7
Sudan	266	248	15·5	13	5·8	5·3

Source: Calculated from U.N. Dept of Economic and Social Affairs, *Yearbook of International Trade Statistics 1969* (New York, 1971), Table A; Table 2a above.

By and large, the countries which conduct the greatest percentage share of their trade with the U.S.S.R. are those with which it has signed payments agreements under which trade does not make use of a convertible currency. It will be argued later that such agreements are likely to stimulate Soviet interest in trade but, in the meantime, one other reason for the correlation of payment agreements and higher levels of trade should be noted: the decision to enter into a fairly novel form of trading arrangement signifies that the African government concerned has given some thought to the matter of developing trade with the centrally planned economies and has decided to take positive steps which it hopes will achieve this. This is most important considering that until the last decade practically all of Back Africa's foreign transactions were with the West so that a tradition of exporting to and importing from certain areas has developed and with it has grown an expertise for facilitating this trade. Left to itself it is doubtful whether private business would have had many dealings with the Soviet bloc. Of course, there are exceptions. In Nigeria businessmen established a Nigeria–U.S.S.R. Chamber of Commerce; in 1967 a Russian organisation concerned with trade in motor vehicles, Avtoexport, formed with Nigerian businessmen a joint-stock company, the West Africa Automobile and Engineering Company (WAATECO) to import Russian cars, heavy vehicles, tractors and agricultural machinery, and by 1971 71 per cent of its shares were owned by Nigerians.[4] In Ghana an enterprising fisherman, Robert Ocran, began acquiring Russian trawlers for his company, Mankoadze Fisheries, in 1962 and from there became a general importer of Soviet sugar, flour, soap and tinned fish, established a subsidiary company, Volga Engineering, to import Soviet vehicles, and became something of a troubleshooter for the Ghana State Fishing Corporation in its own dealings with the Russians.[5] However, these are very much the exceptions that prove the rule and neither African businessmen nor, in some countries, conservative consumers have been adventurous in experimenting with Soviet products. Such conservatism has not been helped by the lack of attention shown in the past to sales promotion by Soviet authorities. At the same time the marketing companies responsible for exporting primary produce have not often taken a lead in promoting sales to the Soviet bloc unless urged to do so by their governments. The Russians have complained that before 1964 the Nigeria Produce Marketing Company refused to sell it any cocoa and as a result the U.S.S.R. had to satisfy its requirements through a third party. Although this was not necessarily a deliberate anti-Communist move by the Marketing Company and can be paralleled by its unadventurous attitude towards other potential new trade partners such as Japan and some African countries, its effect in dampening the growth of Soviet–Nigerian trade is clear. In Somalia until 1970 the country's main cash crop, bananas, was exported by two private enterprises which sold its products almost entirely in Italy, partly, it must be added, because of the bananas received preferential treatment from the Italian government. In view of this widespread conservatism, a number of African governments realised that if trade were to be developed with the socialist countries the state would need to take the lead. President Kenyatta, for one, has argued that '. . . in order to derive maximum benefits from our agreements for mutual trade with the socialist countries it is necessary to establish a single State-controlled agency,'[6] although

TABLE 2.3 Commodity composition of Soviet visible trade with developing countries

Soviet imports	Unit of measurement	1950	1955	1960	1964	1968
TOTAL	million U.S.$	92	231	638	914	1,138
Ferrous metals	,, ,,	—	0	33	13	3
Natural rubber	1,000 tons	70	34	183	186	326
Cotton fibre	,, ,,	37	19	144	138	130
Wool	,, ,,	1	13	17	16	27
Hides:						
large	1,000 units	11	1,071	1,517	616	1,478
small	,, ,,	124	3,320	17,148	19,439	20,787
Tobacco	1,000 tons	2	0	4	52	11
Oil seed	,, ,,	—	7	15	71	56
Edible veg. oils	,, ,,	1	47	13	39	38
Coffee	,, ,,	1	1	19	30	31
Cocoa beans	,, ,,	12	14	58	66	108
Tea	,, ,,	—	—	12	29	22
Rice	,, ,,	—	192	50	308	159
Citrus fruits	,, ,,	—	28	27	66	175
Dried fruits & berries	,, ,,	2	11	47	42	84
Raw sugar	,, ,,	—	206	1,468	1,859	1,749
Cotton fabrics	million metres	—	—	—	6	46
Cotton yarn	1,000 tons	—	—	—	14	16

Soviet exports	Unit of measurement	1950	1955	1960	1964	1968
TOTAL	million U.S.$	32·2	142·2	412·2	1,330·0	2,027·8
Machinery & equipment	,, ,,	0	5·6	133·3	596·7	704·4
Complete industrial plant	,, ,,	—	1·1	71·1	333·3	364·4
Ferrous metals	,, ,,	0	20·0	38·9	60·0	94·4
Non-ferrous metals	,, ,,	—	1·1	6·7	16·7	10·0
Oil & oil prods	million tons	0	2	4	10	66
Timber, paper & pulp prods	million U.S.$	1·1	12·2	34·4	47·8	70·0
Cotton fabrics	million metres	19	93	118	136	157
Chem. prods	million U.S.$	0	1·1	3·3	8·9	25·6
Medicaments sanitary hygiene articles	,, ,,	0	0	1·1	2·2	6·7
Refined sugar	1,000 tons	13	82	139	203	854
Fish and fish foods	million U.S.$	0	0	1·1	5·6	15·6

Sources: *Vneshnyaya Torgovlia S.S.S.R.: Statistichesky Sbornik 1918–1966* (Moscow, 1967); *Vneshnyaya Torgovlia S.S.S.R.: Statistichesky Obzor 1968* (Moscow, 1969).

subsequent political developments conspired to keep trade at a low level. In Ghana, too, the need for State regulation of trade with the socialist countries was recognised and given as one of the reasons for the establishment of the Ghana National Trading Corporation.[7]

Where trade has occurred it has largely been on the basis of Soviet machinery and equipment being exchanged for primary produce (see Table 2.3). Although the Soviet Union claims to do one better than the Western countries where discriminatory tariffs hinder the export of manufactured and semi-manufactured goods from developing countries, Table 2.4 suggests that as far as Africa is concerned it is in a similar

TABLE 2.4 Commodity structure of Soviet imports from selected African countries (in thousands U.S.$ f.o.b.)

S.I.T.C.	Ghana 1970 Exports to U.S.S.R.	Total exports	S.I.T.C.	Nigeria 1970 Exports to U.S.S.R.	Total exports
0	40,046	330,725	0	24,558	234,784
1	—	—	1	—	11
2	496	60,520	2	3	171,862
3	—	654	3	—	713,993
4	—	262	4	—	46,061
5	—	395	5	—	397
6	—	32,536	6	—	54,682
7	—	235	7	—	—
8	—	90	8	—	290
9	—	430	9	15	5,792
TOTAL	40,542	425,847	TOTAL	24,576	1,227,872

S.I.T.C.	Sudan 1970 Exports to U.S.S.R.	Total exports	S.I.T.C.	Morocco 1970 Exports to U.S.S.R.	Total exports
0	—	26,100	0	13,181	236,917
1	—	—	1	—	9,960
2	49,519	262,181	2	575	182,367
3	—	1,040	3	1	1,868
4	—	2,251	4	—	5,273
5	—	82	5	—	10,574
6	—	95	6	216	28,381
7	—	2	7	—	2,421
8	—	24	8	—	10,106
9	—	41	9	—	93
TOTAL	49,519	291,816	TOTAL	13,973	487,960

S.I.T.C.	U.A.R. 1968 Exports to U.S.S.R.	Total exports	S.I.T.C.	Tunisia 1968 Exports to U.S.S.R.	Total exports
0	37,298	140,105	0	645	21,441
1	4,276	7,189	1	—	6,973
2	77,842	293,396	2	702	38,683
3	—	16,227	3	—	31,376
4	—	—	4	3,496	22,948
5	846	7,145	5	—	20,070
6	44,696	126,075	6	30	12,454
7	—	4,141	7	—	1,032
8	9,533	19,880	8	—	1,947
9	94	3,416	9	—	870
TOTAL	174,585	617,573	TOTAL	4,873	157,794

S.I.T.C.	Algeria 1967 Exports to U.S.S.R.	Total exports	S.I.T.C.	Mali 1965 Exports to U.S.S.R.	Total exports
0	2,759	58,475	0	—	9,409
1	4,862	58,924	1	—	92
2	864	20,959	2	579	5,660
3	11	527,854	3	—	55
4	—	487	4	—	76
5	1,100	31,838	5	—	2
6	145	15,025	6	—	234
7	—	8,967	7	33	177
8	48	1,112	8	—	—
9	—	13	9	—	—
TOTAL	9,906	723,654	TOTAL	612	15,705

Sources: U.N. Economic Commission for Africa, *Foreign Trade Statistics of Africa*, series B, vols 18–22; European Commission Statistical Office, *République du Mali, Yearbook 1959–66* (1969).

position to the West. Only a very small proportion of the trade of the given countries is in S.I.T.C. categories 5–8 and where the country concerned is heavily reliant upon a very limited range of exports, its trade with the U.S.S.R. is, if anything, even more limited: 95 per cent of Ghana's total exports are in S.I.T.C. categories 0 and 2, but 100 per cent of its exports to the U.S.S.R. are so delineated.*

* The S.I.T.C. classification of commodities is as follows: 0 = food; 1 = beverages and tobacco; 2 = crude materials (inedible); 3 = mineral fuels; 4 = animal and vegetable oils and fats; 5 = chemicals; 6 = manufactured goods; 7 = machinery and transport equipment; 8 = miscellaneous manufactured items; 9 = miscellaneous transactions.

Not surprisingly, commercial relations with the East have been thought of as an added bonus rather than a solution to all economic woes; not as an alternative to Western markets but as an adjunct to them. This is clear from the actions and statements of responsible African ministers. Even before Kenya's independence its minister of agriculture, Bruce McKenzie, visited the U.S.S.R. and Eastern Europe to find additional markets for Kenya's surplus agricultural production, and when defending his government's policy of selling cocoa to the centrally planned economies the Ghanaian minister of finance, K. Amoaka-Atta, did so in terms of the salutory effect it had had on traditional purchasers.[8]

The countries of Africa are generally reliant upon the export of primary products to provide foreign exchange, and for those whose commodities are derived from plants fluctuations in harvest size can be a major problem owing to the general inelasticity of demand for their goods. It is held that the centrally planned economies can easily alter their import structure and can at short notice import large quantities of a commodity in which trade was formerly rather small, and the Soviet Union's role as an importer of Egyptian cotton in the 1950s is a popular example of such a switch. This flexibility may have been exaggerated. Many of the commodities that the Soviet Union now buys from developing countries are goods that she has traditionally imported. This is true of Egypt's cotton: not until 1959 did Soviet purchases exceed its highest pre-war levels.[9] Nevertheless, despite this caveat, the U.S.S.R. is more able to take deliberate steps to increase imports of a particular good from a particular country than are the market economies. Having decided in the 1950s to buy Egyptian cotton on a systematic basis, the centrally planned economies increased their purchases to 60 per cent of Egypt's exports by 1965–6, and by 1967 Egypt provided 60 per cent of all the U.S.S.R.'s imported cotton.

GHANA'S COCOA: A PARADIGM

In Egypt the need to find new trade outlets was the result of political rather than economic factors. In Africa south of the Sahara there have been similar instances where political considerations promoted trade with the Soviet bloc; Guinea is one such. But these are in the minority. In the main, economic factors have been a more important reason for such adventures.

The major economic issues facing African governments when considering whether to export to the Soviet Union may be stated simply, although the answers are rather more complex. First, does the U.S.S.R. offer a stable market, and if not does its instability counter-balance or exaggerate instability in the market economies? Secondly, does the Soviet Union pay better prices than the market economies, and if not are there any other ways in which earnings will be increased by diverting some exports away from traditional purchasers into the new markets? Third, there is the problem of bilateralism: what are the advantages and disadvantages of agreeing to trade with the U.S.S.R. on a barter rather than a cash basis?

These questions may be illuminated, if not answered categorically, by concentrating initially on the trade in cocoa between the U.S.S.R. and Ghana and then introducing Soviet trade in other commodities and with other African countries when the cocoa horizon becomes too narrow.[10] Ghana and cocoa have a number of advantages for such a role. Cocoa beans are a fairly homogenous commodity, but Ghana produces the prime quality. Soviet imports of cocoa are of long standing, and for most of the period considered in this book Ghana has been its major supplier (see Table 2.5). The trade has been conducted at different times both with and without a payments agreement. During the 1960s a determined effort was made by the Ghana government to increase cocoa sales to the C.P.E.s. Finally, throughout the period 1953–72 the world cocoa market has been unstructured, with no world commodity agreement to complicate the picture.

To a great extent Ghana is cocoa and cocoa is Ghana. Cocoa is Ghana's economic mainstay and in 1968 it accounted for 63 per cent of her total earnings.[11] Ghana is also the world's major producer of cocoa and supplied 30 per cent of total world production in 1971.[12] Unfortunately, the recent history of the cocoa trade has been most distressing from that country's point of view.[13] In contrast to the interwar years which had by and large seen a buyers' market, the 1950s witnessed the emergence of a sellers' market in cocoa and prices rose. However, this good fortune carried within it the seeds of its own demise: on the one hand there was a rapid increase in cocoa production, and on the other traditional buyers reduced their reliance on cocoa by various means. As a result there was a re-emergence of the buyers' market during the 1960s and prices fell steadily and sometimes dramatically. This was doubly unfortunate, since not only did it reduce Ghana's foreign earnings but it also played havoc with advanced planning. Corruption and mismanagement in the Nkrumah government have been rightly criticised for their contribution to the burden of debt which now confronts the country, formerly considered a bright prospect for development, but one estimate attributes 80 per cent of the total deficit on current account accumulated during the 1960s to adverse movements in the terms of trade.[14] It is true that Nkrumah's economic designs were grandiose, but they were formulated in the late 1950s and early 1960s and were not wholly out of line with Ghana's economic prospects as seen at that time. Afterwards these prospects deteriorated, but instead of reducing expenditure Nkrumah's cronies went on a spending spree. However, while there is no justification for such increases in expenditure or for the heavy and corruptly influenced reliance upon suppliers' credits in the regime's latter years, it is very difficult both politically and administratively to alter carefully formulated plans particularly when a government may justifiably believe a bad year to be exceptional; it is Ghana's misfortune that it experienced half-a-dozen such exceptions in a row.

Discussion of a solution to the problems of cocoa centres on four main options: to increase demand in traditional markets, to control supply, to develop new uses for cocoa, or to develop new markets. The first of these options appears in many ways the simplest to attempt, but a major difficulty is that there is an extremely low elasticity of demand in the high-income states of Western Europe and in North America which are the traditional markets. Producers cannot, therefore, have any great confidence in attempts to increase demand in this area by holding down prices; only changes in taste can be expected to effect a major increase in consumption and this is by no means a simple task. An attempt was made in the 1960s to improve Ghana's position by restricting output, but it was found wanting. In 1964 a Cocoa Producers Alliance was formed by Nigeria, Ghana, Togo, Brazil, Ivory Coast and Cameroun which attempted to set a minimum price below which members would not sell their cocoa. In compliance with these regulations the cocoa producers withdrew as sellers in mid-October 1964. Unfortunately, none of the producers were strong enough to withstand this loss of earnings, added to which the 1964–5 crop proved exceptionally large; some producers began to disregard the sales ban. Consequently, the 'cocoa hold-up' collapsed in February 1965 and prices plummeted.

Since producers could not afford to withdraw completely from the cocoa market, a variation on the same theme whereby some cocoa was syphoned off the market to be used in 'non-conventional' processes seemed more likely to succeed.[15] These 'non-conventional' processes included the use of cocoa in the production of margarine, baking fat and cocoa-bread.[16] Unfortunately, to be used for the production of these goods, cocoa had to compete in price with other, much cheaper raw materials, and even at a time when prices for conventional cocoa had slumped to 100/- per cwt they were more attractive than the 35/- per cwt that could be obtained by selling the beans to an oil-seed crusher.[17]

The fourth method of increasing earnings, by finding new markets, had more success, and as the Soviet Union and Eastern Europe represented the largest potential market capable of being tapped in the near future, Ghana proceeded to try to develop it. In this she was successful, and the quantity of cocoa exported to the Soviet Union rose rapidly during the 1960s, reaching a peak in mid-decade (see Table 2.5). Approximately 66 per cent of the Soviet Union's imports from non-socialist developing countries between 1952 and 1972 were industrial raw materials. The remaining one-third were accounted for largely by food

TABLE 2.5   Ghana cocoa bean exports to the U.S.S.R. 1960–72

(1)	(2)	(3)	(4)	(5)	(6)	(7)
			Total			*Value of Ghanaian cocoa*
	Total Ghanaian exports	*Ghanaian exports to U.S.S.R.*	*Soviet cocoa imports*	*(3) as % of (2)*	*(3) as % of (4)*	*exports to U.S.S.R.*
Year						
1960	303	34	57	11	60	20,361
1961	406	19	21	5	90	8,644
1962	423	25	48	6	52	12,152
1963	404	43	53	11	81	13,847
1964	382	33	65	9	51	11,707
1965	494	66	88	13	75	21,161
1966	391	55	56	14	98	16,896
1967	328	57	81	17	70	18,180
1968	329	28	107	9	26	10,853
1969	303	15	97	5	15	7,867
1970	365	51	98	14	52	43,773
1971	n.a.	13	136	—	9	7,332
1972	n.a.	66	130	—	51	40,214

Notes: n.a. = not available.
   (2)–(4) denominated in thousand long tons.
   (7) denominated in thousand U.S.$
Sources: Ghana Central Bureau of Statistics, *Economic Survey* (1962, 1968, 1969); *Vneshnyaya Torgovlia S.S.S.R.: Statistichesky Sbornik 1918–1966* (Moscow, 1967); *Vneshnyaya Torgovlia S.S.S.R.: Statistichesky Obzor 1968, 1970, 1972* (Moscow, 1969, 1971, 1973).

items, of which cocoa formed an important part. As in the case of Egyptian cotton, it is not quite correct to state that Soviet purchases of Ghanaian cocoa are of recent origin. In fact, they began after the completion of the First Five-Year Plan in 1932, but before 1960 such purchases were mainly through brokers and the quantities sold direct were not large. The development of the Soviet Union as a major cocoa importer did not begin until 1960–1.[18] On 4 August 1960 a trade agreement was signed by the two countries and cocoa was mentioned in the attached schedule of goods for export from Ghana to the U.S.S.R. Then, on 4 November 1961, a new trade agreement was concluded which provided that the contracting parties should annually agree on the quantities of goods to be exchanged, and in a protocol this intention was given practical effect by the Soviet Union consenting to increase its purchases of cocoa beans over a five-year-period from 35,000 tons and more in 1962 to 60,000 tons in 1966. At the same time the two countries signed a payments agreement under which trade payments were to be made in non-convertible Ghanaian pounds, and the Soviet negotiators wished these provisions to apply to the cocoa agreement. Such an arrangement was not to the liking of the Ghanaians and it was finally agreed that the cocoa beans should be paid for partly in convertible currency and partly in the form of Soviet goods, with the proportion of the former falling from 55 per cent in 1962 to 20 per cent in 1966.[19]

In the event, the Soviet Union achieved its target a year ahead of schedule in 1965 when it signed a contract with the Ghanaian Cocoa Marketing Board for the supply of 60,000 tons of beans.[20] The year 1965 tells much about the advantages and disadvantages of Soviet trade. The Ghana Cocoa Marketing Company announced the conclusion of the Soviet contract on the 11 February 1965, ten days after the executive committee of the Cocoa Producers Alliance had admitted the failure of their restrictionist strategy and decided to allow Alliance members to resume sales. This news was coupled with the knowledge that the West African crop was particularly abundant, and to quote the authorative Gill and Duffus Cocoa Market Report, 'the market broke sharply in February as throughout the month prices tumbled to reach virtually post war lows'.[21] At first the Ghanaians tried to bluff. On 7 April the Ghana Cocoa Marketing Co. announced to general amazement that they had already sold their 1964–5 main crop, but it later became known that in completing their sales they had negotiated a special collateral deal with a European financial syndicate, which had little use for the cocoa itself, but had agreed to find markets for it. However, in this they were unsuccessful, for by mid-June reports were circulating that a substantial tonnage of this cocoa was once more in Ghanaian hands and, to quote again Gill and Duffus, 'this development naturally weighed heavily on the market'.[22] Ghanaian problems were compounded when their returned cocoa had to compete with other main crop Ghana Cocoa which was apparently being resold by an earlier purchaser.

The experiment in driving up main market prices by sending much of the crop to a European financial institution was clearly a failure, and President Nkrumah announced to Parliament that 'Cocoa which is our main foreign exchange earner will be sold strictly on hard cash basis and no longer on barter basis under bilateral commercial agreements with private financiers and intermediaries.' But, he quickly added,

> There is no question of abrogating our contractual obligations under the Trade and Payments Agreements which we have already signed. These will continue to be honoured and cocoa will continue to be shipped to our trade partners on a bilateral basis as already agreed.*

---

* Ghana, *Parliamentary Debates*, vol. 40, col. 34–5, 24 Aug 1965. Marshall I. Goldman in his important book, *Soviet Foreign Aid* (New York, Washington and London, 1967), appears to have made some confusion here. He states that 'There was some indication that just before his overthrow, President Nkrumah had finally realised the hazards in such a situation (Soviet bilateralism) and was trying to reduce such barter sales to Eastern Europe.' (p. 175). In fact, the barter sales he was trying to reduce were with W. Europe.

Having failed to persuade Europe to buy more, the government turned its attention to the U.S.S.R., and in December 1965 the Soviet Union agreed to purchase 150,000 tons over the following two years and to increase its annual intake to 118,000 tons by 1970.[23] Following this the Soviet Union announced in early 1966 that it had placed a $10 million contract for the supply of a new chocolate and cocoa powder producing plant with an overseas firm; the new factory was to have a daily capacity of 100 tons of goods packed and ready for sale.[24] After the 1966 *coup* which toppled Nkrumah, Ghanaian sales to the U.S.S.R. fell once more, although total Soviet cocoa imports remained substantially higher than they were in 1960.

The experience of Ghana throws light on the questions raised earlier, namely stability, price and bilateralism. Early work suggested that the U.S.S.R. provided a less stable market for the products of under-developed countries than did the West. This is a difficult question, because instability may result from the activities of either trade partner. Neuberger has analysed fourteen raw material exports from under-developed countries to the West and to the U.S.S.R. between 1955 and 1961. He found that the Soviet Union did not provide a more stable market : rather the reverse, and of the fourteen commodities the Soviet market for cocoa was one of the most unstable. Goodman has looked specifically at Ghana's cocoa for the years 1955–64. He also found the Soviet market to be much more unstable than Western markets. However, Hanson in 1971 analysed figures for a longer period, between 1955 and 1967, and found that the stability for the sub-period 1961–7 was much closer to that of the West than Neuberger's and Goodman's figures suggest.[25] The degree of instability that remains can adequately be explained by reference to the activities of the seller rather than to those of the buyer.

The issue of trade stability is an important one. One of the most pressing needs of many developing countries is to be able to predict with some degree of accuracy its likely future earnings. Stability in its pur-chases of cocoa comparable to that of the West is hardly a recommenda-tion for the Soviet Union, since the 1960's saw a period of great instability for that crop, but to have exhibited less stability than the West would have been a black mark against the U.S.S.R.

The next question is that of Soviet pricing. Table 2.11 gives the unit price paid by the U.S.S.R. and by other cocoa producers between 1960 and 1970. When comparing the average Soviet and world prices a great deal depends upon the time period used. If the whole decade is taken then the U.S.S.R. paid on average about $30 per ton less than other consumers. However, this figure is heavily affected by the years 1968 and 1969 when Ghana was not well disposed towards the U.S.S.R. and

TABLE 2.6   Average unit value of Ghanaian cocoa bean exports to U.S.S.R. and other consumers 1960–70

(1) Year	(2) *Quantity exported to U.S.S.R.*	(3) *Quantity exported to all other consumers*	(4) *Total value of exports to U.S.S.R.*	(5) *Total value of exports to all other consumers*
1960	34	269	14,544	116,256
1961	19	387	6,174	132,450
1962	25	398	8,680	125,366
1963	43	361	14,130	121,406
1964	33	349	11,946	124,530
1965	66	428	21,593	114,883
1966	55	336	17,241	85,816
1967	57	271	18,551	112,119
1968	28	301	11,074	174,526
1969	15	288	8,028	210,539
1970	48	349	40,863	259,535
TOTAL	423	3,737	172,824	1,577,426

Notes: (2) and (3) denominated in thousand long tons. (4) and (5) denominated in thousand new cedis.

Average unit value of Ghanaian cocoa exports to U.S.S.R. 1960–7 = (4) ÷ (2) = NC340.

Average unit value of Ghanaian cocoa exports to U.S.S.R. 1960–70 = (4) ÷ (2) = NC409.

Average unit value of Ghanaian cocoa exports to all other consumers 1960–7 = (5) ÷ (3) = NC332.

Average unit value of Ghanaian cocoa exports to all other consumers 1960–70 = (5) ÷ (3) = NC422.

Sources: Ghana, Central Bureau of Statistics, *Economic Survey 1962*, Table 2, *1968*, Table 24, *1969*, Table 24 (Accra, 1963, 1968, 1969); Ghana, Central Bureau of Statistics, *External Trade Statistics of Ghana*, vol. xx, no. 12 (Accra, Dec 1970).

sold to it only as a last resort and, presumably therefore, at a lower than average price. If only the year 1961–7 are taken, then the average price per long ton of exports to the U.S.S.R. is NC333 while the average price to all other destinations is NC328. The years 1961–7 are the period between the signing of the first payments agreement and the great decline in Ghanaian enthusiasm for selling to the U.S.S.R. that came after the fall of Nkrumah and the completion of deliveries under the 1965 cocoa deal.

However, by itself this average figure does not provide an adequate guide to the competitiveness of Soviet buying: it ignores the possibility that, for example, the U.S.S.R. purchased only nominal quantities of cocoa in the years when it had to pay more than the world average, and stocked up when it was paying less. This possibility can be taken into account by weighting the analysis by the quantity purchased. This is done in Table 2.6. The result is the same. If the whole period 1960–70 is taken and the total amount paid is divided by the total quantity purchased, then the U.S.S.R. is seen to pay less than all other consumers. If the period taken is 1961–7 then the Soviet Union pays more. The reason for the differences in Soviet competitiveness if measured over different time periods may be due to the policies of the supplier. It may also be due partly to Soviet prices lagging behind free market prices, possibly because they are based on the preceding year's price. Thus when the free market price is falling, as it was in 1961–5, the U.S.S.R. tends to pay better prices than other purchasers, but when the free market trend is upwards, as it was after 1967, the Soviets pay lower than average prices.

One further refinement must be introduced before the full advantages or disadvantages of the U.S.S.R. as a market for Ghanaian cocoa become apparent. The study thus far has considered average prices, but of more significance are marginal prices. The most important consideration for Ghana is whether the U.S.S.R. paid more or less than other purchasers would have paid for that amount of cocoa at that particular time (and time here may mean hour rather than day, and certainly means day rather than year). The answer to this question does not, unfortunately, appear in the statistical records. However, Ghana's export strategy in the 1961–6 period was such that a Soviet price that was rather lower than the world average could have been acceptable. Returning to the 1965 Soviet–Ghanaian cocoa deal, the price negotiated for the cocoa to be supplied immediately was substantially above that then prevailing on the free market and a figure of £172 per ton has been quoted, but it was below the level to which prices later rose. The Soviet Union has thus been criticised on the grounds that it bought cocoa when the price was low and not when it was high. However, it was inherent in the strategy adopted by the Ghanaian and Soviet governments that this should be so: the former sought to raise prices on the free market by removing some beans from circulation, first by seeking agreement among producers to withhold stocks, then by trying to sell its cocoa for 'non-conventional' uses, then to a European financial syndicate, and finally to the U.S.S.R. Only after the other possibilities had failed was the Soviet Union tried, and Ghana was able to claim with some justification that this last move had effected a rise in prices on the free market.[26] The strategy behind this and other deals was thus for the U.S.S.R. to increase purchases whenever the price was low in order to cause prices on the free market to rise. Naturally, therefore, the Soviet Union can be accused of buying while the going was good, and cutting back when prices rose, but it did so with the approval of the Ghana government. There is evidence that the full implications of the Ghanaian strategy were not understood by all in Ghana. The *Ghanaian Times*, for example, criticised the Soviet Union for adopting the same pricing strategy as the Western countries who were motivated by their 'desire to exploit'.[27] However, the U.S.S.R. was paying a higher price than it need have done, and, after all, the stated principle in Soviet international trade is that it should be mutually beneficial.[28] If the Soviet Union's reputation has been tarnished in some quarters as a result of this operation it will have been because of the extravagant nature of its own propaganda rather than because of what it actually did.

The evidence, from Ghana and elsewhere, is that Soviet negotiators drive as hard a bargain as they can but that there is no reason why they should be able to purchase at a lower price than the supplier could obtain elsewhere at the time of sale and for the actual goods in question, unless the supplier for some reason abandons its normal commercial principles. In the case of the 1965 cocoa deal Ghana had the last word since it actually held the cocoa : after the overthrow of Nkrumah's government and after the world price of cocoa had risen the authorities reverted to their old policy of giving priority to the West and in consequence the delivery of 150,000 tons had to be extended to more than three years. This caused the Soviet Union some consternation since it had to find alternative supplies to meet its planned levels of processing. Moreover, despite the Ghanaian strategy Soviet cocoa purchasers seem to have done no better over the period 1961–7 than they would had they increased their purchases by an equal amount each year. If we calculate an average rate of increase of straight line (least squares) trend values, the total expenditure of the Soviet Union on its Ghanaian cocoa can be compared to the hypothetical sum it would have spent had purchases been increased in a regular fashion from one year to the next (see Table 2.7). Unfortunately, this comparison can only be suggestive and speculative : We know how much the Soviet Union paid per ton for its cocoa, but we do not know if more cocoa would have been available at the same price, or whether had the U.S.S.R. purchased less it would have had to pay a different price per ton. The calculations in Table 2.7 assume that unit prices remain unchanged, but this is a very questionable assumption. Nevertheless, the similarity between the totals of columns (2) and (4) is striking.

If the U.S.S.R. did not greatly benefit from Ghana's strategy, the same should not be said for Ghana itself. During the period in question, Ghana's rivals, the other exporters of cocoa, increased their production of the crop and between 1960 and 1965 world exports of raw cocoa rose from 881,000 long tons to 1,286,000 long tons.[29] This rise in the total amount of cocoa exported had a depressing effect on prices. Thus, in

TABLE 2.7   Actual Soviet imports compared with trend imports

Year	(1) Actual Soviet cocoa imports from Ghana (thousand tons)	(2) Actual Soviet cocoa imports from Ghana (thousand $)	(3) Trend Soviet cocoa imports from Ghana (thousand tons)	(4) Trend Soviet cocoa imports from Ghana (thousand $)
1961	19	8,644	21·5	7,009
1962	25	12,152	28·5	9,918
1963	43	13,847	35·5	11,680
1964	33	11,707	42·6	15,421
1965	66	21,161	49·6	16,219
1966	55	16,896	56·6	17,716
1967	57	18,180	63·7	20,703
TOTAL	298	102,587	298	98,666

Note: (3) shows the size of Soviet imports each year had they increased along a straight line (least squares) trend.
Sources: Tables 2.5, 2.6.

order to maintain its total income Ghana had to increase its own exports and so match the falling unit returns by a rise in the quantity sold. Unfortunately, such an increase in exports would itself depress prices still further, and since Ghana is the major cocoa producer its actions strongly affect the market. By selling to the centrally planned economies, however, Ghana partially managed to break out of the vicious circle. During the period 1960–5 Ghana increased her sales, and her share of total exports rose from 34·4 per cent to 38·4 per cent. But if sales under bilateral payments agreements are excluded, then Ghana's share of total exports in 1965 is only 27 per cent.[30] To a certain extent, therefore, Ghana was able to have her cake and eat it too – she increased her total sales, but was also able to depress the amount of cocoa coming on to the free market. This argument only holds, of course, if sales made under bilateral payments agreements really did remove cocoa from circulation on the free market. While there is no doubt that Soviet imports of Ghanaian cocoa have grown during the 1960s, there have been accusations that these increases were more apparent than real because the Soviet Union re-exported the cocoa it purchased on to the free market. If true this would constitute an unfair practice since not only would it defeat the whole object of the exercise for Ghana, but as trade between the two countries was organised for most of the time on the basis of a bilateral clearing arrangement using non-convertible currency it would also have deprived Ghana of much needed foreign exchange.

The Ghana government was clearly worried lest this sort of thing should occur and several trade agreements be concluded with the Soviet bloc specifically prohibiting the resale of cocoa.

Unfortunately, no definitive statement can be made on this question. The only clear indication of whether the Soviet Union re-exported cocoa beans is to be found by comparing the figures for imports and grindings of beans. Since the main concern here is the resale on to the free market, trade among the centrally planned economies is acceptable and Table 2.8 therefore gives the imports and grindings of the U.S.S.R. and Eastern Europe (excluding Yugoslavia) for the period 1960–70 as we may assume that the policies of these countries are the most strongly co-ordinated of the centrally planned economies. Table 2.8 shows that the shortfall of grindings in relation to imports is quite negligible and

TABLE 2.8   Soviet and Eastern Europe imports and grindings of cocoa beans 1960–70

Year	(1) Imports	(2) Grindings	(3) Imports minus grindings	(4) Cumulative difference	(5) Re-exports
1960	92	71	21	—	8
1961	60	79	−19	2	5
1962	91	89	2	4	3
1963	106	106	0	4	—
1964	124	121	3	7	—
1965	156	134	22	29	—
1966	123	148	−25	4	—
1967	155	160	− 5	− 1	—
1968	190	176	14	13	—
1969	173	170	3	16	—
1970	172	188	−16	0	—

Note: 1 unit = 1,000 long tons.
Sources: Gill & Duffus Ltd, *Cocoa Market Report*, no. 241; F.A.O., *World Cocoa Statistics*, vol. 14, no. 3, vol. 9, no. 3.

that the Soviet Union has only admitted to re-exporting cocoa beans between 1960 and 1962. The difference between imports and grindings is well within the limit of reasonable stocks; during the 1960s the stocks of all consumers averaged around 30 per cent of grindings,[31] and even in 1965 the shortfall of Soviet and Eastern European grindings over imports does not approach this figure. However the figures on Soviet grindings are not necessarily reliable, and the evidence presented here does not rule out the possibility that the U.S.S.R. processed the beans and exported the cocoa butter it produced. This practice would not be contrary to the letter of the trade agreement, and there have been accusations that it occurred, but while such things may have taken place it seems improbable that they did so on any large scale since although cocoa butter is the most sought-after product of the cocoa bean international trade in it is fairly small, as the major consumers produce their own butter. What seems to have been the case is that in the early years after Ghana's independence the Soviet Union possessed only a small capacity to process cocoa and was reluctant to import it; when Ghana pressed her to do so she agreed but may have resold some of the beans on the free market. During the 1960s, however, the U.S.S.R. has increased its capacity for grinding cocoa by 300 per cent, and there seems no reason to doubt that, in general, it now has a *bona fide* interest in the crop. At the same time the Soviet Union's intake of cocoa has on occasion exceeded the planned level of consumption and some cocoa butter may have been re-exported. The Soviet Union is now the second largest consumer of cocoa in the world, while Soyuzplodimport, the all-Union foreign trade organisation responsible for importing it, is the world's largest single buyer. In 1960 the Soviet Union conducted 3 per cent of total world grindings; in 1972 it conducted 9 per cent.[32]

THE INSTITUTIONAL FRAMEWORK AND THE PROBLEM OF BILATERALISM
Thus far, the questions of the stability of Soviet markets and Soviet pricing have been considered; there remains the problem of barter trade. The growing demands of Russian consumers are, of course, an important factor in explaining the expansion of Soviet cocoa imports but they are only a necessary not a sufficient factor. Russian consumers have many demands, not all of which can or have been satisfied at once; the decision to satisfy their demands by increasing the availability of chocolate was in part taken as a result of the promotional role of the Ghana government. One reason advanced by Ghanaians and others for their success is that the trade was, after 1961, conducted on the basis of a bilateral payments agreement under which trade was paid for in non-convertible currency.[33] It is also a stated principle of Soviet foreign trade that preference is given to bilateral pact countries, and Oleg Hoeffding's work on attempts by the U.S.S.R. to achieve a balance in its trade accounts with the non-Communist world between 1963 and 1965 suggests that imports purchased on a barter basis are less likely to be cut back in a balance of payments crisis than are hard currency imports.[34] The evidence of Ghanaian cocoa would certainly bear this out, for it was during the 1963–5 Soviet trade crisis that the U.S.S.R. agreed to a substantial increase in its imports.

Foreign trade in the U.S.S.R. is a state monopoly, a provision that is incorporated into the constitution,[35] and the state exercises its control through a hierarchy of institutions surmounted by the council of ministers and its state planning committee. These two bodies concern themselves only with major problems and delegate the drafting and co-ordination of the foreign trade plan to the ministry of foreign trade. Usually the foreign trade plan is broken down into the import and export plans which are then established in terms of the values to be realised in foreign exchange so that the balance of payments is in equilibrium. These plans are closely co-ordinated with national production plans, material inputs, retail trade and investment plans, etc.[36]

It seems generally true to say that the import plan is the primary element and the export plan essentially an indication of the means available for financing required imports. Beneath the ministry of foreign trade are over fifty all-Union foreign trade organisations which conduct the actual operations of trade and are each responsible for a specified range of commodities. These are the organisations that negotiate directly with the developing countries for the purchase or sale of goods. They obtain imports for Soviet customers on a commission basis and are contractors for Soviet producers for the export of their goods. Most important, from our point of view, they are generally expected to operate on normal commercial principles taking into account price, quality, delivery and payment terms, etc.

While trade can and has occurred between the U.S.S.R. and African countries in the absence of any bilateral legal regulation, it is normally sporadic and at a low level. At the very least, the U.S.S.R. and other Eastern European countries normally wish to conclude bilateral trade agreements which regulate the legal basis of trade, determine the method of payment (normally convertible currency), establish that with the exception of regional arrangements trade will be on a most favoured nation basis, and give an indication to either side of what is potentially available for trade, a point that is obviously important for the centrally planned economies when drafting their foreign trade plans. Such agreements, though they have appended to them a list of commodities available for export, do not in any way bind either side to sell the goods listed therein or refrain from trading in commodities not so listed. From the African point of view they have some political value in that they indicate to African traders that their government approves of the principle of trade with socialist countries. Such approval is by no means of negligible importance in countries where the government is, or has been, hostile to other relations with the U.S.S.R.

Some developing countries have gone one step further in the institutionalisation of trade with the centrally planned economies and have adopted payments agreements. These specify that the central banks of the two countries shall open accounts with each other denominated in a non-convertible clearing unit and that settlements of trade, within certain limits, will be made by debiting one account and crediting the other with the amount involved. The monetary limits within which this system operates, known as the swing credit, are normally stated as are the means by which any imbalance exceeding this level is to be dealt with.* If this last point is left vague it could give rise to difficulties, and so many agreements specify in detail what is to be done. The long-term payments agreement between Hungary and Ghana of 21 November 1961, for example, specifies that imbalances above the swing credit of £G200,000 are to be settled within three months by the delivery of goods and, if still outstanding in a further three months, by payments of convertible currency. In Somalia, where a hybrid form of bilateralism is in operation, convertible currency and goods are specified.[37] Most agreements also carry a gold parity clause to safeguard either side against changes in the rate of exchange of the clearing unit.

A further sophistication is agreement on a trade protocol specifying the quantity of goods to be exchanged similar to that concluded by the U.S.S.R. and Ghana in 1961 (see above). In 1963 this procedure was extended by a protocol that listed the quantities or value £G4.2 million worth of Soviet machinery and equipment and over thirty other goods to be exchanged during that year in order to increase Ghanaian imports from the U.S.S.R.[38] This practice is not widely developed in Black Africa but has been used for the export of Ghanaian cocoa, Guinean bauxite and Somali canned meat.[39]

THE ADVANTAGES OF BILATERALISM

The advantages of such payment arrangements for the Soviet Union and Eastern Europe are that they accord more closely with the set procedures for trade amongst themselves in C.M.E.A. which still forms the bulk of their total trade, that they permit forward planning, and that they save on convertible currency. The last two advantages have also been said to apply to developing countries where fluctuations in primary product prices may wreak havoc with a development plan and where the lion's share of the countries' external assets are normally consumed in working balances for foreign trade (which being on current account earn no interest) and confidence balances (earning a mean return probably somewhat less than that obtainable from development capital formation). However, since trade with the centrally planned economies does not in many cases form a high proportion of total trade, or therefore of

* An indication of the size of these swing credits may be obtained from those granted to Ghana: Albania £G30,000; Bulgaria £G500,000; China (P.R.C.) £G4 million; Czechoslovakia £G250,000; Dahomey £G500,000; G.D.R. £G,500,000; Guinea £G500,000; Hungary £G200,000; Israel £G200,000; Mali £G357,000; Polansd £G500,000; U.A.R. £G100,000; Upper Volta £G500,000; U.S.S.R. £G4 million; Yugoslavia £G350,000. B. A. Konu, Ghana, *Parliamentary Debates*, 5 Feb 1965, vol. 38, col. 750.

total export earnings, the value of bilateral payments for advanced planning is limited. So also is their value as a saver of foreign currency: since the Soviet Union and other centrally planned economies mainly import from the developing countries products which would otherwise have been sold on the free market for convertible currency any savings in hard currency effected by a payments agreement will be offset by a corresponding loss of hard earnings.

This does mean that bilateral trade has no advantages for developing countries. One small point is that it may be possible to make liberal use of the swing credit and run an import surplus; so long as this is kept within the swing limits the goods so imported are obtained at no real cost. The amounts involved are not large, but neither are they negligible: in the case of the 1961 Ghana-Soviet payments agreement, for example, the swing credit was set at £G4 million. However, the major value of bilateral clearing lies in its trade creating potential. Unfortunately, no definitive answer may be given to the question of whether the signing of bilateral payments agreements with the U.S.S.R. is likely to have a significant effect on a developing country's trade. All that may be given is the circumstancial evidence of Soviet statements and historical trends.[40]

At the end of 1968 the Soviet Union had bilateral clearing arrangements with Afghanistan, Algeria, Brazil, Cambodia, Ceylon, Cuba, Cyprus, Ghana, Guinea, India, Iran, Lebanon, Mali, Morocco, Nepal, Pakistan, Somalia, Syria, Tunisia, Egypt, and Yugoslavia, and in the period 1960–7 60 per cent of its total trade with developing countries was conducted with this group.[41] This same feature of giving priority to bilateral partners can be seen in Africa by reference to Table 2.2*a* : of the Soviet Union's major African trade partners only Nigeria and Sudan do not have bilateral clearing arrangements. This does not necessarily mean that bilateralism causes increased trade. The observed correlation between the two could arise because the bilateral pact states have been the most energetic in promoting trade. Although the Sudan and Nigeria are the only exceptions to the observed link, together they form a major exception. On the other hand they are both important countries, particularly Nigeria, which the U.S.S.R. cannot ignore; the same is not true for Somalia, Guinea, Mali or even Ghana. In view of the U.S.S.R.'s stated preference for bilateral payments there is a *prima facie* case in favour of a small African country which wishes to develop its trade in an Easterly direction concluding one, provided that there are no major disadvantages in doing so.

THE PROBLEM OF BILATERALISM

However, many would argue that there are major disadvantages in so doing.[42] It has been objected that bilateral trade between the Soviet Union and the underdeveloped countries is not conducted between equals and that the latter suffer in consequence. This is usually stated in relation to Soviet pricing policy and is not always valid, but in another sense it is valid: the U.S.S.R. is the product of centuries of centralised rule and currently possesses a highly organised economy based on a long tradition of state-directed development; the developing countries, by contrast, are in the main characterised by weak governments, a colonial tradition that has not emphasised active state participation in productive relations, and a civil service educated in this tradition. With the exception of southern Somalia, which was colonised by the Italians, bilateral trade has shallow roots in Africa. As a result, trade has not always operated according to plan; while (as with the non-deliveries of Ghanaian cocoa after the 1966 *coup*) this has on occasion been to the disadvantage of the U.S.S.R., more often it has been to that of the developing countries.

The case of Ghana exemplifies particularly well the organisational problems associated with such agreements. One advantage to a developing country of clearing arrangements is that it may be possible to obtain credit from the swing balance, but in the event the first years of bilateral trading between Ghana and the U.S.S.R., far from seeing the former extract aid from the latter, witnessed the reverse; Ghana ran an export surplus. In December 1962 the balance on the bilateral clearing account with Russia was £G2·8 million, in December 1963 it was £G2 million, in June 1964 £G3·8 million, and in June 1965 £G1·2 million.[43] The figures for June 1964 and 1965 overstate the credit because Ghana's main export, cocoa, is sent during the first two quarters of the year, while the foreign trade organisations of the Soviet Union tend to cram their business into the latter half of the year as plan fulfilment target dates approach. Nevertheless, while within the swing credit margins, the surplus is, to say the least, unfortunate. In part, it was due to the inefficiency of Soviet exporters, who generally lacked finesse in their techniques and were unprepared to alter them to suit the Ghanaians. One particular complaint was that consignments arrived unintelligibly labelled or not labelled at all, and delivery dates were not kept. An indication of the problems experienced is to be found in the Joint Recommendations made by the two governments on the occasion of their negotiations for a commodity credit agreement; Article 5 of the Joint Recommendations states:

In compliance with the wishes expressed by the representatives of the Ministry of Finance and Trade, the Bank of Ghana and the National Chamber, the Ministry for Foreign Trade of the U.S.S.R. shall see to it that the U.S.S.R. foreign trade associations take measure to the effect that:
(a) despatch of commercial and shipping documents to be made that

they would be in the hands of the Ghanaian organisations and firms not later than 5 to 10 days prior to the arrival of the goods at a Ghanaian port;

(b) delivery of goods bought by Ghanaian organisations and firms be so effected that they should arrive in Ghana within the period of validity of the corresponding import licence;

(c) replies to enquiries received from Ghanaian organisations and firms in connection with purchases of Soviet commodities be despatched as soon as possible;

(d) wrapping and packing of exported commodities be improved to meet the requirements of the Ghana market;

(e) all machines and technical goods delivered to Ghana be provided with relative descriptive literature in English;

(f) all consumer goods delivered to Ghana be provided with labels in English.[44]

However, matters clearly did not improve to the complete satisfaction of the Ghanaians and in 1965, for example, in reply to accusations that the Ghana National Trading Corporation was responsible for the shortages of some consumer goods, the managing director, Sir Patrick Fitz-Gerald, claimed that the delays were caused by the improper shipment methods of suppliers in the Eastern countries; he explained that goods which were scheduled to arrive in September, October and November actually arrived in port in December 1964. There were then delays because the suppliers, instead of invoicing goods item by item, always grouped various goods together in one case and as a result customs officials took much longer than normal to sanction deliveries.[45] Nevertheless, the faults were not all one-sided, for Article 2 of the Joint Recommendations requests the Bank of Ghana and the Commercial Bank of Ghana to ensure that 'monies paid in respect of imports from the U.S.S.R. are promptly transferred'.

These administrative problems were exacerbated because the U.S.S.R. at first attempted to persuade Ghana to accept large quantities of equipment. Soviet equipment has not fared well in tropical conditions and there are numerous problems associated with importing it, such as ensuring that there are instructions in English, that there are spare parts, and that the machinery is appropriate to the problems in hand. However, machinery now forms only a small part of Ghana's imports from the U.S.S.R., partly because a more acceptable medium of exchange – oil – has been found, and partly because there are no ongoing Soviet development projects (see Table 2.9).

An associated problem is that of prices: even if both sides have goods which the other desires, bilateralism will function smoothly only if the price at which they are offered is mutually acceptable. When trade is

TABLE 2.9   Percentage share of commodities in S.I.T.C. categories 6, 7 and
8 in the total imports of five African States from the U.S.S.R., over time

Country	S.I.T.C. categories 6, 7 & 8 as a % of total imports from U.S.S.R.		
	1965	*1968*	*1970*
Ghana	56	—	6
Nigeria	69	—	62
Sudan	22	—	43
Tunisia	46	36	—
U.A.R.	43	28	—

Source: Calculated from U.N. Economic Commission for Africa, *Foreign Trade Statistics of Africa Series B*, vols 11–13, 18–22.

paid for in convertible currency it matters little if one side is thought to overprice its products – the aggrieved party has received cash for its exports and can go elsewhere for its imports. Under bilateral trade, however, exports are paid for by one side by appropriate shipments of its own goods; a debtor may, therefore, hold his creditor to ransom, 'either pay the price I ask or forgo the proceeds from your exports!' One scholar, J. R. Carter, has calculated the unit cost of Soviet exports to the industrialised Western countries and to the developing countries in 1958 and 1965, and has concluded that for forty-three items sold in both sets of countries those purchased by the developing countries were 14·9 per cent in 1958 and 13·1 per cent in 1965 more expensive than those bought by the Western countries. This surcharge was particularly marked in the case of machinery and equipment, being 22·6 per cent in 1958 and 34·7 per cent in 1965.[46] Such indexes are interesting and helpful in the study of Soviet pricing techniques, but they are not directly relevant to the question in hand; what concerns policy makers in the developing countries is not whether they pay more for Soviet goods than do the Western countries, since if they do it may be the result of a deliberate lowering of prices to the latter rather than from an inflation of prices to them, but whether Soviet goods are cheaper or more expensive than equivalent Western products. This is not a simple question, for although the stated principle of trade between the U.S.S.R. and the developing countries is that the prices of goods should conform to world market prices, such a 'world market price' is a most ephemeral concept: prices vary from one 'main world market' to another and there is, of course, the problem of comparing commodities; even some raw materials are by no means homogenous. The difficulty of comparison is particularly marked in the case of manufactured goods, and according to Carter's figures Soviet price inflation is most severe here. An attempt will be made when considering Soviet aid projects to determine the cost and quality of Soviet machinery, since most has been imported as part of Soviet aid deliveries. However, it is not only in Ghana that such goods have formed a diminishing proportion of imports from the U.S.S.R., as may be seen by reference to Table 2.9. The trend in trade between the two continents is for more emphasis to be put on articles in S.I.T.C. categories 0–5. In view of this trend Table 2.10 gives the unit price paid by several African countries for a variety of goods which are of fairly consistent quality, in a number of years since independence. Not surprisingly Soviet and world prices have never been identical for the years and commodities considered and, on occasion, the Soviet product has been the more expensive. However, in the majority of instances Soviet prices have been competitive, and extremely attractive in the cases of sunflower seed oil supplied to Kenya in 1968 and fuel oil bought by Somalia in 1967. The figures for crude petroleum are particularly significant since it is currently Ghana's largest import from the U.S.S.R., and it is the most important raw material sold abroad by the Soviet Union and its second most important means of payment after machinery and equipment.[47] On the other hand there are instances of the Soviet Union charging far more than other suppliers as, for example, in 1963 when Mali paid $200 per ton for Soviet sugar and only $145 per ton for its other supplies, although over the six-year period for which figures are available it did not do badly. There is also evidence that the Soviet Union has been charging above the world price for its supplies of white tin to the Las Koreh fish processing factory and the Kisimayo meat canning factory, both in Somalia, which were established and are currently operated with Soviet assistance.[48]

Allegations have also been made that the Soviet Union systematically paid less for African exports than did the Western countries.* Again there is little point comparing the price paid by the U.S.S.R. for its imports from developing countries and from the West because, when the same commodity is involved, the Western supplies will often have come originally from a developing country via one or more third parties who will, of course, take a commission and so raise the price. The most relevant comparison is of the unit price paid by Soviet and other purchasers to a particular African state. The competitive price paid by Soviet importers of Ghanaian cocoa has already been noted above, and in Table 2.11 three other primary products, Nigerian cocoa, Tanzanian sisal and Mali's groundnuts, have been considered; in each case the commodity represents the most important single export of the country con-

---

* J. R. Carter, *Cost of Soviet Aid*, estimates that the Soviet Union pays 15 per cent less than the world market price, although he admits that there are difficulties in making such calculations. See also Oliver von Gajzago, *Der Sowjetische Aussenhandel mit den Entwicklungs Ländern*, Deutsches Institut für Wirtschaftsforschung, vol. 1959, no. 4 (Berlin), p. 435, cited by K. Billerbeck. *Soviet Bloc Foreign Aid to the Underdeveloped Countries: An analysis and a prognosis*, Hamburg Archives of World Economy, mimeo. (1960), p. 39.

TABLE 2.10   Unit prices paid by four African countries for selected imports from the U.S.S.R., in a number of years

a   Ghana – imports of cement (S.I.T.C. 661 200) (£G per ton)

Year	Imports from U.S.S.R.	All other imports
1960	7·65	8·20
1961	7·40	8·05
1962	5·65	6·60
1963	5·25	5·80
1964	6·05	6·55
AVERAGE	6·40	7·04

b   Ghana – imports of crude petroleum (S.I.T.C. 313 010) (new pesewas per gallon)

Year	Imports from U.S.S.R.	All other imports
1967	4·1	5·2
1968	7·1	6·1
1969	7·3	8·2
1970	7·0	6·6
AVERAGE	6·4	6·5

c   Kenya – imports of refined sugar, etc. (S.I.T.C. 061 20) (£ per cental)

Year	Imports from U.S.S.R.	All other imports
1965	1·27	1·32
1966	1·26	1·25
AVERAGE	1·27	1·29

d   Kenya – imports of sunflower seed oil (S.I.T.C. 421 600) (£ per cental)

Year	Imports from U.S.S.R.	All other imports
1967	13	14·5
1968	3·8	12·4
1969	4·5	4·4
AVERAGE	7·1	10·4

e   Mali – imports of sugar etc.
(S.I.T.C. 061 20) ($ per ton)

Year	Imports from U.S.S.R.	All other imports
1962	141	159
1963	200	145
1964	184	189
1965	174	173
1966	216	135
1967*	131	216
AVERAGE	174	170

f   Mali – imports of mueslin and wheat flour
(S.I.T.C. 046 01) ($ per ton)

Year	Imports from U.S.S.R.	All other imports
1964	79	66
1965	90	107
1966	100	96
1967	124	333
AVERAGE	98	150

g   Somalia – imports of fuel oils
(specific gravity less than 0·88 at 15 °C.)
(S.I.T.C. 332 31)
(So Sh per kg.)

Year	Imports from U.S.S.R.	All other imports
1967	0·070	0·366
1968	0·180	0·283
1969	0·204	0·141
1970	0·178	0·221
AVERAGE	0·158	0·253

Note: *1967 – Mali's imports were S.I.T.C. 061 – sugar and honey.
Sources: *a Annual Report on External Trade Statistics of Ghana*, vol. I, Central Bureau of Statistics (Accra, 1959–60, 1961–3, 1964–5).
   b External Trade Statistics of Ghana, Central Bureau of Statistics (Accra, Dec 1967–70).
   c & d East African Customs and Excise, *Annual Trade Report of Kenya, Uganda and Tanganyika* (Nairobi, 1965–9).
   e European Community Statistical Office, *République du Mali, Yearbook 1959–1966* (1969).
   f European Community Statistical Office, *Foreign Trade*, no. 5 (1968).
   g Somali Foreign Trade Statistics (Mogadishu, 1967–1970).

cerned to the U.S.S.R. None of these figures are wholly reliable because there are variations in quality and variations depending upon the time

TABLE 2.11 Unit prices paid by the U.S.S.R. for selected imports from four African countries in a number of years

a   Ghana – exports of cocoa
(S.I.T.C. 072 1) (NC per long ton)

Year	Exports to U.S.S.R.	All other exports
1960	428	440
1961	326	342
1962	348	316
1963	329	337
1964	362	356
1965	327	274
1966	313	256
1967	325	415
1968	395	580
1969	535	730
1970	851	825
AVERAGE 1960–70	413	443
AVERAGE 1961–7	333	328

b   Nigeria – exports of cocoa
(S.I.T.C. 072 1) ($ per ton)

Year	Exports to U.S.S.R.	Exports elsewhere
1964	538	560
1965	557	456
1966	—	—
1967	700	207
1968	720	690
1969	907	829
1970	1,041	952
AVERAGE	744	616

c Mali – exports of groundnuts
(S.I.T.C. 221 12) ($ per ton)

Year	Exports to U.S.S.R.	Exports elsewhere
1962	104	103
1963	—	—
1964	108	165
1965	101	101
AVERAGE	104	123

d Tanganyika – exports of sisal (S.I.T.C. 265 41)
(£ per ton)

Year	Exports to U.S.S.R.	Exports elsewhere
1964	117	108
1965	85	70
1966	66	67
1967	60	51
1968	57	43
1969	63	55
1970	53	50
1971	49	46
AVERAGE	69	61

Sources: *a. Ghana Economic Survey* (1962, 1968, 1969), and *External Trade Statistics of Ghana*, Central Bureau of Statistics, vol. xx, no. 12 (Accra, 1970).
b. U.N. Economic Commission for Africa, *Foreign Trade Statistics Series B*, no. 9, 11, 13, 16, 17; *Nigeria Trade Summary*, Nigerian Federal Office of Statistics (Lagos, Dec 1969, Dec 1970).
c. European Commission Statistical Office, *République du Mali Yearbook 1959–66* (1969).
d. East African Customs and Excise, *Annual Trade Report of Tanganyika, Uganda and Kenya* (Nairobi, 1964–71).

of purchase, but they are nevertheless valuable as general indicators of Soviet competitiveness. Both Nigeria and Tanzania have struck very good bargains with the U.S.S.R. On the other hand Mali has not done so well, and there is also evidence that the Russians have made use of their monopoly position as, until recently, the only foreign consumer of the canned meat produced at the Kisimayo meat processing factory in Somalia, and have been paying less than the cost of production for their imports.[49]

From these admittedly limited examples there is no observable trend to suggest a deliberate Soviet policy of over- or under-pricing. On the contrary, prices seem to be very much a product of individual bargaining. Harking back to the anomaly of the Ghanaian trade surplus in the early years of bilateralism, it does not appear as if Soviet pricing policy can be held responsible for the difficulty. Perhaps it should be emphasised that Ghana's experience was indeed anomalous in the sense of being an exception to the general experience of Russia's bilateral trade partners in the developing countries. Table 2.12 gives total Soviet imports and

TABLE 2.12   Soviet trade with developing countries 1960–7, classified by 'payments agreement' and 'non-payments agreement' blocs (US$ million f.o.b.)

	Soviet exports	Soviet imports	Total trade
Payments agreement partners	7,790·2	4,045·6	11,835·8
Non-payments agreement partners	3,505·9	4,355·1	7,861·0
TOTAL	11,296·1	8,400·7	

Notes: Soviet exports to payments agreement countries as a % of total Soviet trade with them = 65·6 per cent.

Soviet exports to non-payments agreement countries as % of total Soviet trade with them = 44·5 per cent

Source: Calculated from *Approaches to multilateral settlements in trade between the socialist and developing countries,* study prepared by the Institute for Economic and Market Research (Budapest), for the U.N.C.T.A.D. Secretariat, doc. no. TD/B/AC 7/3, Annex II, Table I.

exports from and to the developing countries with which it has payment agreements and those with which it does not. The former group, far from being characterised by a trade surplus with the Soviet Union, in fact experienced the reverse.

Other explanations for Ghana's shortfall of imports are that Soviet products were unfamiliar to conservative Ghanaian importers and consumers, and that import licences were issued inefficiently. An attempt was made to overcome the former problem when the Ghana National Trading Corporation was established 'In order to make full use of these [bilateral] agreements . . .'[50] This was fairly successful although the 1963

Economic Survey still complained that unfamiliarity with their products was one of the factors exerting a downward pull on imports from the bilateral pact countries.[51] Soviet difficulties should, however, be viewed in their context since Ghanaian consumers are noted for both their sophistication and their conservatism.*

The problem of the imbalance of Ghanaian–Soviet trade was made worse because the government lacked the necessary statistical information with which to prepare an adequate plan for increasing consumption. The Abraham Commission of Enquiry into Trade Malpractices in Ghana reported that

> We regret to say that trade statistics and data available for research and planning in the country are either non-existent or unsuitably combined. From the moment when goods enter this country to the time when they are offered to consumers, the Government knows very little about what happens;

it concluded that 'Policies concerning the flow of goods are therefore exercised somewhat in the dark.'[52] The lack of an adequate administrative and planning mechanism initially hindered the issuance of imports licences. In February 1963 preferential licensing was introduced and incorporated into a trade agreement with the U.S.S.R.[53] whereby a list of eight commodities, accounting for 7 per cent of total imports was compiled. These commodities were to be imported only from bilateral trading partners and were chosen because these countries were thought to be competitive in them. In addition, there was a list of twenty-eight commodities, accounting for 10 per cent of total imports, and it was decreed that not less than 20 per cent of imports of these goods should come from bilateral partners. However, these regulations were difficult to enforce and the situation was made worse by the tardiness with which licences were issued. The 1964 *Economic Survey* noted that it had not always been possible to 'issue the licenses in such a way as to enable business enterprises to have time to organise and plan their activities'. It continued, 'This is of special significance as far as trade with the Centrally Planned Economies is concerned because these countries need to

* The latter quality has been felt not only by the centrally planned economies. The G.N.T.C. attempted in the 1960s to introduce a perfectly respectable West German brand of tinned milk but found that for a long time many Ghanaians preferred to pay higher prices at the local market for the products with which they were familiar. The Americans have also fallen foul of the Ghanaian consumer: they sent maize under the PL 480 Programme but unfortunately it was yellow maize, the variety consumed most often in Europe and North America; the Ghanaians prefer white maize, the variety found most often in Africa, and in consequence the food could not even be given away and had, eventually, to be used for animal fodder. N. Uphoff, *Ghana's Experience in Using External Aid for Development 1957–1966: Implications for Development Theory and Policy.* Institute of International Studies (Berkeley, California, 1970), ch. 6, note 97.

be told well in advance what items and in what quantities the country will be importing from them.'[54] This was particularly important in the case of the Soviet Union, because if the notice given was too short the order would nevertheless be accepted as if everything was all right; however, the goods would simply not arrive. In 1964 a new list of thirty-five commodities replaced the two previous lists. Quotas for the listed goods were specified for each particular bilateral partner, and import licences were to be issued accordingly, and to be given for similar goods from non-bilateral sources only if it was found impossible to import them from bilateral countries. The amount set for import from bilateral sources in 1964 was 23 per cent of expected imports, as compared with 14 per cent of total imports in 1963 and 11 per cent in 1962. In order to overcome the problem of timing, Ghanaian import licensing procedures were adjusted so that licences were to be issued at the beginning of each year. None the less, in 1965 the administration of import licences became so bad that in mid-year all licences were revoked when it was learned that already licences for one-sixth more than the total foreign exchange allocations for the year had been issued.[55] Nevertheless, the target set out in the foreign exchange budget of 1965, which anticipated an import surplus with all bilaterial countries of £G8·5 million, was exceeded when the actual import surplus proved to be £G12·4 million. In the case of the U.S.S.R. trade was in equilibrium that year,* and according to the Ghanaian government there were good prospects for further improvements: the minister of finance told parliament that

> Following negotiations conducted in recent months between the Government and a number of socialist countries there are clear indications that we can import in 1966 as much as £G40 million worth of consumer and capital goods from our bilateral trade partners. Against this it is planned to export about £G28 million to these countries thus making available to us a net total credit of about £G12 million from this source.[56]

Unfortunately, we cannot know if this prediction would have been vindicated: two days after this speech was made the government of Kwame Nkrumah was overthrown and the new government suspended all trade and payments agreements concluded with the Eastern socialist countries and the People's Republic of China with a view to reviewing them all in the light of Ghana's interests. In the event, only those with Albania, the People's Republic of China and also Guinea were can-

---

* According to Ghanaian statistics, imports from the U.S.S.R. were slightly less than exports in 1965. See K. Amoaka-Atta, Ghana, *Parliamentary Debates*, vol. 43, col. 655, 22 Feb 1966. According to Soviet statistics, Ghana's imports from the U.S.S.R. were slightly larger than her exports to the U.S.S.R. in that year. This viewpoint is reflected in Table 2.2*a* above.

celled,[57] but relations with the centrally planned economies were strained, no attempt was made to extract aid from the swing credits, and Open General Licences, which could not be used to encourage trade with particular countries, were gradually introduced. In 1969 the new civilian government decided that all bilateral agreements, with the exception of that with the U.S.S.R., should be allowed to lapse when they came up for renewal.[58] The one with the U.S.S.R. was to be retained presumably because it worked relatively simply by bartering cocoa for crude petroleum. However, the government of Ghana changed yet again on 13 January 1972 as a result of a military *coup d'état*. The new government has expressed an interest in renewing bilateral payments agreements with Eastern Europe for much the same reasons as prompted the Nkrumah government.[59]

SETTLEMENT OF BALANCES

In cases where one party to a payments agreement acquires a permanent imbalance, an army of enterprising dealers come on to the scene and buy the clearing currencies at a high discount, take over unwanted goods, find new markets for them and supply the other parties with goods from new sources. This activity is of dubious legality, throws a bad light on the official agreement, and results in high profits (up to 15 per cent of the volume of trade) for the arbitrageurs at the expense of the bilateral partner.[60] To avoid this and interest new countries in bilateral payments agreements, the countries of Eastern Europe have been considering the possibility of multilateral clearing arrangements among payments agreements countries. The triangular settlements of balances may, in principle, be brought about in two different ways: either three countries settle certain deliveries of goods in a triangular fashion on the basis of a prior (*ex ante*) agreement and country A then ships goods to B which sends an equivalent value to C and C to A; or three given countries of whom A has a clearing asset with B and a clearing liability with C agree (*ex post*) that B will pay to C the corresponding amount. In 1966 Cuba made use of the first form of agreement to utilise $24 million of a loan from the Soviet Union to purchase sugar refining equipment from East Germany,[61] while India made use of the second form of agreement in early 1969 when the rupee balances of Bulgaria and Czechoslovakia were transferred to Hungary and East Germany in return for goods sent in the reverse direction.[62]

The C.M.E.A. countries themselves have a system of multilateral settlement which operates through the institution of the Bank of International Economic Co-operation (I.B.E.C.) and the medium of the transferable rouble. I.B.E.C. was created in 1963 on the suggestion of the U.S.S.R. and began operations in January 1964. Members of I.B.E.C. do not have to be in balance with each of their bilateral partners, but only with all their partners taken together. If one member is in surplus with another it builds up a balance of transferable roubles at I.B.E.C. and if in deficit it can be given a short-term credit. The transferable rouble was created at the same time as I.B.E.C. It has the same gold value as the domestic rouble and like the domestic rouble it is not convertible outside Comecon, but unlike the domestic rouble it is convertible within Comecon. Although Article IX of the charter of I.B.E.C. states that other countries may associate themselves with it, and although I.B.E.C. officials have themselves suggested that other states make use of its multilateral clearing, its membership is limited to the members of Comecon.[63] This reticence may be because the developing countries fear that when their debts are transferred they will have to settle with the new partner in 'harder' goods or at a lower price than before, coupled with a belief when they are the creditor party, that the other socialist countries do not have products they want. Another means of settling imbalances that has received more support is for the Soviet Union to agree to accept repayments in kind for economic and technical assistance loans; any export surplus in the African country's balance of trade with the U.S.S.R. can then be used to offset its own liabilities. This procedure has now been incorporated into a number of aid agreements.

THE FUTURE

The future of bilateral trade is obscured by controversy, but while this is so it seems hardly open to doubt that trade either on a bilateral or a multilateral basis between the U.S.S.R. and Africa will increase. The current five-year plans of the Eastern European countries provide for a rapid increase in trade (see Table 2.13). The report of the central committee to the twenty-fourth congress of the C.P.S.U. (1971) notes that more emphasis will have to be put on foreign trade if the Soviet economy is to grow at the desired rate and states that 'additional stress is being given to the need for stability in foreign economic and trade relations, to long-term arrangements and to the harmonisation of economic plans with other countries.'[64]

The emphases in the plans of Eastern Europe are on importing modern equipment, machinery and instruments, and satisfying consumer demands, with an ambivalant attitude towards food and raw materials: on the one hand there is a substantial effort in Eastern Europe to overcome their deficit in some raw materials by joint action, but on the other hand there is a growing awareness that in some commodities importing would be more profitable. In the U.S.S.R. the twenty-fourth C.P.S.U. congress stressed the need to improve the structure of exports, and highly profitable machines and equipment are to take the lead while less profitable products will gradually be dropped from export lists. Methods have now been devised for assessing to some degree the profitability of exports and imports and there is a growing awareness that, in the current drive for efficiency, an orderly pricing system reflecting costs is essential.

All this suggests that trade with the developed market economies will take the lion's share of any increase in trade but that there will be good scope for gains in trade with the developing countries. If trade is henceforth to be put on a more business-like footing this is not necessarily to

TABLE 2.13　Current foreign trade plans of eastern Europe 1971–5 (increases in % over 1970)

Countries	Foreign trade	National income	Industry	Agri-culture	Consump-tion	Invest-ment
Bulgaria	60–5	47–50	55–60	17–20	—	33–4
Czechoslo-vakia	36–8	28	34–6	14	28–30	35–7
G.D.R.	—	26–8	34–6	—	—	28–30
Hungary	40–50	27–30	30–3	15–16	30	30–5
Rumania	55	50–5	50–5	30–5	—	46–53
U.S.S.R.	33–5	40	42–6	20–2	40	37

Source: *Review of Trade Relations among countries having different economic and social systems*, U.N.C.T.A.D., TD/B/359 19 July 1971.

the detriment of the developing countries, many of which have products that the U.S.S.R. really wants. The experience of the 1960s suggests that in its trade policy the Soviet Union did not favour those countries to which it was close politically, except that most of these signed bilateral payments agreements and so benefited from any trade creation so provoked. Mali, Ghana and Somalia all are or have been numbered among the African countries favoured in Soviet pronouncements, yet Nigeria and Kenya, when they were out in the cold, received equally as good and sometimes better prices for their exports and paid no more for their imports. This may appear to be an enigma to those who believe that the Soviet Union's actions are politically determined, since it would appear that Soviet trade policy ran the risk of creating enemies where diplomatic activity sought to create friends. However, while the Soviet council of ministers and ministry of foreign trade, who formulate overall trade policies, may well have expected them to support the Soviet Union's political objectives, the actors who put policy into practice were the foreign trade organisations. The people who run the f.t.o.'s have their own sets of interests which may well differ from those of the ministry of foreign trade planners. Foremost amongst their interests is the need to maximise their undertakings' profitability, and however such profitability is measured it is unlikely to depend upon the happiness of the foreign trade partners. The apparently monolithic structure of Soviet planning masks a battlefield of conflicting interests. There are numerous examples of the Soviet planners' aims being perverted by factory managers and lower rank officials following their own self-interest, and there is no reason to suppose that trade is any different on this score.

3   Aid

The U.S.S.R. has been actively concerned with the provision of economic assistance to the developing countries for about twenty years. The first concrete Soviet proposals for economic assistance to the governments of the Third World were made in 1949 during a meeting of ECAFE; but they were vague, no specific activities or programmes were outlined, and the subject was not broached again for another two years. At the Moscow World Economic Conference of 1952, attended by 500 delegates drawn mainly from the underdeveloped countries, the Soviet Union again declared its interest in providing aid to the developing countries; a year later it expressed an interest in the United Nations EPTA, and in April 1953 it concluded a technical assistance agreement with Afghanistan, its first with a non-Communist developing country. The first such accord signed with an African country was that concluded with Egypt on 29 January 1958; by 1960 the African ranks had swelled to four, by 1966 they were sixteen,* and currently the U.S.S.R. has technical and economic co-operation agreements with forty developing countries in Asia, Africa and Latin America with particular emphasis being given to Afghanistan, Iran, Turkey, India, Pakistan, Egypt, Algeria, Iraq and Syria. But what is aid? Technical and economic co-operation is a much more descriptive term than is the emotive word *aid*. However, economic co-operation occurs between developed countries and need not incorporate any 'aid' at all: aid only occurs when the economic co-operation contains a gift element. To the extent that the Soviet Union charged on its loans a lower rate of interest than the marginal rate of return on its other possible investments, and to the extent that the recipient paid a lower interest rate than that required by alternative potential creditors, the transfer contained a gift element. Thus, while a grant contains an infinitely larger aid element than does a loan, even a loan at a $2\frac{1}{2}$ per cent rate of interest can justifiably be termed as aid. This chapter argues that not all Soviet economic co-operation that masqueraded as aid was aid, but that there was a definite aid element in some of the economic transfers between the U.S.S.R. and Africa.

* Ghana, Guinea, Ethiopia, Egypt, Algeria, Cameroun, Congo (Brazzaville), Kenya, Mali, Morocco, Uganda, Senegal, Somalia, Sudan, Tanzania and Tunisia.

TABLE 3.1   Commitments of bilateral economic assistance by the centrally planned economies 1954–68, by value (U.S. $millions – national currencies converted into dollars at official rates of exchange)

Donors	1954–62	1963	1964	1965	1966	1967	1968*	Total
Total commitments	4,454	341	1,246	646	1,313	621	758	9,379
Bulgaria	20	6	—	—	30	47	35	138
China (P.R.C.)	365	88	305	77	6	—	42	883
Czechoslovakia	468	20	118	43	192	88	200	1,129
G.D.R.	108	—	71	132	—	231	8	550
Hungary	151	14	10	42	52	45	40	354
Poland	332	8	54	22	—	63	20	499
Rumania	112	—	70	—	—	14	45	241
U.S.S.R.	2,898	205	618	330	1,033	133	368	5,585
Recipients								
Total Africa	1,302	242	874	247	46	420	223	3,354
Algeria	—	156	143	—	—	170	—	469
Central African Republic	—	—	4	—	—	—	—	4
Congo (Brazzaville)	—	—	33	29	—	—	—	62
Ethiopia	114	—	—	—	—	—	—	114
Ghana	122	—	22	20	—	—	—	164
Guinea	119	—	—	—	3	—	—	122
Kenya	—	—	55	—	11	—	—	66
Mali	85	—	27	—	—	—	—	112
Morocco	17	—	—	—	—	19	—	36
Nigeria	—	—	—	14	—	84	—	98
Senegal	—	—	7	—	—	—	—	7
Somalia	74	22	—	—	6	—	—	102
Sudan	22	—	—	—	—	27	—	49
Tunisia	48	—	—	—	—	—	55	103
Uganda	—	—	15	15	—	—	—	30
U.A.R.	701	64	517	126	—	120	168	1,696
Tanzania	—	—	51	—	26	—	—	77
Latin America	381	—	—	15	100	107	20	623
West Asia	479	75	97	33	523	64	473	1,744
South & South East Asia	2,292	24	275	351	644	30	42	3,658

Note: * = Preliminary.

Source: *The External Financing of Economic Development 1963–1967*, U.N., E/4652, *1964–1968*, E/4815.

SIZE, DISTRIBUTION AND PROCEDURES

Tables 3.1 and and 3.2 show the size of aid commitments made by the centrally planned economies to countries and regions in the Third World, and the projects being supported by the U.S.S.R. in Africa. This word

TABLE 3.2   Soviet Aid Projects in Africa, by country

Algeria
  (i)   First agreement on economic and technical co-operation signed 27 Oct 1963
 (ii)   Work done as of 1 Jan 1968: agreement reached for 61 projects of which 10 are in operation (i.e. work has begun on their construction)
(iii)   Major projects
        (a) Metallurgical factory at Annabe, cap. 300,000–350,000 tons p.a., with the possibility of extension to 1 million tons
        (b) Thermal power station at Annabe, cap. 100,000 kW
        (c) Factory to produce 'cognac' spirit, cap. 2·5 million bottles p.a.
        (d) Geological survey work
        (e) 21 irrigation canals for irrigating 8,000–10,000 hectares
        (f) Oil and gas institute for 1,000 students, and an oil technical school for 1,000 students*
        (g) Textile technical school with an engineering division
        (h) Industrial and agricultural school centres for 300 and 200 students*
        (i) Lead–Zinc enriching factory
        (j) Mineral enriching enterprise for producing mercury

*Ghana***
  (i)   First agreement on economic and technical co-operation signed on 4 Aug 1960
 (ii)   Work done as of 1 Jan 1968: agreement reached for 20 projects of which 5 are in operation
(iii)   Major projects:
        (a) Gold refinery, cap. 25–30 tons gold p.a.
        (b) Fish processing complex, cap. 25,000 tons of fish p.a.
        (c) Prefabricated–ferro-concrete panel factory
        (d) Geological surveys
        (e) Three school centres

Guinea
  (i)   First agreement on economic and technical co-operation signed 24 Aug 1959
 (ii)   Work done as of Jan 1968: agreement reached for 44 projects, 26 in operation

(iii) Major projects:
  (a) Canning factory at Mamu, cap. 5 million conventional tins p.a.*
  (b) Refrigerator at Conakry, volume 300 tons*
  (c) Airport at Conakry*
  (d) Radio station*
  (e) Polytechnic institute for 1,500 students*
  (f) Sawmill at Nzerekore, designed to expand to a yearly production of 22,500 cubic metres of sawn timber, 6,000 cu.m. of unfinished plywood and 3 million cu.m. of finished plywood*
  (g) 2 cattle breeding farms*
  (h) Geological surveys

Cameroun
  (i) First agreement 12 Apr 1963
  (ii) Work done as of Jan 1968: agreement on 2 projects, of which none in operation
  (iii) Major projects:
    (a) Agricultural school for 200 students
    (b) Forest technology school for 100 students

Kenya
  (i) First agreement 20 Nov 1964
  (ii) Work done as of Jan 1968: agreement on 7 projects of which 1 in operation
  (iii) Major projects:
    (a) Cotton mill at 20,000 spindles
    (b) Radio station
    (c) Fish canning factory
    (d) Factory for processing fruit and vegetables
    (e) Hospital of 200 beds*

Congo (Brazzaville)
  (i) First agreement 14 Dec 1964
  (ii) Work done as of Jan 1968: agreement on 6 projects, of which one in operation
  (iii) Major projects:
    (a) 120-room hotel in Brazzaville*
    (b) Geological surveys

Mali
  (i) First agreement 18 Mar 1961
  (ii) Work done as of Jan 1968: 13 projects agreed, work begun on 6
  (iii) Major projects:
    (a) Cement factory, cap. 50,000 tons cement p.a.
    (b) Geological surveys
    (c) Higher administrative school for 250 students*
    (d) School centre for professional and technical education
    (e) Assistance to assimilate land into the government 'Office du Niger'

Morocco
  (i)   First agreement 17 Oct 1966
 (ii)   Work done as of Jan 1968: agreement on 4 projects, none in operation
(iii)   Major projects:
        (a) Metal processing complex with a school centre for 1,000 students
        (b) Dam on the River Dra, with H.E.P. generator, cap. 5,000 kW

U.A.R.
  (i)   First agreement 29 Jan 1968
 (ii)   Work done as of 1 Jan 1968: 100 projects agreed upon, of which 73 are in operation
(iii)   Major projects:
        (a) Aswan High Dam and H.E.P. plant, cap. 2·1 million kW*
        (b) Coke preparation plant, cap. 280,000 tons coke p.a.*
        (c) Agglomeration plant, cap. 1,000 tons ore per 24 hours*
        (d) 2 oil refineries, cap. 1 million tons of oil p.a. each*
        (e) Factory for producing lubricating oil, cap. 60,000 tons p.a.*
        (f) 3 cotton mills of 45,000 spindles*
        (g) Factory for welding electrodes, cap. 25 million items p.a.*
        (h) Steel works for forging and electro-welding chains, cap. 15,000 tons of forgings and 750 tons of chains p.a.*
        (i) Chemical–pharmaceutical & antibiotics factory, cap. 290 tons of products p.a.*
        (j) Factory for metal-cutting lathes, cap. 725 items p.a.*
        (k) Aluminium cables plant, cap. 1,800 tons p.a.*
        (l) File producing plant, cap. 400,000 items p.a.*
        (m) Factory to produce emery paper & sandpaper, cap. 300 tons produce p.a.*
        (n) Atomic reactor of 2,000 kW*
        (o) Shipyard at Alexandria with a tonnage of 50,000 tons deadweight p.a.*
        (p) Radio factory of 100,000 radio sets & 40,000 T.V.s p.a.
        (q) Thermal power station at Suez, cap. 100,000 kW*
        (r) Works to produce calcium carbide, cap. 5,000 tons p.a., and ferro-silicon, cap. 3,000 tons p.a.*
        (s) Metallurgical complex at Helwan, cap. up to 1·5 million tons of steel p.a.*
        (t) 45 school centres for professional & technical education (41 currently being built)
        (u) 3 milk factories with a total processing cap. of 75 tons of milk per 24 hours
        (v) Enterprise to produce dried onions, cap. 1,000 tons produce per season*

Senegal
  (i)   First agreement 14 June 1962
 (ii)   Work as of 1 Jan 1968: 1 project agreed, but not in operation
(iii)   Major projects:
        (a) Supplying Tuna boats*

Somalia
  (i) First agreement 2 June 1961
 (ii) Work as of 1 Jan 1968: 17 projects agreed of which 6 in operation
(iii) Major projects:
       (a) Milk processing factory, cap. 10 tons milk per shift*
       (b) Radio station*
       (c) Printing works*
       (d) 2 hospitals of 50 beds each*
       (e) Boarding school for 300 students*
       (f) Deepwater port at Berbera*
       (g) Fish canning factory, cap. 6 million conventional cans p.a.*
       (h) Meat processing factory for processing 60,000 large-horned cattle
            p.a.*

Sudan
  (i) First agreement 21 Nov 1961
 (ii) Work as of 1 Jan 1968: 14 projects agreed of which 3 in operation
(iii) Major projects:
       (a) 2 fruit and vegetable canning factories, cap. 3·5 million conven-
            tional cans p.a. each*
       (b) Dried onion factory, cap. 50 tons per 24 hours*
       (c) 2 cereal elevators, volume 50,000 tons & 100,000 tons*
       (d) Milk canning plant for processing 25 tons of milk per shift
       (e) 5 medical institutes
       (f) Veterinary laboratory

Tanzania
  (i) First agreement 26 May 1966
 (ii) Work as of 1 Jan 1968: 5 projects agreed, none in operation
(iii) Major projects:
       (a) Geological surveys
       (b) Factory for fish drying
       (c) 4 refrigerators, volume 50 tons each

Tunisia
  (i) First agreement 30 Aug 1961
 (ii) Work as of 1 Jan 1968: 7 projects agreed, none in operation
(iii) Major projects:
       (a) Land reclamation work
       (b) National technical institute with a yearly output of 160 specialists

Uganda
  (i) First agreement 30 Nov 1964
 (ii) Work as of 1 Jan 1968: 4 projects agreed, none in operation
(iii) Major projects:
       (a) Cotton mill, cap. 4,000 tons yarn p.a.
       (b) Agricultural training centre
       (c) Refrigerators

Ethiopia
  (i)　First agreement 11 July 1959
 (ii)　Work as of 1 Jan 1968: 6 projects agreed, 3 in operation
(iii)　Major projects:
　　　(a)　Oil refinery at Assabe, cap. 500,000 tons of oil p.a.*
　　　(b)　Thermal electric power station at Assabe, cap. 13,500 kW*
　　　(c)　Polytechnic institute at Bahar Dar for 1,000 students*

Zambia
  (i)　First agreement 26 May 1967
 (ii)　Work as of 1 Jan 1968: 5 projects agreed, none in operation
(iii)　Major projects:
　　　(a)　4 diesel electric power stations with a combined cap. of 1625 kW
　　　(b)　Equipping of the medical and engineering faculties of the University of Zambia
　　　(c)　Supply of road building machines and equipment for building tarmac roads

---

Notes: * = in operation (either in part or in full) by 1972.
　　　** = after the military *coup* of February 1966 work on the projects was suspended.
Source: V. S. Baskin, G. I. Rubinstein and B. B. Runov, *Ekonomicheskoe Sotrudnichestvo S.S.S.R. so Stranami Afriki* (Moscow, 1968) Appendix 1.

committed is extremely important: the most significant feature of Soviet aid is that it is normally 100 per cent *tied* in the strictest sense of that word; statements to the effect that the U.S.S.R. and country X have concluded an economic and technical assistance agreement worth £30 million mean that if suitable projects can be agreed upon the Soviet Union will make available up to £30 million worth of goods and services to facilitate their construction. Normally, the economic and technical assistance agreement does not, in the final analysis, bind the Soviet Union to provide anything, and funds promised will only be made available in their entirety if the recipient can put forward a sufficient number of acceptable projects and an adequate amount of finance to cover local costs of construction, although the Soviet Union may supply additional assistance to help with these. Since both these limitations are time consuming, the amount of aid *committed* by the Soviet Union is normally in excess of the amount actually disbursed. Nevertheless, by the beginning of 1971 more than 350 Soviet projects* were in operation in the

---

* These include thirty-two machine building and metal processing plants, nine iron and sheet plants, eleven power stations, twenty-two light and food industry factories, forty-seven agricultural projects, forty-five transport and communications projects, and seventy-seven training institutions.

developing countries, making the Soviet Union by far and away the main donor from among the centrally planned economies, with Czechoslovakia second and the People's Republic of China a poor third. On the other side of the coin, the main recipients were South and South-East Asia in the 1950s and Africa during the 1960s, with over 90 per cent of the aid being channelled into industry and directly productive enterprises rather than infrastructure and social services. This is a higher proportion than for Western donors, as the examples of Ghana and Somalia illustrate (see Table 3.3).

During the period up to 1968 four distinct phases in the history of Soviet aid to the developing countries may be discerned. From 1955–7 the initial aid offers to Asia and the Middle East were made. Then, in the following three years until 1961, the magnitude and distribution of Soviet aid underwent its most rapid expansion with over $1800 million being committed for the development plans of Afghanistan, India, Indonesia, Iraq and the U.A.R.[1] Between 1962 and 1963 there were few new commitments of aid (only $91 million in 1962, the lowest in all fourteen years) both because the Soviet Union had concluded a very high level of agreements just before, including almost all the receptive African countries, and because it was now openly assessing the value of its foreign aid programme. Its conclusions were obviously favourable, for the programme picked up in 1964, but by 1968 the Soviet Union was again concerned over its value, and writings in the U.S.S.R. since then have emphasised the importance of self-generated development and the peripheral role of foreign aid, a stance that contrasts sharply with earlier prescriptions.[2]

The Soviet Union provides two forms of credit for the acquisition of capital goods by foreign buyers: state credits, which are normally available for complete plants and related services, and commercial credits, which are generally used for individual sales of machinery and equipment and are often on slightly harder terms. State credits are typically repayable at $2\frac{1}{2}$ per cent over twelve years. Commercial credits usually require a down payment of 10–20 per cent of the value of the goods, attract a rate of interest of 4 per cent, and are normally granted for periods of up to five years, although sometimes this is extended to seven, eight or more. Thus, Ghana purchased some Ilyushin aircraft, fishing trawlers and agricultural machinery on the basis of a down payment ranging from 10 to 40 per cent, a repayment period of five to eight years, and a rate of interest of up to 4 per cent, while most of its other loans from the U.S.S.R. were at $2\frac{1}{2}$ per cent interest and were repayable over twelve years.[3] In Africa state credits have been reserved for governments, but commercial credits have been available for both government and private concerns. Drawing examples from Ghana again, by 1968 just under $7 million had been received by six private companies from the

TABLE 3.3   Aid projects in Somalia and Ghana, broken down by donor, sector and type

a Somalia**

	U.S.S.R.		Other***	
Sector	Amount*	% of total U.S.S.R.	Amount*	% of total other
Agriculture and related activities	23,016	12	9,387	3
Animal husbandry	—	—	327	1
Irrigation	7,753	4	12,140	4
Industry, power, mining	87,782	45	24,261	7
Basic infrastructure	53,876	28	228,616	68
Social infrastructure	21,444	11	58,975	17
TOTAL	193,871	100	333,702	100

Notes: * = thousands Somali shillings.
    ** = includes projects completed by 1969.
    *** = 'Other' includes E.E.C., U.N., World Bank, West Germany, Italy and U.S.A.

b Ghana*

	U.S.S.R.		I.M.F. countries	
Sector	Amount**	% of total U.S.S.R.	Amount**	% of total I.M.F.
Agriculture	4	14	63	16
Manufacturing	4	14	58	15
Construction	1	4	65	17
Transport and communication	5	18	95	24
Electricity, gas, water	—	—	66	17
Unallocated	14	50	43	11
TOTAL	28	100	390	100

Notes: * = includes the amount outstanding at 1970 on projects funded by contractor finance by June 1966
    ** = million U.S.$
Sources: German Planning and Economic Advisory Group, Dr Hendrikson, *Report on the Progress of Development Projects in the Somali Democratic Republic, 31 December 1969* (Mogadishu and Frankfurt, n.d.), p. 81, Table 4.8; J. H. Mensah, *The State of the Economy and the External Debt Problem*, (Accra, 1970). Information from Bank of Ghana.

Soviet Union, as compared with almost $27 million of medium-term and $11·7 million of long-term credits received by the Ghana government.*

Most of the capital goods transactions between U.S.S.R. and the developing countries are carried out with state credits granted from funds earmarked for that purpose in the state budget, under special bilateral economic and technical co-operation agreements which are negotiated and signed for the U.S.S.R. by representatives of the Committee for Foreign Economic Relations of the council of ministers. This organisation was formed in 1957 with the main task of administering foreign aid, and all important negotiations with the developing countries are conducted by one of its members; it also has responsibility for military aid.†

As with trade, the actual implementation of aid agreements is done by the foreign trade organisations which also administer the granting of commercial export credits. The six foreign trade organisations most closely associated with aid are the ones which specialise in the export of complete plants,‡ but they are all only middlemen in the supply of goods and services. When protocols have been concluded with the recipient specifying which projects are to be undertaken the appropriate foreign trade organisation calls upon over forty 'basic suppliers' and with them prepares technical plans, undertakes geological research, chooses the best location, and executes any other preparatory work. When the plans have been passed the suppliers and foreign trade organisations jointly prepare a detailed list of all the equipment needed, and this is then delivered to the recipient who can strike out any item that it can produce locally. Delivery contracts are then passed on to the manufacturing concerns via the foreign trade department of their ministries. Settlements with the factories are made by the basic suppliers while any guarantees to the customer are given by the foreign trade organisation. This procedure has two corollaries: the first is that the customer is not aware of the actual source of his goods; the second is that the transaction is completed for the manufacturer and the basic suppliers as soon as the merchandise is

---

* Information from the Bank of Ghana. Most of the credit for private companies went to Mankoadze Fisheries, which purchased ten trawlers and one transport ship between 1962 and 1965.

† This aspect of aid will be considered in Chapter 6.

‡ Neftekhimpomexport – plants for oil producing and refining, petroleum and chemical industries; Prommashexport – plants for engineering industry, automobile, machine tools, agricultural machinery, etc; Selkhozpromexport – fodder factories, grain elevators and mills, soil improvement equipment, dams, pumping stations, etc.; Technoexport – cement, bricks and glass plants equipment for light industries and the pharmaceutical industry, airport equipment and installation; Technopromexport – hydroelectric power and thermal power plants, chemical, woodworking and wood processing plants, atomic research centres and laboratories; Tjazhpromexport – complete plants and equipment for ferrous and non-ferrous metallurgy and the mining industry.

taken over by the foreign trade organisation. The first of these explains how African complaints that they are being supplied with second-hand goods can arise. The second may explain why quite a lot of the equipment sent to Africa has been shoddy, since the manufacturers do not appear to suffer directly if the machines they supply do not work and the Soviet Union suffers a political or (if there is a default in debt repayment) a financial setback.

THE NOMINAL AND EFFECTIVE TERMS OF SOVIET ASSISTANCE

The U.S.S.R. often makes gifts to the developing countries of Africa, but they are normally small and do not form a significant proportion of total aid. During 1964–5 the U.S.S.R. committed to Mali $9·6 million in loans but only $1·47 million in grants. Somalia has been a most favoured recipient of Soviet aid, but only 7·1 per cent of Soviet expenditure on completed projects by 1969 was in the form of grants. Kenya appears at first sight to be an exception since 100 per cent of Soviet disbursements have been in gift form, but that is simply because the Kenyan government declined to proceed with the offer of a loan.[4] The great majority of Soviet aid transfers are in the form of loans mostly on terms of $2\frac{1}{2}$ per cent interest and twelve years for repayment, but with some on more commercial terms and some, such as those for Ghana's state farms and its atomic reactor, permitting a longer repayment period. These interest rates may be compared with those charged by Western countries. In 1964 the weighted average interest rate levied by the U.K. on its Official bilateral loan commitment was 4·1 per cent, and that levied by the U.S.A. was 2·5 per cent; in 1968 the figures were 1·3 per cent and 3·5 per cent, respectively.[5] These, however, are global figures and include only official commitments: unofficial Western loans tended to carry a much higher rate of interest, while the comparison of most interest to potential recipients is not of weighted averages but of the actual interest rate being demanded by the potential donors at a particular point of time.

In a number of cases the Soviet Union has agreed to accept repayment in kind either directly, as in the case of Somalia, in the form of exports to the correct value, or indirectly as provided for by the aid agreements with Tanzania and Kenya under which repayments are initially made in convertible currency into a special account, with the Soviet Union promising to use this money for the purchase of goods from the aid recipient.[6] The value of these two arrangements for countries experiencing difficulty in balancing their bilateral trade with the Soviet Union has already been remarked, but there have been criticisms that the aid recipient is hocking its exports, its economic lifeline, for years in advance.[7] To the extent that the developing countries must ensure that the Soviet valuation of their repayment in kind is commensurate with the prices that could otherwise have been fetched on the world market, this is a valid warning, since the Russians tend to act as normal businessmen and drive as hard a bargain as they can when negotiating the day-to-day flow of trade. However, so long as the African negotiators are aware of their interests and actively defend them they have a strong bargaining position. Many such aid agreements now make specific provision for repayment in convertible currency should there be failure to agree on the type and value of goods to be transferred, thus giving the debtor the choice of adopting whichever method better suits the world conditions at the time of repayment, but even where this is not the case the Soviet Union is in the fundamentally weak position of all creditors who do not possess an adequate enforcement mechanism. If the debtor unilaterally abrogates his debts there is very little that the Soviet Union can do; the worst that can happen short of active political interference, which in Africa is unlikely, is the total disruption of commercial links between the two countries, but if relations have already come to such a state that the Russians are believed to be abusing their position this is a small loss to their partner. With the experience of several debt rescheduling agreements behind them, the Russians now know that their partners have this power. Thus Somalia, which would at first appear to be especially vulnerable since it has no option but to make repayment in kind under the provisions of its 1961 aid agreement, in fact made no repayments of any kind in the period under review in this book.

Soviet credits for a particular development project normally cover three items: machinery and equipment not available in the recipient country, technical assistance needed for the construction of the projected works, and the training of local personnel – and sometimes counterpart funds provided by a commodity credit under the terms of which the U.S.S.R. ships to the recipient goods that are unconnected with the project itself but which may be sold for local currency to raise funds to cover the local costs of the project, such as the transport of equipment from port to the construction site, the payment of local labour, or the provision of locally available materials.

However, the nominal terms of Soviet aid – the rate of interest, period of repayment, and similar technical points – are only one aspect of its real value. Also important are the price and quality of Soviet equipment and personnel, the speed with which projects are completed, and their economic feasibility, as well as the size of the contribution that the recipient needs to make. Unfortunately, little systematic research has been conducted on Soviet aid in operation in Africa, and a few spectacular successes or failures have often been generalised to cover the totality of the Soviet performance. In 1961 some observers claimed to have seen snow-ploughs in Conakry where the temperature rarely falls below 80 °F. sent there, or so the story went, as part of a 'complete road building kit' because when such an outfit is ordered in the Soviet Union it automatically includes a snow-plough. Ever afterwards snow-ploughs were popping up here, there and everywhere in Africa, their erstwhile spotters being nothing daunted by the fact that few of them can have had a very clear idea of exactly what a Soviet snow-plough looked like. It seems plain that Guinea, which was the first tropical African country to receive Soviet aid, initially experienced a number of problems: the Russians and East Europeans were in a hurry to make a quick impact and had no experience of local conditions, added to which the Guinean administration, weakened by the mass exodus of the French, was ill-equipped to deal with such highly bureaucratised partners. Cement arrived just before the rains and hardened on the quays, matches became damp and would not light, sugar came too, and was so effectively damp-proofed that it would not dissolve. However, these were early days, and although the secrecy which currently shrouds Guinea prevents an assessment of the present effectiveness of Soviet aid, recent visitors suggest that the quality of Soviet personnel is very high. Nevertheless, a comment such as was made by I. M. D. Little at the conclusion of a study tour in Africa that 'There may be successful [Soviet bloc] projects, but I did not hear of one' requires investigation. According to Professor Little the reasons for this failure were that :

> In the countries which I visited (which excluded Egypt) there was relatively little Eastern money devoted to social and economic over-heads. Russia and the Eastern European countries have concentrated on providing equipment and factories though there has also been some agricultural activity (e.g. Ghana's State Farms). Since such aid has been given with inadequate economic forethought and inadequate technical assistance, both very difficult for the Easterners in Africa, much of this 'aid' has been impoverishing, especially as the equipment often turned out to be very expensive, so that the cheapness of the loan was deceptive.[8]

The first factor to be taken into account in any assessment of the effectivness of Soviet aid is that very little of the aid granted from any source in the past twenty years has been spectacularly effective. To a large extent, therefore, we are comparing shades of mediocrity, and the ability of donors (and recipients) to learn from their mistakes. The second point to bear in mind is that Eastern and Western aid have not, in general, been mutually exclusive competitors; few countries of tropical Africa have relied solely on one side of the Cold War for succour, and where they have it has always been the West that has been favoured. Approaches to the Soviet bloc have usually only been made after it has become apparent that the West is unwilling to satisfy a country's aid requirements as perceived by its leaders, which are not necessarily the same as the country's capacity for absorbing aid. Such moves have not usually resulted in a retaliatory cutback in the aid of Western countries which, while they have on occasion restricted assistance to countries receiving Communist aid, have not done so solely because of the acceptance of Communist aid.*

The experience of Ghana is illustrative of a typical sequence of events leading up to the soliciting of aid from the Soviet Union.[9] During the first two to three years of independence, the new Ghanaian government took little interest in the U.S.S.R. largely because there seemed to be no pressing reason for it to branch out from established international contacts. By 1960 the picture was beginning to alter: in 1957 foreign loans had only been contemplated and were not urgently required; by the end of 1961 Ghana had used £25 million and signed contracts totalling £190 million in loans, which had by then become indispensable to Nkrumah's entire economic and political programme.[10] Ghana's foreign reserves, which had formerly borne most of the brunt of economic development, were dwindling while development needs were growing; at the same time, development activities began to emphasise industrialisation and an expansion of the state sector of the economy. The first of these changes required more foreign investment and aid, while the second made it unlikely that the U.K. and U.S.A. would be willing to provide all the funds. To a certain extent, indeed, Ghana had 'missed the boat' of Western aid. In the 1950s it had not sought aid actively, and an image had developed in the West of a Ghana that did not require assistance.[11]

In 1960, therefore, Kojo Botsio took up a long-standing invitation to visit Moscow, and four months later the two countries signed an agreement on economic and technical co-operation. The following year Nkrumah himself toured the Communist bloc with great success in terms of aid offers received; afterwards Krobo Edusei was deputed to follow up the verbal agreements reached by the Ghanaian president and another agreement on economic and technical co-operation resulted.[12] Similar cases may be found in Somalia, Tanzania and Nigeria where Western aid offers were thought inadequate, while in Guinea, of course, the government had little option but to look to the East for the support that the West at first withheld.

In addition to Western and Eastern official aid, an African state can look for suppliers' credits. Suppliers' credits are loans granted by com-

---

* Ghana and Somalia provide two examples. In 1963 President Kennedy instructed U.S.A.I.D. to extend no further long-term credits to Ghana; Arthur M. Schlesinger Jnr, *A Thousand Days* (New York, 1967). In 1970 the U.S.A. invoked section 620 of its aid legislation prohibiting the granting of aid to a country that trades with the enemy, when the Somali Democratic Republic refused to de-register six ships that flew the Somali flag of convenience and traded with North Vietnam.

mercial firms to facilitate the export of their goods and are guaranteed against a debtor's default in repayment by the exporting company's government. The commercial firm granting the loan is thus in no way inhibited by the economic (un)viability of the projects involved, provided only that it can persuade its government to undertake the guarantee. Such a close relationship between company profits and the initiation of development projects was ripe for corruption, and numerous commissions of enquiry set up by Nkrumah's successors to investigate the misdeeds of his government are replete with examples of Western companies bribing their way into contracts that were either inflated in their price or for projects of doubtful feasibility. This was not a feature of Soviet aid, which made it attractive in principle not only to the government of Ghana but also to the Nigerian administration which specifically referred to the 'gross distortions' caused by the 'side attractions and vested interests' involved with suppliers' credit and made them one reason why the government should make 'strenuous attempts' to attract aid from Eastern bloc countries.[13] On the other hand, while attractive in principle they were not so attractive in practice to those who were doing very well out of the 'side attractions and vested interests', and possibly for this reason many African politicians have been more interested in suppliers' credits than in Soviet assistance.

The advantage of Communist credits over suppliers' credits lies not only in their minimisation of corruption; they were also cheaper, at least in their nominal terms. In what with hindsight can be seen as a catastrophic miscalculation the Ghanaian government believed that because its economy was one of the most advanced in Black Africa and had a fairly well developed infrastructure it could afford to utilise suppliers' credits and reap dividends from the investments thus made soon enough to repay the loans.[14] However, it was inconceivable that, for example, the extension to Tema Harbour at a cost of almost £G6 million could have paid for the servicing of the supplier's credit which required a 60 per cent down payment and the balance to be repaid over two and one-half years at 5 per cent.[15] Whilst this is an extreme case, the typical interest rate for such credits was 6 per cent with repayment normally over three to five years, although just a few extended to eight years.[16] Consideration of all Western credits to Ghana bears out the proposition that Communist aid was more generous in its nominal terms and that it was also better suited for the projects to which it was allocated, in the sense that a higher proportion of Communist financed projects could have been expected to generate income before the loan with which they were financed needed to be repaid (see Table 3.4). As the average repayment period for loans made by I.M.F. members was about five years, only 8.6 per cent of them could have begun to pay for themselves during the repayment period. In the case of the non-I.M.F. loans, the average repayment period was twelve years, and so over 61 per cent could have begun to pay for themselves during the repayment period.*

TABLE 3.4   Contractor financed projects in Ghana, by source and period in which expected to generate income

Source	less than 6 years	Expected to generate income in:			
		6–12 years	over 12 years	Other	Total
I.M.F. million NC	33·7	131·5	177·7	47·7	390·6
I.M.F. %	8·6	33·7	45·5	12·2	100
Non-I.M.F. million NC	4·7	51·2	11·9	23·5	91·3
Non-I.M.F. %	5·1	56·1	13·1	25·7	100

Notes: Includes credits for imports of raw materials and consumer goods as well as projects that do not generate any directly measurable economic returns, excluding the purchase of a frigate, the Drevici Group projects, and the atomic reactor, agricultural equipment, pharmaceutical industry, automobile factory, for which contract prices are not known.

With the exception of Yugoslavia and Czechoslovakia, which are members of the I.M.F., the characterisation of I.M.F. and non-I.M.F. countries is the same as that between Communist and non-Communist.

Source: J. H. Mensah, *The State of the Economy and the External Debt Problem* (Accra, 1970).

If the terms of the non-I.M.F. countries were more favourable to Ghana than those of the I.M.F. states, the same is true of rescheduling agreements since the 1966 *coup*. After the *coup* the new regime exhibited clear anti-Communist tendencies and it was not out of the question for it to repudiate the non-I.M.F. loans completely. Before it fell, the Nkrumah government had negotiated a moratorium on debts owed to the Soviet Union, and after the *coup* this was extended to become a *de facto* moratorium applying to all Eastern debts except those owing to Yugoslavia. Although the National Liberation Council in Accra showed little interest in maintaining friendly relations with the East, it accepted the advice of the I.M.F. and some Ghanaians that it should come to an understanding on the Eastern debts, if only to safeguard the potentially viable Eastern projects still under construction. After negotiating with its Western creditors, who were by far and away the most important, the Ghanaian government turned to its Eastern creditors. The first round of negotiations with the Russians produced no agreement, but thereafter political relations between the two states became less icy and in 1967 a

* The distinction between 'I.M.F.' and 'non-I.M.F.' states is not quite the same as that between 'Communist' and 'non-Communist' states, since Czechoslovakia and Yugoslavia are members of the I.M.F.

rescheduling arrangement was concluded with the U.S.S.R., and later with the other Eastern European countries with the exception of Czechoslovakia, whose debts were unilaterally rescheduled.[17] The rescheduling arrangements were similar to those agreed with the West, except on the question of the moratorium rate of interest, where the non-I.M.F. states were markedly more generous than their I.M.F. counterparts.* Whereas the moratorium interest imposed by the non-I.M.F. states was 16 per cent of the original interest and principal, that of the I.M.F. states was 39·4 per cent of the original (see Table 3.5). This was the cause of some anger in Ghana.

TABLE 3.5   Effects of Ghana's debt rescheduling
           (million NC)

	Original principal and interest (1)	Moratorium interest (2)	Total	(2) as a % of (1)
I.M.F. states	212·6	83·7	296·3	39·4
non-I.M.F.	37·4	6·0	43·4	16·0

Source: J. H. Mensah, *The State of the Economy and the External Debts Problem* (Accra, 1970).

Surely nothing could be better than generous loans, well-suited to the projects they financed. Surely indeed, except that there were two reasons why Communist projects and loans were well-suited: one that the terms were good, the other that emphasis was put on directly productive enterprises. It is herein that the root of much of the criticism of Soviet aid lies. By investing in directly productive industry the Soviet Union was being very ambitious: if successful the factories so created would be tremendously beneficial to the receiving countries and would help them to achieve the stated goal of Soviet aid, that is to develop as quickly as possible; but being ambitious, they were also more liable to failure. If one invests in a road or a railway as the Chinese are doing in Tanzania and Somalia, or in the agricultural extension schemes favoured by the Americans, the

---

* The moratorium interest is a rate of interest imposed on that proportion of the contractual principal and interest that is deferred by rescheduling. Rescheduling extends the period over which the loans are to be repaid so that a smaller amount is repaid each year. However, the debtor does not get off 'scot free', since in addition to the original rate of interest a moratorium rate of interest is charged on the difference between the amount actually repaid each year and the amount that would have been repaid had there been no rescheduling. The total burden of debt is thus increased, but the period over which it must be repaid is extended.

likelihood of failure is much smaller. Once a road is built it simply needs to be kept in good repair; it may or may not act as a catalyst for new investment, it may or may not transform the economic situation prevailing in the localities through which it passes, but these are not the concern of the aid donor who is unlikely to be criticised if the recipient fails to make full use of the project. A factory is quite a different proposition : not only must the building be erected and the machines set in motion but they must also remain in motion, and they must be supplied with raw materials and their products must be conveyed to an adequate market for sale; if the project fails in any of these respects the donor is blamed, and there is little it can do to extricate itself. In Ghana it was agreed that the Russians would not be responsible for the management of the state farms set up with Soviet equipment,[18] but this was to no avail in saving the U.S.S.R.'s reputation: when the state farms failed, responsibility was laid at the Soviet door.

Given the ambitiousness of Soviet aid projects it is particularly important that each item be thoroughly thought out before a start is made on construction. The established procedure for the implementation of Soviet aid promises should give both donor and recipient the power to ensure that this forethought is given. The potential recipient submits a list of projects that it would like to be financed. The Soviet Union then selects those with which it concurs, and finally any differences and difficulties arising are ironed out. In the case of Ghana the original list was long and ambitious, including an iron and steel works, a polytechnic and agricultural college for 5000 students each, eight brick and tile factories, a 400-mile railway line from Kumasi to Ouagadougou, the capital of Upper Volta, a sewage system for Kumasi, Takoradi, Cape Coast and Tamale, and 500 assorted industries. This list was, to say the least, somewhat optimistic and the Soviet Union agreed to finance only a small part of it. However, even had the U.S.S.R. been more accommodating it is doubtful whether Ghana could have afforded to pay the local costs involved in such grandiose schemes. The effect of this procedure should be to ensure that the recipient itself decides whether or not it wants a particular project submitted for consideration, while the donor can continue to reject proposals until only those schemes it feels willing or competent to undertake are left. Of course, if the recipient is not entirely sure what it wants, the donor has scope for suggesting which projects it feels particularly competent to undertake. This last point applies equally to all aid donors and may explain why the Soviet Union is so often 'asked' to build fish processing plants, canning factories, polytechnics and milk factories, and conduct geological surveys, while the Americans are 'asked' for agricultural extension schemes, the British for infrastructure, and the Chinese for experimental tobacco farms and cigarette and match factories.

After the selection of the project to be financed, the next defence against the construction of white elephants is the feasibility survey. Contracts with the U.S.S.R. normally make provision for such a survey, but feasibility planning has been one of the weakest links in aid to Africa of many types. However, while it is clear from the experience of the past dozen years that it was often lacking, not least in the case of Soviet projects, it is not clear where the responsibility for this lies. It could lie with the donor for foisting unviable projects on innocent African states and falsifying the feasibility reports, as is often alleged with projects financed by suppliers' credits, or with the recipients who over-extended themselves and used the unusually great political influence with which they were endowed in the early 1960s to extract whatever they could from the developed world. The ability of poor developing countries to inveigle rich and powerful nations into financing projects for which they do not care might be thought to be limited and, of course, in the final analysis it is. Nevertheless, in the political situation of the early 1960s when the great powers were actively competing with each other for influence, African governments were possessed of abnormal powers of persuasion. This may be illustrated by the case of U.K. suppliers' credits to Ghana: some commentators have seen these as purely a means by which Britain gave a boost to its declining industries,[19] but while this must have been an element in British thinking it ignores the fact that had the British government refused to guarantee a contract already negotiated between the Ghana government and a U.K. commercial firm it would have been widely taken as a political move against the Nkrumah regime; it was a brave government that did such things in the early 1960s. History will no doubt apportion to both sides the responsibility, and the experiences of the Soviet Union in Africa would certainly support such a judgement. The record, so far as it is known, shows not a single, determined and unambiguous posture on the part of the Russians but rather a series of *ad hoc* alignments on project planning issues as they arose: sometimes they were brave and resisted unworkable proposals, sometimes they gave way to white elephantine proposals, and sometimes they appear to have thrown economic rationality to the winds and themselves proposed unviable undertakings.

Distortions in the use of aid may arise from two sources : the intrusion into planning decisions of African political calculations that are incompatible with economic rationality, or the donor's desire to sell as much equipment, machinery and technical assistance, or receive as much short-run prestige as possible irrespective of its effects on the recipient's economy. Taking the first of these, there are a number of political factors that may interfere with economic rationality, such as the desire for prestige (Nkrumah's Soviet-financed atomic reactor project is a suitable example) or the effect of regional rivalries on the siting of industrial projects (like the iron and steel works proposed for Nigeria). In the Nigerian case the Soviet Union has promised £N2·429 million for feasibility and technical studies on the industry and, if these prove to be positive, further help to establish a £N50 million iron and steel complex,[20] but work on this has been delayed because of problems over the choice of site. Both the project and the problem are of long standing: three possible sites, Enugu and Onitsha in the east and Lokoja in the north, were mentioned as early as 1958, and the Nigerian National Economic Council was under pressure from that year to undertake a policy review of the project with a view to determining the most economically favourable location. The various regional lobbies soon got to work and by 1961 both northern and eastern locations had powerful backers, each armed with a suitable consultant's report. There was deadlock. By the beginning of 1964 policy thinking was moving in the direction of establishing two iron and steel mills, even though the economic case for one was marginal. At the sixteenth meeting of the N.E.C. in May 1964 it was agreed to have two plants, one at Idah in the north and one at Onitsha in the east, but these guns were spiked by the withdrawal of the scheme's foreign financial backers. The military *coups* of 1966 and the civil war disturbed the picture, and when the iron and steel complex again emerged it was the Soviet Union rather than Western interests from which external finance was sought, but the problem of siting still remains.[21]

A third example of projects that have their roots in the non-economic considerations of the recipient is the deep water port at Berbera in northern Somalia on which the U.S.S.R. has spent $7·6 million.[22] The port has a greater capacity than its hinterland requires. Yet it is not large enough to form an intermediate or free port, which would require a doubling of its capacity, the installation of bunkering facilities for water and fuel, and cold stores. Even with these additional features it would have to compete with Djibouti and Aden which are both well established in the field.[23] For Somalia the major value of the port is its aid towards national intergration in a country where road communications are very poor.

However, the Soviet Union has not always allowed its protégés to disregard economic prudence entirely, the strange history of the Bui Dam in Ghana being a case in point. The Russians first agreed on 23 December 1960 to give assistance in the construction of a hydroelectric project with an installed capacity of up to 200,000 kilowatts at Bui on the Black Volta river, and to build a transmission line up to 250 kilometres in length away from the project. The work schedule provided for survey, investigation and designing work to be completed by 1962 and material for construction to be delivered by 1966, and left open the date for construction itself.[24] Early in 1962 the Ghana government put up temporary housing for Soviet experts and Ghanaian workers, but by 1963, although the U.S.S.R. was still committed to constructing the dam, the deadline for completion of the survey work had been extended to 1964 and all other deadlines were left open.[25] In August 1965 Nkrumah addressed the national assembly on the subject of the project and the Russian survey, and claimed that:

> this survey has shown that the project is economic and feasible. The Government has therefore decided to initiate discussions on the possibility of implementing the Bui project scheme. In the meantime a start will be made to construct the ancillary work such as access roads in the area.[26]

The Black Volta hydroelectric power scheme was closely linked to the American financed dam on another stretch of the Volta river at Akosombo, to which the U.S. government had committed over $40 million. All the major government backed engineering surveys of the Volta river basin had shown that an H.E.P. project at the Bui Gorge was economic and feasible, but the decision to go ahead with the Akosombo Dam meant that it would be superfluous for many years to come, and in their survey the Russians confirmed this and declined to finance the scheme. However, it appears that Nkrumah felt a need to balance politically the American project at Akosombo, which was viewed with hostility by the C.P.P.s radical wing, and he therefore kept up a pretence that Russian work was to continue although, in fact, none did, save that the Soviet Union obligingly sent a small amount of equipment to the site to embroider the make-believe.[27] By 1968 Ghana was indebted on this score only to the extent of the survey work, which cost some $1,688,145.[28]

This was not the only occasion on which the Russians declined to fall in with the Ghana government's plans. In May 1962 the U.S.S.R. agreed to help establish a textile mill at Tamale in northern Ghana with the aim of developing a cotton industry there. However, differences between the two governments soon arose: the Ghanaian ministry of industry insisted that a cotton gin be attached to the mill, that the mill's capacity be expanded from 6 to 20 million square yards per annum, and that a finer material than the khaki originally planned be produced. It appears that the Soviet representatives in Ghana agreed to the proposed enlargement but were overruled by their superiors on the grounds that the mill would only be profitable using locally grown fibre and that supplies of this were insufficient to feed an expanded mill. In consequence, the project was dropped in January 1966.[29]

However, this attitude of firmness in the face of unreasonable requests appears not to have been typical. Both the foregoing incidents occurred in 1965–6 by which time the Soviet Union was becoming increasingly concerned at Ghana's economic position and had apparently advised in favour of the democratisation of the ruling Convention People's Party and against panic nationalisation in the face of economic difficulties. In January 1966 it had to agree to a moratorium on the repayment of half of Ghana's debts.[30] In such circumstances Soviet leaders were undoubtedly chary of financing any more costly and uneconomic projects with loans which Ghana would be unable to repay.

In other situations the Soviet Union has not been so discerning. On the contrary, there are a number of examples of its active support for projects of dubious value. In Nigeria the Russians have been pushing for the establishment, with their assistance, of a fine new veterinary institute, although the Nigerians would prefer to extend facilities at the existing veterinary research station at Vom, near Jos, and at the Federal Laboratory Service of Lagos.[31] In Somalia the situation is much worse. Over 45 per cent of Soviet aid to projects completed by the end of 1969 has gone to a milk processing factory at Mogadishu, a fish processing plant at Las Koreh, and a meat canning factory at Kisimayo, all of which are financial disasters.[32] It should be added immediately that the problems faced by Somalia are particularly severe and that it is not for nothing that it has been called 'the graveyard of foreign aid'. Nevertheless, while all aid donors and the Somali government have faced many problems and few have succeeded (the Chinese seem to be a notable exception) the Russian approach appears to have recognised none of the problems to be faced. The Soviet project report for the meat factory estimated a capital return period of approximately two years; it did so by assuming 300 working days per year and an eight-hour working shift.[33] In fact, the plant made a loss of $727,985 in 1969 largely because it was operating at only 5.3 per cent of full capacity, and it continues to make a loss.[34] Production is low because insufficient cattle are available and because demand is low : Somalis do not, in general, eat canned meat because it is more expensive than fresh and as yet few foreign outlets have been found apart from Egypt and U.S.S.R., both of whom buy at less than the cost of production. However, no mention of these possibilities appears in the project report which merely explains the operations of the factory under ideal conditions. The report on the milk factory is in a similar vein but the practical problems are the same : it has a capacity of 20,000 litres per day but produces no more than 3000. The fish processing plant also loses money (about 80 per cent of total expenses) basically because it is too big and is poorly sited (although given the political situation in Somalia in the 1960s and the need to provide the north with some investment there is little that could have been done on the latter score). The United Nations Special Fund is now undertaking a survey to investigate the supply of fish, and the Russians are giving help in establishing a fishing fleet, but all this should have been done before the project was started. Clearly no feasibility studies in the full sense of the word were conducted before investments were made in these industries. The results have been particularly dramatic because the economic situation in Somalia is so unhelpful. In Mali, the absence of proper feasibility planning has been less noticeable, but examples are to be found there as well, such as the cement factory at Diamou with a capacity of 50,000 tons per annum for which road and rail outlets have now proved inadequate so that additional ones must be built.

The picture that emerges from these examples is rather jumbled and kaleidoscopic, providing evidence for varying interpretations of the adequacy of Soviet aid planning. Although the weight of the examples inclines to the support of I. M. D. Little's viewpoint that aid was given with 'inadequate economic forethought', their support is not conclusive. Because of the absence, indeed near impossibility, of any systematic and continent-wide research into the administration of foreign aid, and because Soviet aid has been the subject of many political polemics, the 'failures' have been given more publicity than the 'successes'. In Ghana this has been very marked. After the 1966 *coup* all Soviet personnel were repatriated in a period marked by high anti-Sovietism amongst the country's rulers. Save for four state farms no major Soviet projects were completed, although a geological survey and three industrial projects were nearly ready. However, no attempt was made to preserve or utilise the maps, instruments and reports (still in Russia) left behind by the geological survey team, nor were any of the three industrial projects the subject of further work even though the Ghana government considered one of the projects to be an economic proposition and even though the U.S.S.R. expressed a willingness to complete them.[35] It thus appears to the world as though Soviet aid to Ghana has been a complete failure, although this is not necessarily the case.

However, the absence of adequate feasibility planning is not the only ground on which Soviet aid is criticised. Feasibility surveys are stage one of the implementation of aid; stage two is the assembling of the materials required for each project, both those provided by the aid donor and those provided by the recipient herself, and the commencement of construction. At this stage, too, the U.S.S.R. has been criticised on the grounds that it moves very slowly and that its machinery and technical assistance are expensive and of poor quality. Delays there certainly have been: the Kisimayo meat factory in Somalia was planned to start production in 1965 at a cost of $4·2 million, but in fact only began operations in 1969 with a total investment by 1970 of $5·9 million.[36] In Tanzania the Soviet Union promised £8 million of aid in May 1966, and five major projects have been drawn up which should together have utilised one-third of the total sum.* However, by 1970–1 only about £500,000 had been drawn.[37]

As in the case of project planning it is easy to exaggerate Soviet failings. The majority of Soviet aid to Africa was not committed until the early 1960s and much has been offered more recently than that. As the Russians were normally in the field after their major rivals, results have obviously been slower to appear. A timetable for the implementation of Soviet aid is available from Ghana, and while it shows some delays, these are not of any great magnitude.

The first aid agreement between the two countries was concluded in 1960 and it provided a credit of about £14·5 million. However, the projects for which the credit was to be used were dealt with in only the briefest fashion.[38] In December 1960 the two sides met again and drew up a protocol listing ten specific projects for which Soviet assistance would be available.[39] A new aid agreement of November 1961 contained an annex listing ten additional projects, but at the time of the agreements none of them had been fully researched. Possibly as a result of the conclusions reached in the feasibility studies when they were completed, or possibly because of a reassessment of priorities by the Ghana government, only fifteen of these enterprises were included in a new list of twenty-five projects which superseded all previous lists and was attached to the aid protocol of March 1963. In only three cases had preliminary feasibility studies been completed, and two of these three projects – a metallurgical and a tractor assembly plant – proceeded no further. This left under three years before the fall of Nkrumah and the cessation of work on all projects. In the case of the fish processing factory, which was the third project for which feasibility studies had been completed in 1963, production could have begun just before Nkrumah's fall. A contract was signed in October 1963 stipulating that all the equipment was to be delivered within two years, and since the Soviet technicians responsible for erecting the factory were also due to stay only two years it is clear that production was expected to begin in late autumn 1965. In fact the work did not proceed quite according to schedule, but the delays were of only a few months.

The most unsatisfactory features of the Soviet aid in terms of the delays it can create are its provisions for helping with the local costs of projects. These can be very large indeed, sometimes up to two-thirds of the total cost,[40] and the U.S.S.R. has on a number of occasions made available commodity credits, for example to Ghana, Tanzania and Somalia to the extent of $22·2 million, $2·8 million and $10·6 million,

---

* Including a fish processing factory at Kigoma on Lake Tanganyika, with a capacity of twenty-five to thirty tons per day; four refrigeration plants for fish, capacity fifty tons each; geological reconnaisance work; six veterinary centres; an incubator for chickens and fishing gear and equipment.

respectively. These credits are too small to have a general effect on the economy and are merely intended as an aid supplement. They are a rather unwieldly means of assistance, requiring that goods must first be sold before the funds become available, and they are best suited to countries which already possess government owned wholesale or retail stores capable of distributing the goods, such as are found in Guinea, Ghana, Tanzania and Somalia. In Kenya the difficulties of administering commodity credits led to lengthy discussions with the Soviet government. The Kenya government argued that it was not feasible to embark upon the proposed Soviet aid projects without additional assistance for local costs, but that commodity credits were unsuitable for this. To start with they were inappropriate because Kenya was already exporting some of the goods which the Soviet Union proposed to send them.[41] But this was not the only reason. The minister of economic planning and development, Tom Mboya, outlined the government's other economic objections in a reply to a parliamentary question:

> In the first place, there was the time factor. The Kenya Government could never be sure that it would be able to sell all the produce from Russia, nor that the sale of the commodities would fit in with the phasing of expenditure on the Kano irrigation scheme. In addition, the Government had no established machinery for marketing the produce throughout the country nor was there any guarantee that the Russian products would be competitive on the open market with similar commodities from other sources.[42]

It is the contention of Chapter 5 that these were not the only reasons why the commodity credit and, in the end, most of the promised Soviet aid were rejected; and that the other reasons, which were of a highly political nature, were of greater weight in the government's mind. Nevertheless, the problems indicated by Mboya are valid and represent a true limitation on the effectiveness of Soviet aid, although it need not be a very serious one. As noted in Chapter 2 above, the administration of commodity credit should present no insuperable problems for countries that have payments agreements with the Soviet Union provided that the goods so supplied are easily saleable. Similarly, few difficulties should be experienced by countries with state owned importing agencies provided, once again, that the commodities can find a ready market, such as exists for petroleum and petroleum products.*

The most serious criticism of Soviet aid is not that its implementation, whether commodity credits are used or not, is too slow, but that the price

---

* The U.S.S.R. supplies petroleum on a cash basis and has recently agreed to sell it to Somalia on a credit basis. *Somali National Bank Bulletin* no. 27–8 (July–Dec 1971). pp. 20–1. The U.S.S.R. is to supply $3 million of petroleum products to be paid for over five years.

and quality of machines and personnel supplied under aid programmes are, respectively, too high and too low. Officials in Ghana's geological survey department, with whom a team of Soviet geologists worked, complained that Russian vehicles consumed too much fuel, while a civil servant sent to Moscow to sign a contract for Soviet machinery for the Ghana state farms objected that much of it was unnecessary or unsuitable.[43] It is difficult to evaluate these criticisms: while there has certainly been some difficulty in adapting Soviet machinery, particularly vehicles, to African conditions, similar difficulties have been experienced by other suppliers and may owe much to the absence of adequate maintenance facilities. Some complaints have been made that equipment was second-hand, in contravention of specific provisions in most of the agreements, but this is hotly denied by the Soviet government, although the method by which the U.S.S.R. administers its aid programme means that the recipient can never be sure. What may be safely concluded is that, in general, Soviet equipment is less sophisticated than equivalent Western products. One estimate puts the frequency of breakdown of Soviet engineering machinery at three to four times that of the United States.[44] In a difficult tropical environment these differences may be magnified.

The criticisms levelled at Soviet personnel are that they are expensive and sometimes inefficient. Soviet experts are used to prepare feasibility studies and working drawings, to help construct industrial units, and to give their local counterparts on-the-spot training. Not all of this is covered by Soviet credits. The contract for the fish processing complex at Tema in Ghana, for example, provided for the cost of design work and the supply of equipment to be met by the credit extended in the 1960 aid agreement. However, in addition to this, the Russians were to supply thirty-two experts, of whom nine were to train Ghanaians, five were interpreters, and the remainder were to supervise construction. The five interpreters were provided free, but for the others the Ghana government had to pay salaries ranging from £G92 to £G147 per month. Not all were to stay for the full estimated construction period of two years, but the total wage bill came to £G30,656. These salary scales were quite moderate; but, nevertheless, it was an extra cost to Ghana. At first salaries had been higher: a team of Soviet agricultural specialists sent to inspect possible sites for pilot schemes to produce rice, maize and cotton in 1961–2 were paid £G250 a month and all expenses, including first-class air travel to and from Ghana; the head of the establishments secretariat calculated that the Soviet experts were 50 per cent more expensive than personnel hired direct.[45] Nor was this an isolated case: each member of a team of Soviet geologists in Ghana was given £G285 per month, all travel (first-class) to and from Ghana, accommodation, household furnishings, cooking and travel within Ghana; since a senior expatriate geologist earned at the most £G210 per month and had to pay for tax, rent and domestic help out of this, his net income was about half that of these Russians.[46] In 1961 a correspondence passed between Nkrumah and Khrushchev concerning the payment of expatriates, since Western personnel were often paid for by their governments. A compromise was reached whereby the U.S.S.R. paid half the salaries and the full cost of installation allowances, insurance, baggage and transport. Nevertheless, the Russian geologists continued to receive their inflated salaries until 1963 when they were cut to £G130 per month following the personal intervention of Nkrumah.

The immediate cause of Nkrumah's intervention throws light on another feature of Soviet personnel: their aloofness. The Soviet geological survey team (S.G.S.T.) began work in Northern Ghana in March 1962 and did so quite independently of the Ghana survey department (G.S.D.). After nine months of operation during which visible results were few they indiscreetly announced the 'discovery' of gold near Nangodi, without first referring the matter to the G.S.D. This proved rather an embarrassment when it was pointed out that their gold had originally been uncovered in 1922–3.[47] Thereafter the S.G.S.T. was placed under the jurisdiction of the G.S.D, but it still worked autonomously. This is typical of Soviet technical assistance personnel in Africa and is one of their attractive features for governments which do not wish their own citizens to form too close an attachment with foreigners. However, in Ghana and probably in other countries where there are established experts in the field in which the Soviets are operating, such exclusiveness was easily taken for contempt, and a natural resentment developed.

The aloofness of Soviet personnel can breed not only bad relations but extra expense. A report on the Las Koreh fish processing factory in Somalia recommends that more emphasis be given to training Somalis to take control and points out that such training has been hindered because there is only one interpreter in the factory.[48] In Ghana it was in the state farms that Soviet personnel proved most costly in terms of effects on production, and where personal relations were at their worst. This is not surprising since the state farms were so beset with political, administrative and economic problems that Soviet rigidity could only make things worse. The State Farms Corporation was originally established for purely technical reasons although it later developed strong political overtones. It was also essentially a self-generated Ghanaian venture, for although the Russians agreed to finance four farms and the Israelis two, this was a very small proportion of the 105 state farms that nominally existed at one stage. The Soviet offer of assistance came some six months after the first political announcement leading to the establishment of the state farms. In an aid protocol signed on 23 December 1960 the Russians specifically agreed to give assistance in the setting up of two rice growing and one maize growing state farm of 2400 hectares apiece, and a survey of the economic feasibility of setting up a cotton growing state farm of the same size.[49] In September 1961 an agreement was signed with Technopromexport for the four farms.[50] A team of experts arrived shortly afterwards, and by the time they had left in January 1962 four locations had been picked.*

Although the State Farms Corporation had been intended originally to operate on commercial lines,[51] the aim of providing employment soon became overriding. The number of farms expanded rapidly, and many who were not farmers by experience or choice were drawn in, lines of authority and communication were confused, and the results were a dismal failure.[52] The failure of the Soviet and Israeli farms, therefore, is not solely attributable to the donors' mistakes. This said, however, the activities of the Soviet specialists did little to improve the situation. When, in 1966 new accounting techniques were introduced to the State Farms Corporation making it possible to extract deficits for individual farms, it was found that for the year ended 31 December 1966 the average deficit of the four Soviet farms was C59,405 before depreciation and C177,315 after depreciation, compared with an average loss to all state farms of C13,500 before and C27,520 after depreciation, due partly to the considerably greater than average size of the state farms.[53] Many of the Soviet failures appear to be due to rigid practices and poor-quality assistance. It is possible that experience would have taught them to be less rigid, but they were not given this opportunity after the fall of Nkrumah. The Soviet team growing cotton at Zongo–Macheri had to obtain permission from their embassy in Accra for such routine actions as the uprooting of diseased plants. The first rice crops at Afife and Adidome were total failures because the Russians had incorrectly calculated that natural precipitation would provide adequate moisture. Soviet agricultural equipment used two to three times as much fuel as equivalent Western machines, and many of the tractors and bulldozers were too light for the job and broke down. The average gross yield per acre for maize at Adidome, Afife and Branam considered together was 66 per cent of the national average for traditional agriculture, and the average gross yield for rice was 18 per cent of the national average.

Soviet assistance to state farms has had little more success in Somalia, where $27 million has been provided by the U.S.S.R. for two state farms at Gelib and Tugwajalleh. Only the latter has so far been established, and it is 1500 hectares large and employs fifty-six people and one project manager. It was originally intended to produce wheat for import substitution but has since changed to growing maize and sorghum. It is not very successful partly because of a high level of corruption before the 1969 *coup*, and partly because of bad planning: there is, for example, no

* At Adidome, Afife, Branam, and Zongo–Macheri.

drinking water within eighteen miles of the farm, and a tanker has to be sent daily to the nearest well. The Somali ministry of agriculture has plans to bring it into the 'crash programme' of self-help farms established after the 1969 *coup* and discontinue its state farm status.[54]

SOVIET EDUCATIONAL AID

In addition to machinery and technical assistance at the project site, the Soviet Union has provided educational aid in the form of teachers and sometimes schools, and scholarships for African youth. Of these, the scholarships are by far the most important both in terms of the numbers of countries and the numbers of people involved, and in terms of their implications for African governments. One of the most marked effects of colonialism in Africa has been the deification of education.[55] Education was popularly associated with social prestige and economic power. In such circumstances many young Africans were determined to secure an education wherever this was possible. For English speaking students Britain or America were normally the first choice: for the francophone Africans it was France. Those who could not obtain their first choice would go wherever they could, and this often meant to the Soviet Union which at first claimed to be able to educate anyone, irrespective of his qualifications.

Figures on the number of African students in the U.S.S.R. are most difficult to obtain. Scholarships were often made available through a wide variety of institutions – Soviet friendship societies, trade unions, political parties or individual politicians – in the early years of independence and before, when some African governments disapproved of their young citizens going to Communist countries or, even if they approved, had not the institutional apparatus to co-ordinate Soviet scholarships. Since then most African governments have formed their own scholarship board, and it is often mandatory on students to travel only under its auspices. In order to gain some idea how many of their nationals are in the Soviet Union, a number of governments have instituted a system of extra allowances which are paid to students who register at their embassy. This system has produced some startling results: when the Nigerian government introduced such allowances it discovered that there were at least three times as many Nigerian students in the U.S.S.R. as it had supposed. In recent years the control of students travelling to the Soviet Union has been much greater, due largely to the U.S.S.R.'s own policy. Her original claim to be able to educate anyone brought a great deal of trouble. Students who obtained their scholarships through a trade union, political party or an individual politician might not and frequently did not have any scholastic aptitude, and were travelling abroad for the prestige and excitement. When they found the excitement to be less than anticipated and the course work exacting they were disconsolate. Around 1963 there were a number of disturbances involving African students in the Soviet Union. The precise reasons for this are not known but probably included the lack of scholastic ability among some students, Soviet inexperience, some racialism coupled with good old-fashioned jealousy because African students were often better off than their Russian colleagues, and African dislike of Soviet austerity. Since then the U.S.S.R. has been keen to co-operate with African governments in regulating the awarding of scholarships.

Despite the inaccuracy of statistics it is clear that the U.S.S.R. is a major provider of scholarships for some countries. In 1970 it was the second largest source of foreign government scholarships for Ghana, providing 204 as against the 347 of West Germany, 171 of the U.K. and 112 of the U.S.A.[56] As of March 1969 there were 289 Ghanaian students known to be in the U.S.S.R., distributed among some seventy institutions. The largest group were at the Lumumba People's Friendship University, specifically built to accommodate Third World students, but this group was nevertheless only thirty-six strong, and was only slightly larger than the group attending the Kharkov Medical Institute (thirty-one in number). The great majority were on five- or six-year courses. Almost half were studying medicine, while a further eighty-one were studying various types of engineering or agriculture and related subjects; only two were studying economics, two journalism, and ten international law.[57] In 1970 the U.S.S.R. was the fourth largest provider of foreign government scholarships to Kenya, but with 297 fell a long way behind the U.K. (with 1560), the U.S.A. and India.[58] In 1972 there were 678 Nigerians on Soviet scholarships, as compared to 51 on American government awards.[59] Such figures overstate the proportion of a country's students studying in the U.S.S.R. because many Africans have private finance or scholarships provided by non-governmental foundations to study in the U.K. and U.S.A. However they do indicate that any problems with Soviet education need to be taken seriously by the African governments.

The most serious problem from the African governments' point of view is the comparability of standards. This was particularly marked when the flow of students was uncontrolled and persons of low calibre departed for the Soviet Union, returning a few years later with some letters after their name. The problem of standards has tended to become enmeshed with problems of prejudice and discrimination: in Kenya, for example, many of those who studied in the U.S.S.R. have been of the Luo tribe, and it has been hard to tell either whether in fact they have been unable to obtain employment, as some of them claim, or whether this failure, if it exists, has been the result of tribal or scholastic considerations.[60] In Ghana, some Soviet trained medical doctors who returned after the fall of Nkrumah were re-examined by the Ghanaian medical authorities and found wanting. Some said that their training was inadequate, others that

it was different from that received in the West but of the same standard.
The new military government has now resolved the issue by decreeing
that all Ghanaians qualified as doctors, engineers, and technicians in
Eastern Europe are to be accorded equal treatment with their Western
trained counterparts, subject to whatever 'orientation' may be considered necessary.[61]

THE AFRICAN CONTEXT

Despite these failures it is very easy to exaggerate the extent of Soviet
error and underestimate local responsibility. There was a widespread
feeling among many who advocated the use of Soviet aid (and other aid
for that matter) that it would disburse itself and would generate economic
development without too much effort on their part. There was even some
thought, among Ghanaians at least, that the loan terms of Soviet aid
were merely a formality and that repayment was not really expected.
This attitude was not limited to Africans, and, although it is unfair to be
too critical on the basis of hindsight, it is remarkable how many economic
development plans drafted with expatriate assistance accepted the
structural inadequacies of the developing economies but assumed a perfectly functioning polity. In fact, the polity was far from perfectly
functioning and for a variety of reasons failed to keep a firm control on
the aid it received.

This is particularly striking in the case of Somalia. Somalia is a poor
country by any standards, and during the colonial period it was
neglected; yet within a couple of years of independence it found that its
strategic position at the mouth of the Red Sea brought aid donors in
droves to its doors. President Abdirashid Ali Shermarke summed up his
govemnment's attitude towards its suitors in the aphorism: 'if a hungry
man is offered food, it is useless to warn that he risks indigestion. First
he will sate himself, then consider how to avoid possible digestive
trouble.'[62] The first Somali five-year plan called for public sector development expenditure of $196 million financed entirely out of aid. The
ambitiousness of this target may be judged by considering that the
ordinary budget (which averaged $23 million during the first two full
years of independence) could only be balanced by means of grants-in-
aid, mainly from Italy.[63] The planned expenditure targets were not, in
fact, achieved, but nevertheless by the end of 1969 Somalia had received
some $179 million in loans and grants from foreign governments and
international organisations.[64] With an estimated population of 2·3
million, this works out at approximately $78 per head over the nine
years; the gross national product is in the region of $60 per head. The
plan itself was coy about its aims and noted that 'Considering the needs
of the country, the Plan is no doubt modest and its targets realistic',

although it did go on to concede that 'Nevertheless, it is sufficiently large
to present many difficult problems in its implementation,'[65] and that:

> There is always a danger that the limited administrative and tech-
> nical resources of a country may be spread thinly by attempting too
> much. This can result in very poor performance, waste and frustra-
> tion. No more should be attempted than what is feasible.

But it assured the reader that 'This consideration has been kept constantly in view in drawing up the Plan.'[66] In fact, the description of the
document by one commentator as 'a bold and ambitious example of
planning without facts'[67] is absolutely correct. Great reliance had to be
put on donors preparing their own studies on development priorities and
individual development projects.[68] The results have been fairly gloomy
all round, and the austere military government that took power in 1969
is emphasising the need for self-reliance.

Instances of new governments over-reaching themselves are certainly
not limited to Somalia, which is only given as an example because the
barren physical, economic and social background is slow to forgive. Suc-
cessive disclosures of gross corruption at all levels have led the cynical to
believe that aid was sought merely to oil certain pockets, but the root
causes seem to be deeper than this. The exaggerated aura surrounding
government was mentioned in Chapter 1 as a source of the interest
shown in the continent by the great powers. The influence of this
chimera was not restricted to foreign powers. Writing of Nigeria, where
it might be remembered the phrase 'planning without facts' first arose,
James O'Connell has put the argument in a form that makes its relevance
to this discussion clearly apparent. The Nigerians were greatly impressed
by the ability of British officers to rule huge slices of territory.

> This impression led them to magnify the power of government – a
> power that was already linked in their minds with transforming
> modernisation in society. It led them to over-estimate what political
> control might achieve. It was only when they had held power them-
> selves for some time that the Nigerian political class began to appre-
> ciate how scarce were the resources that a government in a poor
> country could mobilise, and how few in numbers and how thinly
> spread through the country was the administrative service that had
> once looked so all-pervasive. But before they had made those shatter-
> ing discoveries, Nigerian politicians had over-committed their re-
> sources and personnel. They had also opened Pandora's box of
> aspirations with welfare schemes that whetted people's hopes at least
> as much as they fulfilled their expectations.[69]

Thus it was that the Somali government, and many others too, threw
themselves into the world of international aid where a thin veneer of

benevolent humanity frequently masked self-interest. One is not here referring only to the use of great-power aid to further macropolitical objectives, but also to the micropolitics of those who administer the aid. The United Nations is one donor which attaches to its aid no obvious 'strings' such as demands for military bases, preferential investment laws or the like, yet it is no longer rare to observe that many U.N. aided projects appear to exist more for the benefit of the specialised agencies that operate them than for the country which plays the host. This is because too many people, from the technical assistance man who cannot obtain a comparable post in his own country upwards, have an interest in seeing that the bureaucracy continually expands. A grain marketing project in Somalia has twice been suspended by the government on the grounds that it is not sufficiently useful, but it has been repeatedly resurrected and is currently in operation once more.

This does not mean that aid is of no value – even limited results are better than none – but what it does suggest is that aid whether Soviet, Western or multilateral, must be firmly controlled by the receiving government. The record shows that Soviet aid can be useful if properly supervised. On a number of occasions in Ghana, for instance, anomalies existed largely because no one did anything about them, and they continued to exist until Nkrumah himself became involved. Unfortunately, as he was clearly unable to deal with all the everyday aspects of development, and as his style of government hindered the frank expression of criticism, he did not become involved very often.

The record also suggests that for some countries there should be a different sort of aid. In a country like Somalia what is needed is both assistance in establishing industrial and agricultural projects, and financial aid to keep them functioning after they have been established until such time as local expertise and backward and forward linkages in the economy have developed. This is the essence behind the Kenyan and Ivoirien strategies of encouraging private development by expatriate companies, but unfortunately this mode is costly, not least because of the large profits that the companies normally wish to repatriate, and it is not equally beneficial for all countries. The Russians are singularly ill-equipped to give this sort of financial assistance as the nearest they can manage to cash grants are commodity credits which, while valuable under certain circumstances and in small amounts, are limited by the absorptive capacity of the recipient's market.

4 'Beautiful Feathers': Ghana, Guinea and Mali

However famous a man is outside, if he is not respected inside his own home he is like a bird with beautiful feathers, wonderful on the outside but ordinary within.

Ibo proverb

In Chapter 1 it was argued that during the 1960s the Soviet Union was prepared to establish cordial relations with practically all tropical African countries which so desired. However, its appearance as a benefactor was not welcomed in all quarters. Not all African countries have conducted a similar amount of trade with the U.S.S.R., nor have they all received similar amounts of aid. These differences flow largely from the varying responses of African governments to the Soviet advances. The previous two chapters have looked at the general features of Soviet trade and aid policy towards Black Africa as a whole as evinced from examples culled from all seven of the countries given special attention in this book. This chapter and the next, by contrast, concentrate on five particular countries: in this chapter it is Ghana, Guinea and Mali; in Chapter 5 it is Nigeria and Kenya. This does not imply a rigid categorisation of these five states into two ideological–political groupings. At one time, commentators split Africa into the rival moderate – Monrovia and radical – Casablanca groups and attributed a number of similarities to the states so classified. This is not the case here: it is simply that these five states acted in different ways on the particular issue of relations with the U.S.S.R., and it is convenient to divide them into two groups while analysing this issue. It is for this reason that the two chapters have been accorded broadly evocative, literary appellations rather than tightly descriptive titles.

Ghana, Guinea and Mali have been chosen as representatives of those states that responded enthusiastically to Soviet overtures. The relationship that existed between these three and the U.S.S.R. was an integral part of their broader foreign and domestic policies, which won for them continent-wide and international attention. Like the hero of Cyprian Ekwensi's novel, Ghana, Guinea and Mali all had beautiful feathers and cut a bright figure in world affairs. They appeared to many, both in

Africa and elsewhere, to be brilliant manifestations of the potential of Africa unbound. Their relationship with the Soviet Union was largely a 'marriage of convenience' from their point of view. 'Seek ye first the political kingdom,' Nkrumah had said, 'and all will be added unto you,' and the governments of these three countries all began assiduously to use their new found political power as a means to other ends. These ends included African dignity, African unity, and, above all, economic development, a prerequisite for the first of these three ends and a corollary of the second. Sékou Touré might declaim that 'We prefer poverty in freedom to wealth in slavery,' but what he desired even more for his country was wealth in freedom.

Their search for economic development brought them into contact with the Soviet Union which, during the period following their independence, was developing its position as an apparently benevolent *grand frère* to the Third World. However, its largesse, as indicated in Chapters 2 and 3 above, would not simply fall into the laps of supplicants. To derive the maximum benefit from what the Soviet Union had to offer the recipient had herself to undergo a certain reorganisation. Trade was more likely to grow if it was structured, and this involved active state participation in commerce. Soviet aid was given largely to governments rather than to private enterprise, and so its utilisation involved the state in directly productive industry. This increased role for the government in economic affairs, in turn, emphasised the need for effective planning, and here the experience and assistance of the centrally planned economies seemed relevant.

Ghana, Guinea and Mali were encouraged to undertake this reorganisation both because a number of external factors made the diversification of their economic contacts a matter of urgency, and because such changes were in line with policies already held by their leaders. In Guinea, the post-independence rupture with France made it imperative that new trade and aid partners be found, but other Western countries were clearly reluctant to present themselves. Following the break-up of the Mali Federation, the former French territory of the Soudan, which retained the name of the defunct federation, felt that its dignity required it to break away from France and to find new economic partners. In Ghana, the steady fall in the world price of cocoa led to a similar diversification of economic relations. In addition to such stimuli there were others stemming from the leadership's estimation of its own power position. Claude Meillassoux has argued that the Malian bureaucracy required an economic power base from which it could overcome the opposition of the traditional 'aristocratic' elite; the extension of the state's role in economic affairs provided it with such a base.[1] Nkrumah, it seems, saw the matter in a similar light. Emmanuel Ayeh-Kumi, who served as his economic adviser, told a press conference after the 1966 *coup* that the ex-president 'informed me that if he permitted African business to grow, it will grow to the extent of becoming a rival power to his and his party's prestige, and he would do everything to stop it, which he actually did'.[2] The West was at best indifferent to a rapid growth of state economic activity, and at worst hostile towards it. The socialist countries, by contrast, positively welcomed it, believing that it might strengthen the 'progressive forces' within these countries; and they were prepared to provide assistance towards this end.

Besides being a 'marriage of convenience' the relationship was also a 'union of hearts'. To a certain extent Sékou Touré, Modibo Keita and Kwame Nkrumah all felt that the history of the U.S.S.R. incorporated some lessons that were of value to them; the Soviet Union seemed to present a model of development that was in many ways more suited to the requirements of Africa in the 1960s than were alternative Western ways. Such feelings generated a lot of talk. Socialism became a byword. The socialism talked about had little in common with the orthodox philosophy of the U.S.S.R., and in many cases could be said to be synonomous with industrialisation and a welfare state. Its origin can be seen in a moral desire to avoid the social disruptions felt to be associated with capitalism, and also in more immediately practical considerations. To the first Malian planning minister socialism was the only feasible option open to the new state for, as he said, 'You cannot be a capitalist when you have no capital.'[3] Yet, despite its non-Marxist origins the talk did produce a small amount of action which tended to reinforce the changes brought about as a matter of convenience.

The Soviet Union, for its part, showed a great deal of interest in these three countries. As early as 1962 they were placed in a special category as states that were particularly well situated for the construction of socialism.[4] The years 1961–6 were ones of great ferment among Russian academics concerned with Africa. They were also the years when these three countries had embarked upon a course of action that was viewed very favourably within the U.S.S.R. and had yet to experience any major setbacks. The 'convenience' derived by the Soviet Union from the relationship is not easily defined, and indeed it is the object of the whole book to suggest what tangible benefits the U.S.S.R. has received from over a decade of contact with Black Africa. Africa's impact upon Soviet philosophy is more simple to describe. Marxism–Leninism has always distinguished between the subjective and objective features of a situation. In respect to Africa, the former included the views and attitudes of those in power, while the latter covered the economic and social basis of the state. From the U.S.S.R.'s experience in Ghana, Guinea, Mali and other countries outside Black Africa, it was inferred that some new states already possessed the subjective preconditions for socialism. At first it was felt that because the objective preconditions, in the form of an economic and social situation that could support socialist development, were missing, any attempt to set off on the road to socialism would be premature and would be undermined by imperialist counter-measures. However, by 1964 a new idea was winning acceptance: it was possible to embark upon socialist construction before the full maturation of the objective situation because the might of the world socialist system was at hand to support the young states against imperialism. The early innovations of Ghana, Guinea and Mali were an important influence on this intellectual development, while their later failures were similarly influential in provoking its demise.

While the relationship was a 'marriage of convenience and of hearts', it was not a union without its difficulties. The reorganisation required of the African partners involved considerable use of their political power to force, rather than merely to register, changes in social and economic conditions. 'Political Power' may be, as Nkrumah asserted, 'the inescapable prerequisite to economic and social power'; but the 1960s showed that in Africa, although it may be a necessary prerequisite, it is not yet a sufficient one. By the end of the decade the early stars appeared to be more like brilliant but transitory meteorites, and it seemed that despite the beautiful feathers they were quite ordinary within. It was suggested in Chapter 1 that an overestimate of the leverage available to the incumbent of the seat of government in Africa was a contributory factor in explaining early Soviet interest. It is now suggested that a similar overestimate contributed to the failures experienced by Ghana, Guinea and Mali and to the disappointments suffered by the U.S.S.R.

It is important, therefore, to look fairly closely at what happened in these three countries and to suggest why it happened. Other Black African states have developed close economic and other ties with the Soviet Union, and some have experienced the same problems faced by Ghana, Guinea and Mali. These three West African states were, however, the first to push their new political power to its limits in an Easterly direction, and they did so in a particularly formative period for the opinions of Africa, the West and the Communist world. This inevitably involves a danger of distortion. The experience of a country which illustrates particularly well an aspect of the relationship is stressed: when considering the organisation of domestic commerce, for example, emphasis is given to Guinea's many administrative changes and reforms; when the weaknesses of attempts at rigorous planning are under discussion, it is Mali's performance that receives most attention. The harnessing of three countries together in one chapter implies that the experiences of one are reproduced to a greater or lesser degree in the others. In most cases they are, but a difference in degree may sometimes be so great as to be a difference in kind. Such distortion is aggravated by the practical problems of amassing information. Ghana provides the lion's share of data used in this chapter simply because far more primary and secondary information is available concerning it than is available concerning Guinea and Mali where, whether from obsessive secrecy or from a real poverty of information resources, the governments publish far less material. The possibility of such distortion could only be removed by ignoring these two francophone states, and this seems much too drastic. It is felt that the dangers of distortion do not invalidate the approach adopted here. Provided that they are treated with caution, the qualified generalisations made should rather act as a beacon for future research efforts.

FIRST MOVES

Both Guinea and Mali came to independence in somewhat dramatic circumstances which help to explain why they responded so readily to Soviet overtures. In Ghana, however, it was not like this: the 'model colony' became the 'model Commonwealth member', with the Queen at its head, a British general in charge of its armed services, and Nkrumah sporting the title of privy councillor. Yet by the 1960s Ghana was vying with its partners in the ephemeral Ghana–Guinea–Mali union for the radical leadership of the continent, and all three had substantial political and economic contacts with the Soviet bloc. The developments of 1960 and 1961 appeared to come out of the blue, and to be in stark contrast to the first three years of Ghana's independence during which Ghana's foreign policy was clearly orientated towards the West. However, during these first years changes were occurring which make the events of 1960 and 1961 less startling. These changes were not popular with all Ghana's politicians. Because of the comparatively open arena in which foreign policy debate took place, a study of the years 1957–9 reveals not only what the changes were, but also provides a clear illustration of those forces which supported them and those which opposed them.

The dominant policy followed during these early years was a natural extension of Nkrumah's pre-independence statements on foreign affairs. In 1954 he told a press conference that it would be useless to kowtow to either the East or the West. 'In my opinion,' he said, 'the Gold Coast should follow a middle course maintaining the balance between East and West. I really believe in a Third Force.'[5] But this balancing of which he spoke was not to be taken as meaning that the Eastern connection should be upgraded to a parity with that with the West. For, a few months earlier, he had declared:

in the present struggle between the Eastern and Western Democracies ... we regard our country as being wedded to the democracies that are friendly to us. To those who are familiar with our development plans this should be patently obvious . . . As we would not have British masters, so we would not have Russian masters, or any other masters for that matter. It is not our intention to substitute one Imperialism for another.[6]

These sentiments were, no doubt, influenced by Nehru's burgeoning philosophy of non-alignment, and were tempered by the practical realities of an independent Ghana's world position,[7] not to mention the practical realities of the C.P.P.s position in the non-independent Gold Coast with the events in British Guyana fresh in their minds.*

In 1957 the C.P.P.'s dilemma was resolved by independence, but Ghana's position in the world changed only slightly. Prime Minister Nkrumah summed up the position in a statement to the national assembly.

> . . . our international policy must be realistic. Ghana is too new and too small a country to presume to judge between the great powers on an ideological basis. Our relations with the United Kingdom must of necessity be close because of the very many economic and historic ties that bind us together. Of the other great powers France is our neighbour and we are on all sides surrounded by French territory, and it is therefore in both our interests to maintain close and friendly relations. The United States of America has always taken a lively interest in the development of the emergent states of Africa. In the present stage of our development, investment from the United States will be of great assistance to us. Nevertheless, although we have those *special* relationships with these three great powers, I am sure that they would be the first to appreciate the realistic reasons why we, as a small country, should endeavour to preserve *normal* relations with the two other great powers of the world today, the Soviet Union and China.[8]

Ghana was thus to have 'special relations' with the West as contrasted with 'normal relations' with the East. The Soviet Union for its part seemed to reciprocate this attitude and prepared to enter into a 'normal relationship' with the new state. Three weeks before Ghanaian independence the Soviet foreign minister, D. T. Shepilov, presented his biannual foreign policy review to the supreme soviet, but he did not consider the coming event in West Africa to be worthy of mention.[9] Despite this omission the Soviet Union was represented in Accra on independence day, but only by a low-powered delegation led by I. A. Benediktov, the minister of agriculture, who was then on the verge of disgrace. The delegation's departure received only scant attention in the Soviet press.[10]

* In April 1953 the first elections to be held with universal suffrage brought Dr Cheddi Jagan's People's Progressive Party to power. The British colonial authorities considered Jagan to be too radical, and in the following October the constitution was suspended 'to prevent communist subversion'.

In contrast *Pravda* had, three days previously, devoted an entire page to the 'growing struggle of peoples in colonial and dependent countries against the imperialist yoke' and specifically referred to Indonesia, Goa, Algeria and Cyprus, but not to Ghana.[11]

Relations between the two countries remained 'normal' until the 1960s. For the first years of its existence Ghana trod carefully in its relations outside Africa, and its foreign policy, in the words of one of its creators, was 'based on pragmatism and a desire to feel one's way in the maze of international jungle'.[12] Soon after independence, Ghanaian delegations attending international conferences were advised to support the Indian line in debate and voting.[13] Not unnaturally, this attitude of caution and consolidation was evident in several fields, including economic development, an area that was to prove to be closely related to foreign policy.*

Underlying this policy were a number of developments that give perspective to the changes of 1960 and 1961. From the first, Nkrumah took a prime interest in external relations and until November 1958 held the foreign affairs portfolio. This was partly a consequence of the low interest in international affairs shown by many C.P.P. M.P.s and partly the result of Nkrumah's own burning interest in foreign, and particularly African, politics. Michael Dei-Anang, who was principal secretary at the ministry of foreign affairs and then head of the African affairs secretariat has told us that 'From the beginning his [Nkrumah's] personality dominated the field of Ghana's external relations, because he felt that he had a specific mission for Africa which could be fully realised only under his control at the helm.'[14] Under his direction the country adopted a vigorous African policy. A Conference of Independent African States was convened in Accra in 1958, and later in the year the same city played host to the first All-African People's Conference at which many of the future leaders of Africa met each other, often for the first time.

These conferences reinforced the head start that its early independence had given Ghana as a diplomatic leader of the continent. To make its position secure the government felt the need of a wide ranging network of diplomatic missions. By June 1962 it had forty-four embassies and twenty-nine others in prospect, which would give it more missions than Australia.[15] However, in its early stages this development was hindered by administrative problems, and Ghana's diplomatic priorities were made clear. In the first year of independence diplomatic missions were opened in the top priority capitals: London, Washington, Paris, New Delhi and Monrovia. The following financial year (1958–9) plans

---

* Although the First Five-Year Development Plan was substantially completed by June 1957, the Second Five-Year Plan was not inaugurated until March 1959, the intervening period being covered by a Consolidation Plan. *Second Development Plan 1959–1964* (Accra).

were made for a big expansion to open missions, mainly consulates, in Africa and a few European capitals, including Moscow. Unfortunately, limited personnel and other resources prevented the target being fulfilled. When it became necessary to retrench, Moscow was one of the capitals to be dropped and the Ghana embassy there failed to get fully under way until 1960.[16] The rapid spread of missions outstripped the supply of trained career diplomats and required the use of political appointees. However, this was no hardship to Nkrumah, who distrusted the British trained foreign service.[17] Pre-independence training for the new foreign service had been limited and, of course, strongly oriented towards British practices. Nkrumah was not keen on the British orientation of this training, but there was little that he could do about it. Soon after independence, however, he began to make use of Indian offers of assistance in this realm.[18]

The opposition United Party held different views about the correct international posture for Ghana. They attacked the government's policy on two grounds. The first was moral. They rejected outright any form of non-alignment. Joe Appiah summed up his party's attitude when he told the national assembly:

> '. . . we on this side of the House want to make it quite clear that in the so-called conflict of East and West we declare unequivocally that we stand with the West because we believe that values are at stake and those values must be preserved . . .'[19]

In the opposition's opinion, the government's limited contacts with the Soviet bloc were straws in the wind and revealed the true nature of their sentiments. Later in the same debate another opposition speaker, R. R. Amponsah, claimed that talk of non-alignment notwithstanding the C.P.P. 'in their heart of hearts' were 'committed to an alliance with the East'.[20]

However, in addition to this moral argument there were criticisms of a more practical nature. Nkrumah's policies were expensive and the expected return uncertain. Joe Appiah, for one, was not convinced that the hard taxed cocoa farmer was receiving value for money. 'The big powers somewhere in Europe and Asia', he said, 'can afford the *luxury* of so-called positive neutrality . . .', and he went on to outline the gradualist thesis that was being heard in Nigeria and elsewhere and was the hallmark of those who had no use for closer, or even more numerous contacts with the Soviet bloc:

> We believe that a foreign policy for a country such as ours must be evolved from the known to the unknown, that we must seek to produce a foreign policy of solid alliance with the things and people that we

have tried and known – the norms and concepts that we have inherited.[21]

In support of its gradualist policy, the opposition criticised the speed with which the government was opening up diplomatic missions throughout the world.[22] It argued that missions should be established mainly for the promotion of trade and economic relations. At the time they made their point this meant limiting diplomatic contacts to the West, but their argument was turned against them when the government made deliberate attempts to foster aid and trade relations with the centrally planned economies and therefore required an extension of its diplomatic network.*

But frugality and morality were not the only reasons for the opposition's stance, for in their opinion domestic and foreign policy were closely interrelated, and their desire for a particular foreign policy stemmed from the belief that it would contribute to a favourable domestic policy. They feared that the government's eye was lingering too long on the repression practised by Communist regimes against their own domestic opposition groups, and they therefore shied away from any closer contacts with these countries. One opposition member, M. K. Apaloo, argued that 'Some people have already begun to discount the forms of democracy and perverting the spirit of democracy in this country and they are on their way to that form of democracy known as the Eastern type of democracy – a democracy of compulsion . . .'† To counter this danger the opposition put its faith in the distaste of Western governments for undemocratic and dictatorial regimes. Ghana, they reasoned, should concentrate on its relations with Europe and North America, and in order to extract the maximum advantage from this connection it must organise its domestic affairs on a free and democratic basis. In arguing for Western alignment the opposition was thus arguing for its own survival.[23] Nkrumah, however, had a better appreciation of the situation, for, as he pointed out, foreign investors were less interested in the democratic organisation of a country than in other features. 'The foreign investor looks for stability, and my Government are determined to maintain a stable administration in this country.'[24] The government therefore continued with deportation and detention laws aimed at suffocating the opposition out of existence.

* Hints that this was an element of the government's foreign policy were made from the earliest days of independence. See Ghana National Assembly, *Debates*, vol. 7, cols 310, 312, 29 Aug 1957.

† Ghana National Assembly, *Debates*, col. 2173, 4 Sep 1958. A curious sequel occurred when Apaloo was himself implicated in a plot to overthrow the C.P.P. government by force.

THE SOVIET UNION AND THE CLOSED ECONOMY: PLANNING

These trends that were becoming apparent in Ghana accelerated sharply in the 1960s when Ghana found itself with economic problems similar in some respects to those of Guinea and Mali. The stability engendered by Nkrumah's policy does not appear to have satisfied foreign investors, and between 1957 and 1961 there was a net outflow of private capital to the tune of £6·5 million.[25] This despite the fact that Ghana's development strategy at this time was under the joint supervision of W. Arthur Lewis and K. A. Gbedemah, both of whom set great store by an orthodox financial policy to encourage foreign private investment.

The political thrust towards the Soviet Union was closely related to economic changes within the three African countries. Indeed, the two cannot be satisfactorily isolated from one another. They were related not in the sense that economic problems caused the political change, but in the sense that economic developments reinforced and sustained political measures that had been introduced for a whole host of reasons, many of which had nothing to do with economics at all. It is convenient to refer to Ghana, Guinea and Mali as passing from an 'open economy' to a 'closed economy' at the turn of the decade. The concept of these two forms of the economy and the transition from one to the other has been well elaborated and applied specifically to Ghana.[26] The 'open economy' is characterised by a fully convertible, highly backed currency, few quantitative restrictions on imports, and relatively low tariffs. This type of economy responds readily to external influences, and its long-term growth rate is largely dependent upon the external elasticity of demand for its exports and the domestic income elasticity of demand for its imports. Such a situation characterised pre-independence Ghana and to a lesser extent Guinea and Mali, where there were restrictions on trade outside the franc zone. However, the 'open-economy' does not endure long after independence. The combination of increasing political demands for development and the stagnation of exports brings about its demise. The open stage may be prolonged by a number of short-term expedients – depletion of reserves, mild tariff increases, etc. – but this cannot continue indefinitely, since export proceeds show a distinct tendency to lag but no such dampening can be expected of the political demands for development. Governments may concede general wage increases to reduce political tensions but this may hamper exports and will probably increase imports. As the foreign exchange crisis deepens loans become harder to float abroad, foreign private capital may take fright, and domestic private capital tends to seek safety overseas. Sooner or later a crisis develops and the open economy loses its capacity to cope. The conservative reaction to this will be to press for a return to extreme financial orthodoxy in order to restore foreign confidence. But politicians who fear serious social consequences following any reduction in public expenditure will tend to favour a solution involving import restrictions to reduce purchases of inessential goods, an autonomous banking system to prevent capital leakage and reduce dependence on the monetary policy of a foreign country, a non-convertible currency and perhaps the rationing of imported essentials. As the crisis develops support for such a 'closed economy' will be reinforced while that for an 'open economy' will not.

Guinea's abrupt launching into international waters put a heavy strain on the economy, but until March 1960 no major effort was made to alter the traditional structure of trade. In the interim the private companies and the banks practised a systematic policy of withdrawing their capital from the country. The landmark of the state's retreat into a closed economy was its withdrawal from the franc zone on 1 March 1960. In Mali, too, the creation of an independent unit of currency on 1 July 1962 was an unmistakable sign of the transfer. In Ghana the clearest indication that such a movement was afoot, if it had not been clear before, was the 1961–2 budget, which was the first to be prepared within the office of the president rather than the ministry of finance and represented a defeat for Gbedemah's views.

It soon became apparent that the 'closed economy' might also entail a 'closed polity'. All three countries experienced violent political dissent which was either caused or exacerbated by the new economic measures. In Ghana the movement to a closed economy was accompanied by a strike in the major industrial centre of Sekondi–Takoradi which swiftly spread to other towns. In Mali it was followed by street demonstrations from traders and the gaoling of opposition politicians, while in Guinea fifty-three days after introducing the new franc, Sékou Touré announced the discovery of a monstrous plot in which he implicated the French and nineteen people were condemned to death.

During the period of the 'open economy' the Ricardian concept of comparative advantage and Western models of development held sway. But in the 'closed economy' this is no longer the case. No longer do the needs of development co-exist happily alongside the demands of consumers. Planning assumes a more rigorous appearance, since the plan must now allocate foreign exchange in a rational way among competing activities, and ensure co-ordination between import licensing and the various sectors of the economy. 'To plan is to choose,' as Julius Nyerere has remarked, and in planning the experience of the Soviet Union could not but appear particularly relevant. E. H. Carr is right to number the popularisation of planning among the major achievements of the October Revolution, but it was not just in the sphere of plan preparation that the Soviet system offered guidance. The October Revolution not only put the question of priorities and allocation at the forefront of political discussion, it also created a system of government that was able to cope with the discontent that planning amid scarcity engendered.[27] Likewise, the Soviet model of development, based on the infant industry argument of protection rather than liberalism's comparative advantage and free trade, appeared more relevant to a 'closed economy'.

Again, because of the open nature of its political system, Ghana provides the best illustration of this movement from an open to a closed economy which was to have such marked implications for the U.S.S.R. As far as any two years can be, 1960 and 1961 are a turning point in the history of Nkrumah's regime. From then until the *coup d'état* of February 1966 the government made a determined vocal and to a certain extent an actual attempt to move from the situation bequeathed it by over half a century of colonial rule. In foreign affairs Ghana's voice became steadily more radical; in domestic matters state intervention in the economy and rapid industrialisation were the watchword, and an attempt was made to transform the C.P.P. from a mass party into a vanguard party. The Soviet Union was closely involved with these changes: it was a beneficiary of the new foreign policy, and its example and its cash were an important influence on the domestic transformation. In turn, Soviet miscalculations concerning the effectiveness of Nkrumah's plans played their part in the development of Soviet thinking about Africa.

It would be wrong to attribute all the changes that took place in Ghana's foreign and domestic policies to developments in its economic position. Nkrumah understood and enjoyed politics far more than economics, and when his immediate political objectives – leadership of Africa, strengthening of his position within Ghana, etc. – differed from Ghana's economic requirements, the latter were normally cast aside. The growing radicalism of his foreign policy pronouncements owed much to increasing competition in Africa. 1960 was a great year for African independence, for in that year seventeen countries moved on from colonialism. Before then Ghana had to compete for the limelight in Black Africa with only Ethiopia, Liberia and after 1958 Guinea. It took no great radicalism to appear more progressive than the first two of these, while Guinea's post-independence weakness enabled Ghana to maintain its position as a leader of the new Africa. After 1960 it proved more difficult to make such an impact on the African stage. At the same time, Nkrumah found himself being outflanked by countries like Guinea and Mali which appeared to be more radical and discovered that the greatest resistance to his plans for continental unity came from the states he considered to be conservative. Under the impact of these three new features of interAfrican politics, Nkrumah's statements became ever more radical and unrestrained.

Such radicalism need not have led Ghana to the U.S.S.R. However, as

Ghana entered the 1960s economic considerations encouraged the strengthening of relations with the Soviet bloc. When they departed, the British left Ghana with reserves of £200 million, one of the best examples of state machinery in Black Africa, a well developed (perhaps over-developed) education system and infrastructure, some foreign exchange earning primary products, an extensive service sector involving 23 per cent of the active population in 1960, but a poorly developed industrial sector which in the same year employed only 13 per cent of the working population. Ghana's problem was that of a rich underdeveloped country: it was reaching the limit of possible development given the existing socio-economic structure and had to embark upon the difficult path of industrialisation. There were political as well as moral imperatives for such a course, with the increasingly ominous example of the grossly unstable Dahomey, once known as 'the left-bank of French West Africa', to remind leaders of the danger of letting the growth of education outstrip the expansion of the economy.[28]

The 1950s were a good period for Ghana. The cocoa boom enlarged the country's foreign reserves, and in the expectation that it would continue the government was able to launch a large investment programme without having to impose restrictions on private income, save to the extent that the Cocoa Marketing Board withheld from farmers a proportion of their cocoa earnings. By 1960 the situation was becoming less favourable. The foreign investment needed to supplement domestically generated reserves failed to materialise. Partly as a result of this and partly as a result of poor management, foreign exchange reserves ran low.[29] At the same time the price of cocoa began to fall. In the seven years before 1960 the average price of Ghanaian cocoa beans on the London market had been NC618 per ton; in the seven years 1960–6 it was NC374 per ton.[30]

Not surprisingly, government thinking did not immediately adjust to the new position. The Second Five-Year Plan, far from sounding a note of caution, optimistically encompassed two plans, a 'small coat' involving £G132 million worth of projects, and in addition a 'large coat' bringing the total up to £G350 million, to be implemented if the 'small coat' objectives were exceeded. However, it became increasingly clear that growth at the rate planned by the government was not possible without restrictionist measures on consumption, fresh sources of foreign assistance, and new markets for cocoa. The first required a more active government involvement in the economy, while the second and the third, in so far as they involved commercial contacts with the centrally planned economies, required changes in the government's administrative system. As Ghana moved towards a closed economy, the administrative system bequeathed it by Britain began to appear unsuitable in a number of respects.[31]

Until after the Second World War the primary goal of British colonial administration in Africa had been the maintenance of law and order. Until 1929 there was no necessity to establish an administrative framework to absorb public investment from abroad since the British government did not make available any public funds for development purposes. Commercial development was left to private enterprise, and for infrastructure the territories had to rely on local revenues or loans floated on the London market. Grants-in-aid of the budget were available in cases of extreme need, but were administered under the vigilant and penny pinching eye of the treasury. The Colonial Development Act of 1929 provided £1 million annually for agricultural and industrial development schemes, but the depression dealt a severe blow to attempts at economic development. The Colonial Development and Welfare Act of 1940 made colonial development an end in itself for the first time, but little was done under its auspices until the end of the Second World War. Thereupon a new Colonial Development and Welfare Act was passed which made possible long-term planning. There was even talk of 'state socialism'. However, as one observer has put it, ' "state socialism" in the colonies frequently meant little more than the administration's right to preserve and protect the colonial people from developments which it considered undesirable, and to promote industry and commerce which seemed acceptable'.[32] The result was that government activities tended to be restricted to the provision of public utilities that formed a framework for the operation of private capital. In the Gold Coast these framework providing activities were incorporated into a Ten-Year Plan for Economic and Social Development, launched in 1951. The plan was modest in its terms of reference, being basically a public expenditure programme, or 'shopping list', whereby each government department prepared a list of its preferred projects which were then totalled, compared with the funds available, and pruned accordingly. Thus, no account was taken of the private sector or of interrelationships within the economy. The rationale of the plan was set out in its second paragraph :

> In a world of uncertainties and constantly changing circumstances it is impossible to lay down a plan for future years which states in minute detail all that it is hoped to achieve. No one can foretell the trend of future world events in the political and economic fields. The most that can be done, therefore, is to set down a statement of objectives which, if circumstances allow, should be attained in the years ahead, and that is what this plan sets out to do.[33]

This was the atmosphere in which Ghanaian civil servants acquired their experience.

When soon afterwards Nkrumah was made leader of government business it was decided to shorten the plan to five years, and on its expiry there was a two-year period of consolidation. Thus it was that the Second Five-Year Plan, the 'two coat' plan, was introduced in 1959. Though it was more ambitious than its predecessor in its targets, in its methodology it was similar, for it, too, used the 'shopping list' technique. However, as E. N. Omaboe, then government statistician, has noted :

> It is only fair to point out that both in the case of the first and second plans, even if the planners had wanted to use better planning methods they would not have been able to carry the exercise far in view of the poor state of the country's statistical data.[34]

But statistical deficiencies or no, this second plan was abandoned two years after its inauguration in favour of a Seven-Year Plan which made far greater claims to rigour. No official explanation was given for this move, but it occurred shortly after Nkrumah's successful 1961 tour of the Soviet bloc and China, which he made in the company of several leading Ghanaian radicals, and it was widely felt that his action was designed to make Ghanaian planning more like that practised in the centrally planned economies. E. N. Omaboe, for one, has suggested that when the Ghanaian delegation saw sophisticated Soviet planning in action, 'It is likely that they came to the conclusion that their plan was no plan at all.'[35] Planning is an area in which the 'union of hearts' with the U.S.S.R. was especially apparent. It is central to the economic organisation of the Soviet bloc countries and, as they became closed economies all three African states adopted plans that bore a resemblance at least in their intention to those in use in the socialist countries. Socialist economists were brought in to supervise the drafting of these plans – Dr Joseph Bognor in Ghana, Professor Bernard in Mali, and Professors Bettelheim and Bernard in Guinea; the first was a Hungarian while the other two were members of the French Communist Party. In all three cases it was intended that the new plans would not only be drafted along socialist lines but would also develop the economy on socialist principles.[36] But the two objectives of development along socialist lines and rigorous socialist planning were in any case not separable: the first was not possible without the second. Socialist planning implied wide ranging and tightly controlled government economic activity. All three governments realised, even when they had faith in the 'natural socialism' of traditional African life, that there were many people with a vested interest in retaining and developing a capitalist economy, and that unless the government played a major role in economic life through the institution of the plan their socialist intentions would be undermined.

Yet the plans, the centrepieces of the edifice, were the weakest links. While they previewed wide ranging government activity they provided no adequate mechanism for it to be tightly controlled. The Ghanaian seven-year plan, when it emerged, did not appear to have taken full consideration of the need to choose between competing projects, and it candidly admitted that 'Much work remains to be done in working out detailed programmes of implementation and in planning individual projects.'[37] Those projections and targets that were detailed in the plan were based on out of date statistics.[38] A very high-powered State Planning Commission was established in 1964 with the power to vet the expenditure plans of the spending ministries, but the latter resisted the innovation and continued to operate autonomously.[39] Guinea was no more successful in this respect. The rigour with which its plan was applied is evident from a comparison of the distribution of planned and actual expenditure. 47·6 per cent was allocated to productice projects, but in the event only 29·1 per cent was spent in this sector, with agriculture particularly suffering. By contrast, infrastructure (including administration) took 57·4 per cent instead of 35·9 per cent allotted to it in the plan.[40]

Despite their grandiose claims, these 'socialist' plans were little different in substance from those being drafted elsewhere in Africa. Their weakness is of great importance. They were the most ambitious aspect of attempts to 'borrow' from the socialist countries' experience, and they were central to the three governments' attempts to alter economic conditions by political decree. In Mali the four-year plan was drafted at great speed and its subsequent performance illustrates rather well the difficulties of ambitious planning in the current African context. Its fundamental principles were outlined at an extraordinary congress of the Union Soudanaise on 22 September 1960. Three months later the plan was ready, even though the government economists also had to give considerable attention to the effects of the rupture with Senegal. Inevitably, it was a list of objectives and possible means for attaining these ends rather than a catalogue of specific actions to be taken, for which neither the time nor the information were available. It was ambitious, seeking an 11 per cent increase in production per year (compared with an actual growth rate of just over 3 per cent per annum in the previous fifteen years) and a doubling of exports by 1964. For its success it depended upon great administrative austerity, heavy taxes on production, and a highly efficient public sector. To avoid *immobilisme* the administrative austerity had to be accompanied by the development of vague sounding 'revolutionary new formulas' based on the mobilisation of the masses and a breaking away from colonial forms in order to make education, social services and administration less costly.*

* Samir Amin, *Trois experiences*, pp. 106–7. This belief that the government machine would become miraculously more efficient is found elsewhere. In Ghana, the seven-year plan foresaw a reduction in spending on administration from £G9·1 million (or 17 per cent of total expenditure) for 1959–63, to £G3·5 million (or 5 per cent of expected expenditure) in 1964–70; A. Krassowski, *Development and the Debt Trap*, p. 63.

Despite these questionable assumptions and preconditions for success, the plan was accepted by government and party in January 1961, although its time limit was extended to five years. During the first half of 1961 it was revised in the light of new information and government *faits accomplis* such as the creation of the highly expensive Air Mali. It was hoped thereafter that the plan would be adhered to, but the minister of the plan had insufficient authority to ensure this and was hardly aided by the vagueness and optimism of the document itself. When in July of the following year Professor Bernard studied the *tendances spontanées* that were developing, he found that FM20 milliard of additional investment on projects of debatable priority had been made since January 1961. His criticisms appear to have had some effect, for not all that was planned was actually put into effect, and in September 1962 the left-wing Seydou Badian Kouyaté was replaced as planning minister by the much more conservative Jean-Marie Koné, who was granted stronger powers over the spending departments. Nevertheless, the improvement was not marked.

In the following November a fresh five-year plan was introduced to replace the old, and it was accepted by the national assembly on 25 January 1963. The new plan had similar objectives to the old. It accounted for 80 per cent of total national investment and gave heavy emphasis to directly productive investment (see Table 4.1).

TABLE 4.1   Mali's five-year plan 1963–8: planned investment, by sector

	% of planned investment
Directly productive investment of which:	65·2
Agriculture	25·4
Industry	14·0
H.E.P. schemes and geological surveys	11·3
Transport and other	14·5
Non-directly productive investment of which:	34·8
Administration, education and health	10·8
Transport and communications infrastructure	18·0
Housing	6·0

Source: Samir Amin, *Trois expériences africaines de dévelopment* (Paris, 1965), p. 120.

The greater part of the finance for all this, totalling FM47·6 milliard, was to come from abroad, but in addition FM30·6 milliard was to be generated domestically, with public sector commerce providing FM1·7 milliard annually by 1967.[41] In the event, the forecast proved wildly optimistic. The index of activity in the secondary sector (energy, industry, public buildings and works, etc.) increased appreciably from 100 in 1959 to 175 by June 1968, but this still fell far short of the plan target. The primary sector (agriculture) and the tertiary sector (transfers, services, commerce, etc.) were more stagnant : their indexes increased from 100 in 1959 to 116 and 113, respectively.[42] Professor Amin has listed the reasons for this failure.[43] Exports grew at only half the rate expected, thus preventing some investments from occurring and upsetting the schedule of others. After the creation of the Mali franc in 1962 these balance of payment difficulties were no longer masked by membership of the franc zone. Rural mobilisation was less successful than anticipated, both because of the quality of the agents used and the atmosphere within which they had to operate. Some of the newly created enterprises did not operate effectively, and the required administrative austerity did not materialise.

Part of the reason for the poor performance of 'rigorous planning' in these three countries was that the governments concerned were simply overreaching themselves: they had neither the cadres nor the statistics for such a task. Nor, it seems, did they possess the required amount of dedication to planning. The decision to experiment with socialist planning was more an affair of the heart than of the head, and there were too few considerations of solid self-interest to back it up. Whilst certain members of the administrations were no doubt sincerely convinced of the need to allocate expenditure according to the plan, others had excellent reasons for ignoring it. Such reasons were not always venal : circumstances change rapidly and may make the plan appear irrelevant, while ministries that are denied funds in the plan may sincerely believe that they are performing vital functions and should be allowed to expand. Well intentioned or not, however, the net effect was to undermine planning. A plan that is not put into practice is no plan at all.

THE SOVIET UNION AND THE CLOSED ECONOMY: COMMERCE

A new attitude to planning was not the only change that accompanied the development of the closed economy and involved the U.S.S.R. In other areas of their economic organisation these three governments found solid reasons of convenience for making adaptations along Soviet lines. If their response to Soviet planning methods was largely an act of faith, their introduction of new forms in commercial organisation reveals a ready appreciation of necessity. Nevertheless, even in the commercial realm their innovations introduced for reasons of necessity were sometimes encouraged and extended when the socialist countries offered advice which reinforced their existing predispositions. These changes were largely concerned with providing a suitable administrative framework for the conduct of bilateral trade. In Ghana the possibility of developing bilateralism was first mooted seriously in 1958 when proposals were received from Israel, the U.A.R., Czechoslovakia, the G.D.R. and

Poland. The government accepted the first two of these but declined the others. At this time the Israeli and Egyptian agreements were considered to be exceptional, so that only *ad hoc* arrangements were made by the Bank of Ghana to deal with them.[44] Indeed, they were exceptional, for when Ghana concluded its first trade agreements with the U.S.S.R. and Czechoslovakia neither included a bilateral payments agreement. The one with Czechoslovakia reaffirmed the principles of G.A.T.T. to which both signatories adhered, while the one with the U.S.S.R. was based on the reciprocal granting of 'most favoured nation' treatment in respect of all matters related to trade between the two countries. The following year, however, marked a major conversion to bilateral trading on the part of the Ghana government. Between May 1961 and January 1962 fifteen payments agreements were signed. While the agreements were with both Communist and non-Communist, I.M.F. and non-I.M.F. member states, the main impetus for the conversion clearly came from the centrally planned economies.*

The conversion to such a highly structured form of trading was a major innovation for the ex-British colony. The only comparable experience of any duration had been during and for a few years after the Second World War, when most of the export trade of the British dependencies was compulsorily directed to Britain under bulk purchase agreements in which the U.K. government was the purchaser. In the ex-French colonies, however, there was more experience of controls and structured markets. In the 1950s the French government introduced a series of measures designed to support primary produce from the franc zone. When, therefore, Guinea and Mali signed bilateral trade and payments agreements with the U.S.S.R. in 1959 and 1961, respectively, they were not breaking new ground in quite as marked a way as was Ghana.

However, they had other problems connected with their currencies which did not trouble Ghana. Both belonged to the franc zone. The first of the two to break away was Guinea, but it was not done without some heart-searching.[45] The Soviet Union did its best to overcome such doubts and gave the reform loud vocal support, terming it the most important aspect of Guinea's economic changes.[46] In addition, practical help was given by Czechoslovakia, who minted the new currency.† The centrally planned economies benefited from the reform in a direct way, since it provided a great strengthening of trade relations with them. The French reaction to the move was swift and vigorous, and led to a dramatic

* The Communist countries were: Albania, Bulgaria, People's Republic of China, Czechoslovakia, Hungary, Poland, East Germany, Rumania, U.S.S.R. and Yugoslavia.

† J. Suret-Canale, *La République de Guinée*, p. 180. William Attwood claims that the Czechs overprinted the banknotes and issued surplus ones to Czech technicians working in Guinea, with the result that the authorities probably never knew exactly how many were in circulation. *The Reds and the Blacks* (London, 1967), p. 70.

decline in commercial relations between the two countries and their replacement by links with the eastern bloc. The full force of this change-over may be appreciated from Table 4.2. Despite the severity of Guinea's

TABLE 4.2   The direction of Guinea's trade 1958–62, by zones and per-centage

Imports	*1958*	*1959*	*1960*	*1961*	*1962*
Franc zone	77	74	48	18	20
Sterling zone	5	1	4	5	4
Dollar zone	7	8	7	8	12
Eastern countries	—	9	45	42	38
Others	11	8	6	27	26

Exports	*1958*	*1959*	*1960*	*1961*	*1962*
Franc zone	76	51	41	30	34
Sterling zone	7	8	4	2	—
Dollar zone	9	8	10	12	13
Eastern countries	1	16	23	28	30
Others	7	17	22	28	23

Source: B. Charles, 'La Guinée', in A. Mabileau and J. Meyriat (eds), *Décolonisation et Régimes politiques en Afrique Noire* (Paris, 1970).

break with its metropole in 1958, its trade ties with the franc zone remained predominant through 1959. However, after the currency changes, imports from the franc zone slumped from 73·7 per cent of total imports in 1959 to 38 per cent in 1960 and a mere 18 per cent in 1961. The Eastern countries were the clear beneficiaries, increasing their share from 9·3 per cent in 1959 to 45 per cent the following year. In the realm of exports the change was less marked, largely because of the pre-dominant position of minerals mined by expatriate companies. Of the centrally planned economies the U.S.S.R. did particularly well: in 1958 the value of its exports to Guinea was negligible; in 1959 it was GF134 million, by 1961 it was GF2000 million, and by 1962 GF3000 million, making it Guinea's most important single source of imports.[47]

To produce this effect the French government had forbidden the transfer to Guinea of money and all exports that were not paid for in advance in currencies other than the Guinean franc. The violence of these reactions was quite unexpected; as in 1958, the Guineans had under-estimated the general's ire.* Although the Soviet bloc moved in to fill the gap they were unable to supply all the essential goods that had

* J. Suret-Canale, *La République de Guinée*, p. 181. Edward Mortimer cites several illustrations of Guinean underestimation of the gravity of their 'No' vote in 1958. 'How can a mother abandon her children?' Sekou Touré asked a British journalist; a few days later he found out. *France and the Africans 1944–1960* (London, 1969), p. 330.

previously been obtained from France, and this, together with the responsibility for civil and military pensions which France had suspended in 1958, posed heavy difficulties for the young republic and proved seriously inflationary. The Guinean franc soon lost its parity with the C.F.A. franc, smuggling was encouraged, and a black market in 'hard' currencies flourished with transactions discounting the Guinean unit by 75–80 per cent. Added to these troubles was a lax control on the supply of money which increased between 1961 and 1964, the period for which figures are available, by about 23 per cent per annum. The authorities have, however, refused to devalue, and the Guinean franc is currently estimated to be about three to four times over-valued, thus stifling the country's trade on the free world market.[48]

On 1 July 1962 Mali followed Guinea's lead and created its own unit of currency. As with Guinea, the U.S.S.R. gave the move strident support, listing it as one of the reforms that put the country on the road to non-capitalist development.[49] As in the case of its predecessor the move was prompted by a feeling that the arrangements of the franc zone hindered the development of trade with the countries outside, and were an affront to African nationalism. However, the change did not lead to any marked increase in trade with the U.S.S.R., and following severe inflation the Mali government decided that the move had been a false one. In early 1967 a mission was sent to Paris and agreed on a three-stage reintegration of Mali into the franc zone. Although the process has not yet been completed, since 29 March 1968 the Mali franc has, in effect, been convertible.

In the organisation of commerce the interests of the African leadership in these three countries and the requirements of bilateral trade were complementary. In view of the marked reluctance of many private importing firms to develop the new commercial contacts with the East, all three African governments felt compelled to enter directly into the commercial sector and created strong state trading organisations. Such concerns also strengthened their power base, both by taking commerce partially out of the hands of potential rivals and in more direct ways: Nkrumah, for example, was found to have benefited by £750,000 from the purchase of A. G. Leventis, a company which formed the core of the Ghana National Trading Corporation (G.N.T.C.).[50] The specific, overt tasks of these organisations were to conduct trade with bilateral partners, help control the 'mix' of imports and exports and, hopefully, earn profits for the nation. However, there was also the possibility that they might incur losses. Their performance held important implications for the U.S.S.R., since their success or failure affected the Soviet Union's ability to strengthen and develop its bilateral trade with its African partners. In addition, they represented to some extent an application of the experience of the socialist world to the needs of Africa. Like currency reform, the 'nationalisation of trade' was welcomed by Soviet writers as a potential step on the non-capitalist path.

The state trading corporations have experienced a mixed history. The most successful commercially has been the G.N.T.C., set up in 1961 with a major objective of trading with bilateral partners.[51] While this was its major initial objective it has never been solely concerned to deal with the centrally planned economies, and neither has it been at any stage the only company operating in this field, although at its peak it handled 30 per cent of all imports from these countries, including all those associated with commodity credits. The new organisation grew rapidly, and by 1965 it had 210 branches throughout the country. To help it in competition with established trading firms it was given a monopoly over the importation of milk, rice, sugar, flour and cement. Initial problems of combining the component organisations into one unit contributed to a loss of £66,000 on a turnover of £5·5 million during the first year of operation. Since then, however, with the exception of 1967 when the Cedi was devalued, the corporation has returned a profit out of which it had, by 1970, paid NC4·5 million to the government.

In Mali and Guinea state commercial enterprises have been less successful. The Société Malienne d'Importation et d'Exportation (S.O.M.I.E.X.) was formed in 1960. Like G.N.T.C. it had a prime and at some periods an exclusive concern for importing from the centrally planned economies and has been helped by having a monopoly over the import of certain essentials.* Unlike G.N.T.C. it has, with two other state enterprises O.P.A.M. and S.O.N.E.A., a monopoly over most exports. The import side of S.O.M.I.E.X. work has been hindered by a loss of FM1 milliard in depreciation of stocks, while the export side has been dogged by smuggling. So bad did the latter become as a result of the state monopoly and the currency reforms that the government had eventually to give *de facto* recognition to the situation by the introduction of two sorts of import licences: 'licences avec règlement financier' and 'licences sans règlement financier'. The former were for the purchase of essential goods and carried an official allocation of foreign exchange. The latter permitted the import of non-essentials but provided no foreign exchange thus recognising, in effect, that the holder possessed a supply of 'hard' currency across the border. So unpopular was the state monopoly that one of the first acts of the military government that overthrew Modibo Keita in 1968 was to limit the scope of state commerce.[52]

In Guinea the history of state commerce has been particularly convoluted, and it illustrates some of the difficulties of this path. Between

---

* Sugar, salt, flour, milk, oil, green tea, soap, matches, cigarettes, cement and sisal. Private enterprise was given limited rights to trade with the centrally planned economies in 1964. *Elements du Bilan Economique 1964*, Chambre de Commerce, d'Agriculture et d'Industry de Bamako (Mar 1965), p. 18.

1959 and 1961 there was a moderate level of state intervention; from 1961 to 1963 emphasis was put on regionalism; 1963-4 was marked by a liberalisation of the commercial regime, but in November 1964 the controls were severely reintroduced. Since then the trickle of information emanating from Guinea suggests that the system of controls remains in force.

The first phase coincided with the belief prevailing within the party and government that the fundamental conflict facing Guinea was an external one : that between the international exploiters – the imperialists – and the international exploited – the Third World. Little weight was given to the danger of internal conflict between the exploiting bourgeoisie and the exploited masses. There was thus felt to be no need to adopt a commercial policy which vigorously curtailed the power of the bourgeoisie, besides which the government's capacity immediately after independence was decidedly limited.[53] The policy adopted inclined to the immediate decolonisation of commerce, with beneficial results for the bourgeoisie who were admitted to sectors whence they had formerly been excluded by expatriate competition. The state reserved to itself a semi-monopoly on imports and exports, a monopoly of the wholesale trade, and a participation in the retail sector where, for example, it established model shops to illustrate the 'correct' prices. One of the government's first moves in establishing such a position was in the field of trade with the centrally planned economies. In 1958 a mixed company in which the government held a 50 per cent stake, the Société Africaine d'Expansion, was established to develop trade with the socialist countries.[54] On 24 January 1959 it was absorbed into a new and wider-ranging organisation, the Comptoir Guinéen du Commerce Extérieur (C.G.C.E.), which held a complete monopoly over trade with the East and, after June, a monopoly on the import of rice, sugar, flour, cement, beer and matches and gave priority to imports of these goods from the centrally planned economies.

The policy of giving preference to the socialist countries was to a certain extent a reaction to fears that flowed from Guinea's isolation. Numerous French enterprises had withdrawn or were operating at a reduced level, and many expatriates had left the country. This was partly due to French pressure and partly due to fears of mass nationalisation.* The result was widespread unemployment, and the immediate need to feed those who were without work was met by food imports from the socialist countries.[55] In addition, there were fears that France and its allies would use a trade boycott as a weapon to undermine the new republic. Thus, for example, it was decided that petroleum imports,

* In the summer of 1959 all firms operating in Guinea were required to register their headquarters in the country by the end of September. *West Africa*, no. 2208, 26 Sep 1959, p. 773.

which came from international companies and were refined in France, should henceforth be supplemented by imports from the U.S.S.R. so as to outflank any attempts to cut off Western supplies. By the mid-1960s imported petroleum was exclusively Soviet or Cuban.[56]

The new policy met with initial success. The prices of many imported goods were lowered, for the prevailing prices in the franc zone were above world market levels, and the price of exports rose. However, the tasks entrusted to the C.G.C.E. were too great for it. It had multifarious roles: importer–exporter, wholesaler, food retailer, concessionaire for vehicles, banker and hotelier. The result was *un courant générale d'anarchie*, made worse by the hostility of private enterprise.[57] Following the creation of the Guinean franc, the conflict with private enterprise was ameliorated, but only because of the drastic action of the large expatriate concerns, such as C.F.A.O. and Niger France, that closed most of their establishments.

On 11 May 1960 the Comptoir Guinéen du Commerce Interieur (C.G.C.I.) was formed with a network of state shops to engage in the retail trade. It was intended that the new organisation should handle the sale and servicing of C.G.C.E. goods, market research and price fixing. However, problems remained and the supply of goods to the interior was irregular. The two organisations were too unwieldly and too hastily constructed. Bookkeeping was poor, as was planning. In 1961, instead of the planned level of FG11·1 million imports, the bill came to FG15·7 million with the increase largely being accounted for by consumer goods.[58]

On 25 August 1961 both the C.G.C.I. and the C.G.C.E. were abolished and a new set of institutions was created with the emphasis on functional specificity and regionalism. The C.G.C.E. was replaced by a series of specialist import and export corporations: Guinexport was given responsibility for agricultural exports and Prodex for the export of other local products, and there were fifteen separate organisations for imports. The functions of the C.G.C.I. were redistributed between some large national stores and a series of regional *comptoirs* which engaged in the wholesale trade under the guidance of the regional administration. The state shops were either let out to private concerns or closed.

This limited liberalisation met some internal opposition, and shortly afterwards there occurred the events which culminated in the expulsion of Ambassador Solod. However, the decentralisation did not bring about the required improvements. The regional authorities abused their position to buy goods on credit, and by October 1963 they owed the regional *comptoirs* FG2·6 milliard. It was therefore decided to liquidate the regional experiment, and a period of greater free enterprise was ushered in. The state monopoly on exports was abolished and retail trade was liberalised, although an attempt was made to restrict the development of a mass of petty traders. Unfortunately, the new methods proved no more successful than the old. Despite a 10 per cent price cut, widespread hoarding and smuggling to neighbouring countries pushed up the price level. A very large number of small traders appeared and corruption and stealing became even more marked. The main beneficiaries were the bourgeoisie who had consistently improved their position since independence.* In line with their enrichment, party thinking began to move against the domestic bourgeoisie, and the tenets of scientific socialism were taken more seriously. In 1964 the situation came to a head. The *loi-cadre* of 8 November 1964 was designed to curtail abuses and satisfy the left-wingers, who had been disturbed by what they regarded as concessions to capitalism and the West.[59] The regional *comptoirs* were re-established under a new name but were placed directly under the control of the minister of internal trade. Subject to their financial viability, some state shops were reopened, and consumer co-operatives were encouraged. At the same time all the privileges accorded to private traders were withdrawn, a series of new controls was imposed, and at attempt was made to give preference in what remained of the private sector to 'legitimate' traders, i.e. those established before 1958. The state monopoly on foreign trade was reimposed and there was a doubling of customs and border guard officials. The reimposition of the monopoly on foreign trade was, in fact, a formal rather than an effective change, for state control had never really been removed. Although the state monopoly had officially been relaxed in 1961, the private trader still had an obligation to operate through a state corporation and to obtain from the government an import or export licence. After the *loi-cadre*, principle was brought into line with practice and Guinexport was given the formal and actual monopoly of exports (Prodex had been abolished in 1963), while the fifteen specialist concerns retrieved their monopoly over imports. The effects of the *loi-cadre* were dramatic. In the region of Gueckédou, for example, with 135,000 inhabitants, only three private traders were left as officially recognised operators. They were joined by U.R.C.O.M.A., a regional consumer co-operative which had seven district co-operatives controlling sixty-five shops.[60] Four years later Guinexport's powers were again trimmed, but not as part of any more liberal experiments. It had been guilty, according to the newspaper *Horoya,* of cavalier behaviour regarding certain countries. It had been giving preference to some buyers at the expense of the socialist countries in return for what *Horoya* rather primly described as 'considerations which, while currently accepted in Western business circles, are felt to be incompatible with State officials'. Henceforth, the choice of market for the country's exports was to be made under the supervision of the appropriate ministry, with Guinexport

---

* Rivière, *Les Consequences* p. 83. Evidence for this is that in 1961 imports of textiles and shoes were 99 per cent higher than planned, and motorcycle imports were 104 per cent above planned levels.

merely executing the accords so contracted.[61] Guinexport also lost its powers to purchase goods for export direct from the consumer co-operatives and private traders.

The reaction of private traders to the November 1964 *loi-cadre* was sharp. Attempts were made to form a new political party, the Parti de l'Unité Nationale. The government's counter action was equally decisive, and it arrested the leaders of the movement. The French were accused of complicity, and relations, which had been improving, cooled. While it was able to deal with political opposition, the government was less able to remove the deficiencies of economic organisation. Prices rose but wages remained stagnant. Between 1960 and 1969, according to one estimate, prices rose on average 100–20 per cent but labourers' and lower white-collar wages increased by only 10 per cent.[62] Together with this inflation came a poor distribution system: not only was the supply of goods irregular but it was also uneven, with Conakry and the main towns being relatively well provided, to the detriment of the interior. In 1968 it was felt necessary to establish a Commission Nationale de Distribution to assure a just and rational division of the goods.[63] The overall situation does not appear to have improved since then. In early 1973 Sékou Touré, speaking at a national economic conference, called for a radical shake-up in the economy, with the closing of state enterprises that were not making good. He added, indicating that smuggling is still a major problem, that the systematic closure of frontiers would continue and that markets which were usually held close to the frontier would be moved farther away from it.[64]

It is quite correct to note, as do Suret-Canale and others, that all this does not add up to a state of misery for the majority of the population. Notable advances have been made in some areas, particularly education, and even in the realm of distribution it is largely imported goods that are affected (and these are rarely essential to traditional life). It is hardly a satisfactory situation that prevails in some of Guinea's neighbours, where the shops are full of goods but only a tiny minority of the population can afford them. Nevertheless, it must be noted that a number of administrative experiments have been tried in Guinea and none appear to have proved satisfactory. The penalty of this failure is greater than just the opportunity cost of time spent on these schemes. Guinea's exports stagnated during the decade 1960–70. In 1960 they were worth $55 million, in 1970 $56 million. Part of the reason for this is undoubtedly the high rate of smuggling of produce into neighbouring states. In addition to this, the cost of operating these state controlled schemes and the parallel anti-smuggling measures is high. Close to 70 per cent of Guinea's recurrent expenditure goes to personnel, compared with 45 per cent in neighbouring Ivory Coast where Adam Smith's 'invisible hand' is given a freer rein.[65]

THE SOVIET UNION AND THE CLOSED ECONOMY: PRODUCTION

State corporations were not only established in the commercial sphere. They were also formed to give the government an *entrée* into productive sectors of the economy and were regarded as a means of spreading socialism. Besides these functions, they were an essential accompaniment to Soviet and Eastern European aid. While the centrally planned economies do make loans to private enterprise (see Chapter 3 above), such credits are normally confined to individual pieces of machinery and correspond more closely to Western commercial credits than to official aid. Complete factories and other projects which form the bulk of Soviet commitments are very rarely sent on credit to private concerns. To the extent, therefore, that Ghana, Guinea and Mali wished to increase their capacity to absorb Soviet aid it was necessary for them to extend the area of direct state involvement in economic life. All did so. Guinea, for example, nationalised its diamond mining industry in March 1961 and formed a state mining company (E.G.E.D.) which used Soviet geologists for exploration. By 1968 Mali had thirty-four state corporations of which eleven were involved in industry. Some were profitable, some were not: the four most important made profits, out of which they supported the government's development effort in 1969 by FM210 million paid in indirect taxes, but the others lost FM45 million that year.[66]

The creation of such state corporations was strongly supported by the Soviet Union. Soviet writers recognised that 'state capitalism' was not necessarily progressive; it all depended on who controlled the state. Under colonialism and in some nominally independent African states, for example, 'state capitalism' was merely a tool for exploiting the masses. However, Ghana, Guinea and Mali were deemed to have state sectors that were among the most progressive outside the socialist world.[67] The experience of these three countries in extending the scope of state enterprise both illuminates the modalities of implementing Soviet aid, and reflects on the validity of the development prescriptions offered by the U.S.S.R.

It is from Ghana that the greatest amount of information is available on the functioning of these bodies. By March 1965 Ghana had forty-seven state corporations of which twenty-four were industrial concerns, and the share of gross manufacturing output coming from state enterprises rose between 1962 and 1966 from 12 to 20 per cent.[68] In supporting the policy of extending the sphere of government activity, the level of public expenditure trebled at constant prices between 1958 and 1965 and the proportion of government employees rose from half to three-quarters of the recorded wage labour force.[69]

Nkrumah's desire to spread state enterprises did not spring solely from his socialist convictions. It is clear that economics was not Nkrumah's strong subject. Krassowski has argued of Nkrumah that

> his own writings suggest that he had a good grasp of Ghana's major economic weaknesses; but they suggest, equally, that his conception of the industrial Ghana to which he aspired was vague . . . He appeared incapable of conceiving any intermediate position between the Ghana he knew and the industrial countries which he knew . . . For Nkrumah, therefore, restructuring was not so much a strategy as an objective which could be advanced by the simple device of spending money on roads, harbours, power stations, schools and such like, which would, in turn, bring industrial, commercial and agricultural development.[70]

When it did not, in fact, bring immediate development, Nkrumah could only conclude that the private sector was lacking in enterprise. This lack had to be made good by the state's initiative.

Nevertheless, there were ample signs that what was envisaged was not so much state capitalism as state socialism, even if the distinction between the two was only hazily understood. The first indications were that the government expected the state corporations to spread socialism not only by enlarging the public sector of the economy but also by introducing new, non-capitalist principles into the conduct of their business. In 1961 the minister for industry, Mumuni Bawumia, explained that

> The measure of the success of a capitalist venture is direct and clear-cut – 'Income minus Expenses = Profits'. This is, however, not the true measure of the success of the I.D.C. [Industrial Development Corporation] Subsidiary Companies. They are State-owned and are committed to operate on the socialist pattern to spread maximum benefit directly and indirectly to the masses.[71]

However, this proved to be rather an expensive operation. When launching the seven-year plan in March 1964 President Nkrumah insisted that, in their socialist pattern of operations, the state corporations should not depart too far from the 'Income minus Expenses = Profit' formula:

> I must make it clear [he said] that the State Enterprises were not set up to lose money at the expense of the taxpayer. Like all business undertakings, they are expected to maintain themselves efficiently, and to show profits.[72]

The ambivalence between profitable operations and social welfare was an important source of difficulty for the new structures, and was partly responsible for a more serious disharmony which developed between politicians and civil servants. This lack of rapport appears to have been particularly marked concerning projects, plans and ideas that had some connection with the Communist countries. Michael Dei-Anang has referred to it in the foreign ministry, and there is considerable evidence that it existed elsewhere.[73] The civil servants would reply that any differences were the result of politicians' prejudices and had no foundation in fact.[74] Indeed, it would be a gross overstatement to argue that the civil service sabotaged the politician's plans. The problem was partly that many prominent people in civil service and other 'non-political' occupations had distinctly political backgrounds and had formely been opposed to the C.P.P. Sir Tsibu Darku, a chairman of the Cocoa Marketing Board, had bitterly fought the C.P.P. before independence. Sir Charles Tachie Menson was the chairman of the civil service commission, but he had earlier been an opposition M.P. In addition, the civil service attitude of mind was not conducive to rapid change in the direction proposed by Nkrumah. This manifested itself in a general predisposition against projects and ideas from the Soviet bloc, and also some specific instances of foot dragging and opposition in relation to individual Soviet–Ghanaian schemes.

A Committee for Economic Co-operation with Eastern Countries had been established in June 1961 to co-ordinate the growing number of transactions in this field.* When in 1963 it discussed the anomaly of Ghana's favourable balance of trade with the U.S.S.R., the suggestion was made that imports of American and Canadian flour be blocked in favour of supplies from Russia, but one principal secretary argued that such a proposal would upset established trade relations with North America and that on these grounds it 'should be ignored'.[75]

Bilateral trade was an innovation fraught with difficulties in the early stages, a leap in the dark made even more drastic by the speed at which the conversion to barter trade was made. No enthusiastic welcome could be expected from the civil servants, who must also have looked askance when the Russians delivered reports on their proposed aid projects which described their operation under ideal circumstances, and then called these 'feasibility studies' (see Chapter 3 above). Rigorous but slow moving analyses of Soviet assistance which emphasised all its inherent defects, coming on top of an atmosphere of distrust, must have appeared as deliberate sabotage to politicians eager for success.

Such fears were fuelled by specific instances of anti-Communist prejudice intruding into attitudes. Nkrumah was hardly convinced that his advisers were devoted to socialist planning when J. H. Mensah, chief architect of the seven-year plan and the senior civil servant member of the state planning commission, wrote an article arguing that Marxism was irrelevant to Ghana.[76] Before this relations between Mensah and Nkrumah had been excellent, but after the article was attacked in the

---

* It was an influential body consisting of seven ministers (at a time when there were only eleven ministers in the cabinet) and a secretariat of four high-level civil servants.

Spark the state planning commission ceased to function until it was reborn in June 1965 under a new executive director.[77] The ill-feeling between the Ghana geological survey department and the Soviet geological survey team has been noted in Chapter 3. Relations were no better in the State Farms Corporation. The origin of the state farms idea had nothing to do with the U.S.S.R. and was essentially an extension of technical experiments from the colonial period.[78] However, the designation 'state farms' and the fact that the first major policy statement leading to their creation was made the day after Ghana became a republic and was swiftly followed by Soviet offers of assistance, gave the whole scheme political overtones. Norman Uphoff records J. H. Mensah as being of the opinion that civil servants were biased against everything Russian and resisted the state farms as 'Communist'.[79]

The effects of this civil service reticence was to add further fuel to Nkrumah's distrust and encourage him to dispense with their advice. The civil service official who complained from Moscow that much of the equipment he was being offered was unnecessary or unsuitable received in reply a curt directive from Accra to sign the order and have done.[80] The speed of change in the arrangement of government functions was often so fast as to hinder any attempt to secure technical competence.[81] In 1961 the ministry of agriculture was organised almost out of existence, and Nkrumah has been recorded as stating that the ministry of foreign affairs ought to be burned down.[82] Parallel lines of authority developed radiating from the president. At the height of this, in 1962–3, there were twelve secretariats in the Flagstaff House compound and twelve ministries elsewhere in Accra. The result was that co-ordination, never very good, became almost impossible, and Nkrumah came to rely on his cronies, who unfortunately showed themselves interested only in private financial gain. It appears that towards the end of his regime the president had become totally isolated and unaware of the true state of the economy.*

The rapid and widespread introduction of state enterprises would have presented difficulties in the most favourable situation. Often the statistical information needed to make effective decisions was lacking, as were the necessary administrative cadres and working capital. After 1965 twenty-four of the state enterprises, those involved directly with industrial production, came under the general supervision of the state enterprises secretariat, which was essentially a separate government department. The other corporations – service, commercial, agricultural,

---

* In March 1965 he met all his most qualified financial advisers, who reported Ghana's near-bankruptcy. Nkrumah seemed stunned at the news and resolved to put the economic house in order, but this resolve was soon undermined by his cronies who persuaded him that the civil service was painting a gloomy picture in order to slow down the rate of transformation. N. Uphoff, *Ghana's Experience*, Chapter 8, n. 8.

constructional and trading enterprises – continued to operate under the aegis of various appropriate ministries. Administrative control under such an arrangement was diffuse, uncertain and sometimes confusing.[83] However, such problems were greatly exacerbated when the political leadership mistrusted those administrative cadres that it did have. As a result, despite the claims of the president that the state enterprises were to be run on commercial lines, the 1963 *Economic Survey* warned that few of them had been able to justify their existence and recommended that they all be examined with a view to being put on a sound business line.[84]

The State Farms Corporation revealed this disharmony in a particularly striking fashion. The seven-year plan had recognised that the corporation was 'most liable to run into difficulty through inadequate organisation and insufficiency of management', but nevertheless expansion was pushed ahead rapidly.[85] Up to October 1962 the corporation had acquired only twenty-six state farms, but it was then compelled by presidential directive to absorb 10,000 people put out of work by a reorganisation of the ministry of agriculture; its complement of 'farms' rose from twenty-six to 105.[86] This influx of workers who were not state farmers by experience or choice did little to help the venture. Krobo Edusei, when minister of agriculture, complained characteristically that 'The state farmers sit down and drink palm wine when they should work', and the Abrahams commission of enquiry remarked in more measured terms that on the state farms 'There is a definite hour to begin work and a definite hour for closing. These hours are, unfortunately, not necessarily related to the demands of farming.'[87] In addition, management and co-ordination were complicated by the existence of three separate chains of authority. Agricultural officers, who were in charge of technical matters, were responsible to the ministry of agriculture. Executive officers, who were responsible for administration, were employees of the State Farms Corporation. On top of this, the Israeli and Soviet advisers on their farms reported directly to their ambassador, who might persuade Nkrumah to overrule ministry or State Farms Corporation decisions. There was a running battle between the agricultural and executive officers, with the former regarding the latter as party hacks and in turn being considered arrogant and unrealistic civil servants.[88]

When introducing the State Farms Bill into parliament, Krobo Edusei had assured members that he had 'sufficient powers in the draft Instrument of Incorporation of the Ghana State Farms Corporation to see to it that its finances are properly managed and husbanded'.[89] Nevertheless, the resulting disorder was most conducive to mismanagement and corruption. One thousand tractors, for example, were ordered without competitive tendering; they were surplus to requirements and cost the government over 10 per cent more than the sum originally voted by parliament.[90]

Even the G.N.T.C., which was one of the most commercially successful of the new corporations, experienced conflicts over political and economic objectives. At the national level it sometimes had to import goods that the government felt it politically necessary to import. At the local level it was liable to be used as a source of political patronage.[91] Other examples could be multiplied. One which closely affects the U.S.S.R. is the State Fishing Corporation. It purchased Soviet trawlers but has never operated them successfully, and they now lie idle. Its privately owned rival, Mankoadze Fisheries, bought similar craft and used them with profit.[92]

The Balance Sheet

This account of the relationship between Ghana, Guinea and Mali, and the U.S.S.R. has emphasised the 'marital problems'. The failures are all too evident and have received much attention. It should, therefore, be emphasised that the picture is not entirely bad. It is too easy to equate prosperity with the volume of goods to be found in the shops of capital cities. With specific reference to relations with the U.S.S.R., although much that was 'borrowed' from Soviet experience has proved inappropriate, there are notable successes. Soviet assistance and commerce enabled Guinea to survive the first difficult years. Bilateralism is now recognised as an important part of Ghana's trade strategy, and the payments agreement with the U.S.S.R. has survived three different post-Nkrumah governments. Further, the events since independence provide a wealth of experience for all the new African countries showing both the advantages of experimentation and its limitations.

Nevertheless, the overall result has been disappointing. Socialism was seen as a means to industrialisation, but by December 1965 agriculture accounted for 55 per cent of Ghana's G.D.P. as against 52 per cent in 1957.[93] Socialism was to promote equality and forestall class divisions, but in Guinea the marked colonial differentials in salaries have been maintained in state enterprises, and the workers and peasantry have been ill-equipped to withstand inflation.[94] The blame for the failure of the development plans, according to Samir Amin, lies with the politicians who wasted scarce resources on prestige and luxury projects. There can be no doubt that such costly white elephants exist and that, as in the case of 'Job 600' in Accra, they may be the final straw on the camel's back. But man does not live by bread alone. Some, although only some, of the prestige projects were possibly an essential accompaniment to calls to austerity, but planners seem to have overlooked such political realities.

One of the factors underlying the experiments of the early 1960s was a belief in the supremacy of government, not only in the legal but also in the practical sense, and in its ability to force the pace of economic and social change. This view was explicitly stated by the U.S.S.R. with its distinction between subjective and objective factors and the growing belief in the possibility of revolution from above. The process of extending the sphere of state economic activity was assisted from the Soviet Union by aid and trade and, if the statements of Soviet politicians and scholars are any guide, by advice. While less explicitly stated, there seem to be grounds for believing that the Africans held similar views. A. Zolberg has suggested that Africans in this period had a very mechanical view of the political community : they conceived the state as a set of levers with which to apply direct pressure on the polity in order to achieve the government's goals.[95] Certainly Guinea's attempts to organise commerce, for example, leave the impression that those in power saw success in terms of finding the 'right formula' for their decrees; when the formula remained elusive the only explanation left to the government was the activity of 'saboteurs'. To the extent that they held similar views as to the strength of political power in Africa the two sides no doubt reinforced each other, encouraging each other in their course of action.

However, the motives behind the extension of the state sector by these three African governments were not solely concerned with creating an anti-colonialist, socialist revolution from above. They also involved considerations of more immediate, parochial self-interest. The need for the African governments to secure a power base has already been introduced. Before independence the colonial authorities provide a *raison d'être* for the nationalist movements and their leaders. After independence this justification was removed and new methods of securing support had to be devised. The public sector in the new states became an object of high esteem in which employment was eagerly sought; it was also the sector over which the government had the greatest degree of control. It was, therefore, to this sector that the rulers looked for a source of patronage. As the need for patronage grew, so did the public sector. This fact does not appear to have been fully appreciated by Soviet commentators until after the failure of their protégés in Ghana and Mali forced a reconsideration.

Those drawn into the public sector were thus not necessarily socialists in the Soviet use of this term. Neither were many of those whose task it was to effect the revolution from above. Many found opportunist reasons for appearing to have the correct views. The novelist Ayi Kwei Armah has summed up the later Nkrumah period in the sentence 'Men who know nothing about politics have grown hot with ideology, thinking of all the money that will come.'[96] Few concrete measures were taken to alter this situation by the African leaders, and little assistance could be given in this sphere by the U.S.S.R. In 1961 Nkrumah 'purged' the 'conservatives' from his government and replaced them with men of a more radical disposition, but within a year the 'old guard' had returned to office. In 1967 Modibo Keita reformed his administration by creating a National Council for the Defence of the Revolution, but in the November of the following year it was overthrown by a military *coup*, provoked, at least in part, by the increasingly radical style of its rule. Attempts were made to 're-educate' the governors and educate the youth along socialist lines, by such means as the Ideological Institute established by Nkrumah at Winneba. The Soviet Union could and did give assistance to education in the form of buildings, teachers and scholarships, but there is no evidence that it produced any marked effect in popularising scientific socialism.

Perhaps the major lesson to be drawn from the relationship that developed between the U.S.S.R. and Ghana, Guinea and Mali is that it emphasises the constraints that exist to limit freedom of manoeuvre. Economic co-operation offered one of the most fruitful lines for developing contacts between Africa and the socialist bloc. It was fruitful in the sense that it could benefit both sides and in the sense that there was scope for it to mature from simple, loose ties to the more complex commercial relationship that the U.S.S.R. has, for example, with India. However, trade and aid have been a double edged prize, for it was in their quest that the most serious constraints to the further development of Afro-Soviet relations were experienced. For Africa, bilateral trade involved organisational problems which, while not insurmountable, suggest that it cannot at present successfully form more than a small part of total trade; state involvement in productive industry often achieved little for the G.N.P. and may have exacerbated existing tensions between different elements of the administration.

The lessons for the Soviet Union were clear, and have clearly been taken. It has had to recognise that limitations exist in African countries even where there is a leadership that is anxious to overcome them. Such a proposition is well-known to Marxism–Leninism, but in the middle 1960s it was overlooked by those who argued that the strength of the Soviet bloc could be used to help progressive leaderships overcome the constraints of their situation and imperialist subversion. In arguing this viewpoint, they were exaggerating either the power or the determination of the Soviet bloc. In none of the three countries has the Soviet bloc been the major provider of aid (if U.S. public and private activity in the Guinean mining industry is included). Thus all three tried to build socialism with capitalist funds. As for support to regimes under attack, the Soviet Union has been even less forthcoming. When the armies of

East Africa mutinied in 1964 the British sent in troops to restore order; President Mba's government in Gabon was saved by the timely arrival of French paratroopers; but when Nkrumah and Keita were overthrown, the U.S.S.R. did nothing. It seemed by the close of the 1960s as if the objective situation was important after all.

5 Measure for Measure: Nigeria and Kenya

Not all African countries have reacted favourably to the prospect of closer ties with the U.S.S.R., and not all have considered that they had anything to learn from the centrally planned economies. Some countries, like Ivory Coast, have managed to maintain very cool relations with the Soviet Union ever since independence, despite a brief experiment with a Russian diplomatic mission in Abidjan. More common, however, has been a changing relationship. Sometimes the changes have been brisk, like those following the *coup d'état* in Zanzibar in 1964. In addition to these easily observable jumps in the diplomatic barometer, the years since independence have seen a continuously changing relationship between the Soviet Union and the African continent : countries which once stood aloof have since begun to pay some heed to Soviet wooing, while some who responded early have since turned their backs and walked away. Such changes are evident in Nigeria and Kenya, two countries which within ten years appeared to have changed places completely. While the flamboyant gestures of Ghana, Guinea and Mali have caught the public eye, the subtle changes exemplified by Nigeria and Kenya perhaps provide a deeper insight into the nature of the Soviet–African connection.

NIGERIA

The Colonial Background
Of all the countries in Africa few can claim to have exhibited less interest in foreign affairs before independence than Nigeria. The overriding goal of the Nigerian nationalist parties, as with other such groups, was the attainment of independence and how to cope with it, both of which were essentially domestic matters. They also had more experience in domestic affairs since it was not until 1957 that the federal prime minister began to exercise some influence in foreign affairs and only after 1959 was this influence particularly marked. The regions did have a degree of competence in quasi-foreign affairs in the form of commission offices in London from which they vigorously promoted their own interests and competed with the federal government for industrial development con-

tracts. This activity was to provide valuable training for the politicians of the Western Region, who, after independence, campaigned for a more radical foreign policy, particularly since their region was the most independent of the three in its London activities. However, this was foreign affairs in a very limited form although, as it was largely concerned with promoting economic development, it did reinforce in Nigerian eyes the close relationship between foreign policy and economic development.

What interest there was in foreign affairs was normally expressed in 'moderate' terms. One scholar has attributed the difference between the Nigerian and Ghanaian approaches to the world by reference to the class from which the respective countries' leaders were drawn.[1] Nigeria was ruled during the first half of the 1960s largely by an old-established elite, a group that had been defeated by the 'verandah boys' of the Convention People's Party in Ghana during the run-up to independence. Certainly there is a similarity between the foreign programmes of the Nigerian government in this period and the opposition United Party in Ghana, and certainly the old elite had more reason to be in sympathy with the U.K. than the 'new men' who formed the Ghana government. However, while these factors created the right conditions for a radical or moderate foreign policy to develop they required a positive catalyst before they could come into effect. In Ghana it was a combination of political and economic factors that led to the increasing radicalisation of foreign policy, while in Nigeria it was domestic political considerations that led Chief Awolowo of the Action Group, an 'old elite' politician by any standards, to espouse policies similar to those of Nkrumah, and economic pressures were what forced the government to adjust its stance of cold aloofness to the Communist countries.

Whatever the reasons for these changes, there is no doubt that in the 1950s Britain's proposals for an independent Nigeria's foreign policy met with widespread acquiescence. These proposals, as they were outlined in 1956, were that foreign affairs should remain a rather peripheral matter for the Nigerians with great reliance being put on the U.K. government for many years to come. One of the most explicit statements of British intentions for the foreign services of its African colonies was framed with specific reference to Nigeria:

Even when the Federation assumes responsibility for its external relations it will not be necessary for it to be represented diplomatically in every country where some Nigerian interest is involved. Representation on that scale would be prohibitively expensive in men and money. There are many countries in the world where the older Commonwealth countries such as Canada and Australia, as well as those which have come more recently to full Commonwealth status such as India, are content to leave the diplomatic representation of their interests to Her Majesty's Government in U.K.[2]

In pursuance of this policy, provision was made only for full diplomatic representation in London, Washington, Khartoum, and one Western European capital, together with consulates in Jeddah, Fernando Po and Libreville, a U.N. delegation, and a small ministry of external affairs in Lagos.[3] After independence the government defended the slow rate of establishing diplomatic missions in Communist countries on the grounds that the foreign service was too small to cope with a more rapid expansion. But this defence obscured the fact that when the foreign service was being created a policy decision was taken by Britain with Nigeria's acquiescence in favour of a small diplomatic service and against immediate diplomatic ties with the Communist world.

This attitude towards foreign affairs was not confined to Nigeria, and similar instances may be found in other parts of the continent.[4] Such a policy of reliance upon British diplomatic missions and the British security service had obvious advantages for the U.K., and these must have been a factor in British calculations.* However, it also represents a 'common sense' attitude based on the gradualist ethos of colonialism. Unfortunately, for both the policy and the ethos, the world is not run on common sense principles. Nevertheless, the proposals for a limited Nigerian foreign service judged well the mood of the times. In the debate on the white paper in the Nigerian house of representatives there was a small amount of criticism of its limited scope, but after a short debate it was approved without a roll call.[5] The following year the chief secretary complained that the major difficulty with even this limited programme was that there were too few qualified applicants.[6] Two years later Jaja Wachuku raised the point that while foreign service trainees had been sent to various Western countries to gain experience, none had been sent to Moscow. However, the prime minister declined to respond on the grounds of a technicality and Wachuku did not pursue the matter.[7] The Nigerian government and, it seemed, all the major political parties accepted the gradualist thesis. One year after independence Wachuku was once again speaking to the house on the question of diplomatic ties with the U.S.S.R., but this time in his new capacity as minister of foreign affairs. He agreed with a questioner that Russia was

* However, this has turned out to be a mixed blessing. Those who give loyalty expect loyalty in return, and no small part of the federal Nigerian fury that was directed against Britain's equivocation during the civil war may be attributed to this. During the 1960s, Nigeria acted as the old dominions of Australia and New Zealand had acted before the First World War and, to a lesser extent, between the wars: they, as they thought, built up a bankable balance of 'good will' by adopting foreign policies close to Britain's own; this balance, they thought, could be drawn upon in time of need. When events proved that it could not automatically be drawn upon, there was a natural resentment of 'betrayal'.

a very important country, but objected that Nigeria could not open an embassy in Moscow because there were no Russian speakers in the diplomatic service. The language problem had not risen with Britain and the U.S.A., of course, and so missions had been established there. He continued, 'You must start from what you know and progress towards what you do not know. Because, for us to rush into Russia without first preparing the ground would, I think, be to commit political and diplomatic suicide.'[8] Not only was there a low level of interest in foreign affairs generally, but also none of the three major parties felt inclined to espouse in particular the cause of closer relations with the Soviet bloc. In the pre-independence period the N.C.N.C. could be regarded as traditionally the most sympathetic towards the Soviet Union, largely because of its association with the Zikist movement. The movement was, broadly speaking, socialist and anti-colonialist. It was formed independently of the N.C.N.C. but, during its first three years of existence, it operated largely as the party's youth wing. However, in 1948 the N.C.N.C.'s campaign against colonialism began to wane and the Zikist movement took on an independent existence, organising strikes, boycotts and other forms of positive action. Despite the use of party leader Azikiwe's nickname, the movement did not carry either him or the bulk of the N.C.N.C. with them and succumbed to colonialist counter-moves. In the 1950s the N.C.N.C. adopted more active tactics, but on the boat home from the constitutional conference of May–June 1957 its leaders agreed 'to play the game according to the rules laid down by the Colonial Office'.[9] These fluctuations earned the disapproval of the U.S.S.R., where Azikiwe was described as an 'unsteady figure', a characterisation that can have done little to make him enamoured of the Soviet Union. Nevertheless, the N.C.N.C. still appeared to be the Soviet Union's most likely ally. The Action Group, by contrast, presented a solidly pro-Western front. It had firm roots in what Sklar has described as 'probably the largest and wealthiest compact business group of Africans in Africa',[10] and many of its leaders had taken the title *Chief* although they had no traditional functions to perform. As a result, the Action Group was dubbed by Soviet writers as a party under the rule of 'feudal marionette princes of Yorubaland' which was committed to 'monarchical institutions'. Its views on Nigeria's foreign service preparations were summed up by one of its deputy leaders, Chief S. L. Akintola, who argued 'In the diplomatic service Britain leads and all others follow' and insisted that Nigeria should 'cherish' the British connection.[11] In his autobiography the party's leader, Chief O. Awolowo, roundly condemned non-alignment when he wrote that 'In the present world context, when atheistic materialism is threatening to destroy or stifle all that is best and noblest in man, neutrality in international affairs, whether passive, positive or independent is an unmitigated disservice to humanity . . .';[12] and it was on such a foreign policy platform that the Action Group fought the 1959 pre-independence election. This platform earned the rebuke from Azikiwe that it was 'calculated to endanger the existence of Nigeria by antagonising certain powers and by abdicating the sovereign right of Nigeria to exercise initiative in its foreign policy'.[13]

Within two years this debate was to sound extremely ironic as Awolowo shifted his ground drastically and began to attack the foreign policy of the N.C.N.C./N.P.C. government for its conservatism. The central focus of Awolowo's attack was the Anglo-Nigerian Defence Agreement. This agreement gave Britain some limited military rights on Nigerian soil, enabling the R.A.F. to operate a 'second route' to the Indian Ocean should the normal route via North Africa become blocked. However, it was not the specific provisions of the agreement but its symbolism of the closeness of Anglo-Nigerian relations that gave rise to most criticism. When Awolowo began the attack, it was revealed that he had initialled the revised agreement during the 1960 constitutional conference in London. His reply was that Britain had used 'barefaced, unabashed and undue' pressure to extort the signature: he was led to believe that Nigeria would not get its independence without the document, and so, he claimed, he decided to compromise his principles on foreign policy in order to speed the advance of independence. This was hotly denied by Prime Minister Abubakar Tafawa Balewa.[14] The most significant feature in this context is that Awolowo felt no visible qualm at subordinating foreign policy to domestic ends.

Balewa's party, the Northern People's Congress (N.P.C.), was completely unsympathetic to the development of ties with the U.S.S.R. Its horizon was less the world of East–West competition than the brotherhood of Pan-Islamism. There was nothing in its outlook to encourage it to favour the U.S.S.R. and much to discourage it, such as deep seated fear that Communism would upset the established order and a belief that any connection with the Soviet Union would further the Communist cause.[15] In its 1959 election manifesto the party said that it would 'rule out completely any idea of adopting a policy of neutrality in international affairs'.[16]

The various pressure groups and movements outside parliament that might have been expected to press for closer relations with the U.S.S.R. were for a variety of reasons neither strong nor persistent in their support for this cause. The Nigerian 'left' has always had an ephemeral and ever changing appearance, with new groups rising and occasionally pulling off a minor (or sometimes even a major) victory before subsiding into insignificance, its members dispersing and re-forming again into new groups. Some of its leaders have achieved a brief prominence before returning to obscurity; others, like Sam Ikoku, have kept bobbing around the surface of politics. About the only continuing thread in these groups, apart from some of the leaders, has been the faction ridden trade union movement. In contrast to the francophone African colonies where until the mid-fifties the French Communist trade union, the C.G.T., was firmly established, the position of Communist workers in British territories was very weak. Most of the anglophone trade unions, including Nigeria's, followed the lead of the British T.U.C. when it broke with the Communist-dominated World Federation of Trade Unions (W.F.T.U.) in 1949. Elements within the Nigerian labour movement sought to re-affiliate throughout the fifties but they were consistently out-voted. In 1956 they tried to force the issue: the fourth annual congress of the All-Nigeria Trade Union Federation (A.N.T.U.F.) voted in favour of international affiliation but narrowly against affiliation to W.F.T.U.'s main rival, the anti-Communist International Confederation of Free Trade Unions; later General Secretary Gogo Chu Nzerebe tried to argue that this amounted to implicit support for affiliation to W.F.T.U. However, the only result of his tactics was that those opposing affiliation to W.F.T.U. withdrew from A.N.T.U.F. to form a new group, the National Council of Trade Unions of Nigeria. This was the first of several ideological splits that were to plague the Nigerian workers' movement in the years to come and to engage the energies of those who might otherwise have been more vigorous in their criticisms of the government's foreign policy.

Awolowo Changes Sides

The determination of foreign policy issues therefore fell largely to the three major political parties who, judging from the 1959 election, seemed content to let the issues pass by default. There was the squabble between Awolowo and Azikiwe over non-alignment but this amounted to very little. K. J. W. Post, in his comprehensive survey of the election campaign, covering some 450 pages, devotes less than two of them to foreign policy debates.[17] However, the results of that election injected a vital new factor into the situation. Before the election all three parties had been confident of victory and quite prepared to go along with anything that the British government might suggest on the rather peripheral matter of foreign policy, in order to speed the attainment of full domestic power. The election gave victory to the N.P.C., clearly the party least interested in changing Nigeria's foreign outlook; to the N.C.N.C. it gave a share of power, but to the Action Group it gave nothing at all at the federal level.

In its new position as the opposition the Action Group began to search for a new role and a new policy. As it searched it became clear that the steadfastly pro-Western platform it had presented to the electorate concealed divisions within the party. These divisions though profound were by no means obvious, and Sklar records that 'there are many members and some leaders who do not even know that the Party houses deeply antagonistic ideological groups'.[18] But the strains that followed defeat made these cleavages apparent to all. Before independence the dominant themes of Action Group domestic policy had been fairly conservative: at a congress in 1958 it had been suggested that it would be appropriate to describe the ideology of the party as 'constructive socialism', by which was meant that the principles of social welfare and economic development should take precedence over doctrinaire nationalisation; this idea met with general approval and was labelled by one delegate as socialism 'not to the left but to the right'.[19] The right wing and the conservative centre of the party was formed from the business elite, professional groups, and the progressive element among the traditional chiefs. But there was also a left wing which drew its support from some of the Marxists whose hopes of forming an independent force in Nigerian politics had been dashed in the early fifties. The left wing influenced the party to some limited extent before independence, but after the 1959 defeat Chief Awolowo began increasingly to lend it his support. This was not to the liking of all sections of the party, and in 1962 Akintola dismissed a set of working papers on 'democratic socialism', prepared by a group of young party leaders at Awolowo's request, as 'the work of revolutionary babes who haven't the astuteness to gain the party a single vote'.[20] These ideological disagreements were one of the ingredients in the great Awolowo–Akintola rift that destroyed the Action Group as an effective political force.

This shift in the balance of power within the Action Group produced its most dramatic effect in the field of foreign policy. Almost overnight, it seemed, Awolowo was transformed from a supporter of close ties with the West in general and Britain in particular, and a forthright critic of neutralism, into an advocate of non-alignment and a more radical foreign policy. The occasion of this sharp reversal was a visit he paid to Ghana in June 1961. On his return he issued a statement in which he advocated Nigerian membership of the Ghana–Guinea–Mali Union and condemned the Monrovia conference because it was convened through the financial backing of the Western powers. This statement marked the start of a vigorous campaign for a more radical foreign policy. The exact reasons for Awolowo's turnabout are still uncertain; to what extent it was a matter of personal conviction, and how far it was due to an appreciation of political tactics, is still a matter of speculation.

From the perspective of political tactics, the Action Group's new policy had much to recommend itself. It was above tribal divisions and so could aid the party in achieving Awolowo's ambition of winning support outside the Western Region. It was a well chosen weapon for weakening the governing coalition, whose official policy of non-alignment was clearly a child of compromise born of the necessity to provide a common umbrella for the two parties whose views on foreign affairs had been the most at variance prior to the attainment of office. It was, however, a rather fragile umbrella and very vulnerable to attack, particularly since the N.C.N.C. was given little part in the formulation of its practical aspects. Until July 1961 Balewa himself held the foreign affairs portfolio, which he then handed on to the former head of the Nigerian delegation to the U.N., and N.C.N.C. M.P., Jaja Wachuku. This appointment was welcomed on all sides of the house,[21] but as it became clear that Wachuku was merely a mouthpiece for a predominantly N.P.C.-dominated *status quo* policy, his popularity soon fell away. He chose to remain in the government, but his defence of its policies became, on occasion, transparently thin and he became so unpopular that when Balewa again, after 1964, took up responsibility for foreign affairs it was a popular move.[22] Not only was the government vulnerable to attack on foreign policy, but also the Action Group had had some experience in this field through its commission office in London. When Nigeria House was expanded the other regions moved in with their offices, but not the Western Region, which maintained an independent position and was the most vigorous of the three in promoting its own interests. Although the 1958 constitutional conference limited regional activities and subordinated them to the federal high commission, this was more of a theoretical than a practical constraint.[23]

The main thrust of the Action Group's attack was against the Anglo-Nigerian Defence Pact in particular, and Nigeria's pro-Western policy, including its cool relations with the U.S.S.R., in general. The official foreign policy of the government was one of flexible independence. In a ministerial statement Balewa told the house:

> We shall, of course, endeavour to remain on friendly terms with every nation which recognises and respects our sovereignty (hear, hear) and we shall not blindly follow the lead of anyone; so far as it is possible the policy on each occasion will be selected with proper independent objectivity in Nigeria's national interest. (hear, hear.) We consider it wrong for the Federal Government to associate itself as a matter of routine with any of the power blocs.[24]

In pursuance of this policy the government was very forward in advocating the admission of the People's Republic of China into the United Nations, and it supported a Soviet-sponsored U.N. resolution on decolonisation.[25] However, this independence and flexibility of outlook did not extend to more concrete relations with the Communist countries. China was not invited to the independence celebrations, and a minister of state, M. T. Mbu, admitted that 'it is common knowledge that Nigeria has shown and will continue to show a preference for assistance from the Western bloc.'[26]

The attitude towards Soviet advances was, if not openly hostile, at least highly non-committal. After a number of small incidents, including the reception of Soviet guests to the independence day celebrations by only minor officials because the others were all with Princess Alexandra, Balewa proclaimed publicly that 'Nigeria will not be bullied' by Soviet demands. He claimed that the leader of the Soviet independence day delegation, Y. Malik, had handed him a note from Khrushchev in which he 'insisted on opening an Embassy forthwith'. Balewa continued, 'I told him protocol must be followed and we would consider an application in the proper form. We have just now received a letter from the Soviet Ambassador to Ghana making a formal request which is being considered, but we are dealing with applications in due order in accordance with Nigeria's interests.'[27] This unsubtle approach by Khrushchev must have reinforced all the doubts the N.P.C. leaders already had as to Russia's intentions in Africa, and it soon became apparent that in the view of the government Nigeria's interests did not require haste in the establishment of diplomatic relations. Permission for a Soviet embassy was given in March 1961 but a limit was placed on the number of staff. The advance party of Soviet diplomats had difficulty in finding permanent accommodation in Lagos, and since the federal government declined to assist them they spent their first year in the Federal Palace Hotel.[28] Finally, sixteen months after independence the first Soviet ambassador, F. P. Dolya, arrived.

While it agreed to the establishment of diplomatic relations, the government was more reserved on the question of any fuller contacts between the two countries. Before independence there had been a policy of restriction on travel to Communist countries; this was fully endorsed by Balewa.[29] After independence he informed the house that this general policy no longer applied but that individual passports might not be endorsed for any country 'where there is reason to believe that the purpose of travel is not in the best interests of Nigeria'.[30] These restrictions appeared to work in the opposite direction also. In 1961 two Russian radio correspondents were refused entry because their documents were not in order. Since Nigeria's affairs were handled in Moscow by the British embassy, which had issued the documents, there was concern lest the negligence had not been accidental. The rationale behind the proposals of 1956 that the British government handle Nigeria's affairs in many parts of the world was that there was a clear distinction between policy and routine administration, that most of Nigeria's affairs in these countries would be concerned with the latter, and that specific orders could be made when the former was in question. Incidents such as the one involving the radio correspondents raised doubts about the validity of this distinction and increased demands for a Nigerian mission at

Moscow. Nevertheless, the government remained adamant and maintained a pre-existing ban on Communist literature.[31]

Awolowo and part of the Action Group began to attack this reticence. In November 1960 the man who had only months earlier written that 'atheistic materialism is threatening to destroy all that is best and noblest in man' now complained that 'It is obvious from the utterances of Government spokesmen that the Government is mortally afraid of the growth and spread of Communism or Communist doctrine in this country,'[32] and this he deplored. Critics, including some members of the N.C.N.C. and N.E.P.U. (a northern party in alliance with the N.C.N.C.), argued that the defence pact and Nigeria's restrictions on contact with Eastern countries made a mockery of its professed non-alignment. Two dominant themes appeared in their arguments. One was that there was an economic cost in slighting the Soviet Union. In his autobiography Awolowo had written disparagingly of states that, in their quest for economic and technical assistance, 'adopt the tactics of wooing the nations of the two blocs at the same time . . . I consider these tactics to be both disreputable and dangerous.'[33] But he now argued that 'we have no right, if we want to foster our aspirations scientifically, economically and culturally, to discriminate against the countries of the Eastern bloc.'[34] This point was taken up by Chief Enahoro, who asked specifically why no efforts had been made to send students to the Soviet bloc.[35] However, perhaps the most telling criticism was the other line of attack: that Nigeria was losing the place, given it by its size and wealth, at the forefront of African politics, and that this place was being taken by young upstarts like Ghana. W. O. Briggs complained that Ghana was 'stealing the show' and that 'African people all over the world are coming to regard Ghana as the symbol of a new dynamism, a new nationalism,' and although Balewa replied that it was 'shameful' to compete with Ghana the taunt clearly carried a sting for many.[36] In Ghana, Nkrumah was winning continent-wide and world-wide recognition, if not acclaim, by his independent and ambitious foreign programme. His ministers were fêted in the capitals of the Communist and radically non-aligned world; questions were asked about him in Western legislatures; he seemed to be making the former colonialists stand up and take note; his policies breathed excitement. Not so those of Nigeria: the government might claim that they were sensible and down to earth, but it could not argue that they were exciting. Yet there was a need for some excitement, some degree of glamour, some evidence that Nigeria was making a mark on the world. Such a mark was found during the civil war when the Federal Military Government decided to purchase Soviet weaponry. 'RUSSIAN VISIT CAUSES ALARM', blared the banner headline of the *Nigerian Observer*, 'Hurried meetings in Europe and the U.S.'[37] But under the civilian regime there was little about foreign policy that could be popularised. The opposition continued to push this theme, and one M.P. even claimed that when he went abroad he discovered people who thought Nigeria was a part of Ghana![38]

However, concern with foreign affairs in the house of representatives was still low. Throughout 1960–2 a group of M.P.s pressed for the creation of a parliamentary committee on foreign affairs. This demand culminated in a full-scale debate on a motion proposed by the government deputy chief whip and another government whip, neither of whom were N.P.C. members. Jaja Wachuku's counter-arguments were dubious in the extreme but he nevertheless carried the day.[39] In 1964 the matter came up for discussion again, and again it was opposed by the foreign minister, this time with arguments which bordered on the absurd.[40] Nevertheless, he again won the vote and no parliamentary committee on foreign affairs was established.

With their parliamentary prospects so barren, the movement for a radical change in foreign policy looked to the *congerie* of radical, semi-organised groups outside parliament for their support. These were groups like Cyprian Ekwensi's fictional Nigerian Movement for African and Malagasy Solidarity. The most substantial of them was the Nigerian Youth Congress led by Dr Tunji Otegbeye, a physician, and his largely middle-class, intellectual associates. These groups were unable to challenge the three major parties. Attempts by Otegbeye to turn the N.Y.C. into a political party merely resulted in a cracking of the whips by the major parties and a mass exodus from the N.Y.C. However, they did provide an important thrust to the radical movement, particularly over the abrogation of the Anglo-Nigerian Defence Agreement in which the N.Y.C. played an important part. They also pressed the cause of better relations with the socialist countries. Otegbeye, himself, formed the Socialist Workers' and Farmers' Party, an avowedly Communist organisation, and in his capacity as its leader he attended the 1969 Conference of World Communist Parties in Moscow and was arrested for his pains on his return to Nigeria.

Support for the radical cause came also from the international environment, where Nigeria soon found its independence questioned by some of its neighbours. While Balewa showed little aptitude for quelling domestic criticism of his foreign policy, he quickly learned the subtleties of interAfrican politics. As a carefully calculated concession to radical opinion, the government in October 1962 lifted its restrictions on the export of columbite and later specifically added it to the list of goods available for export attached to its trade agreements with the Soviet Union and Eastern Europe. Columbite is a strategic raw material, being an additive used to harden steel in nuclear and space devices, and Nigeria currently produces 64 per cent of non-Communist supplies. At the time of the Korean War strict controls were imposed, making export to the Soviet bloc impossible. These regulations were tightened up in 1954, but this was not really necessary since the U.S.A. was rapidly stock-piling the material. Exports soon trebled in volume and increased sixteen-fold in value, but during the second half of the 1950s purchases fell off, surplus stocks were released, and prices slumped. By permitting export to the Communist countries Nigeria was falling foul of the U.S. Battle Act of 1951, which specifies that all forms of U.S. assistance are to be terminated if a recipient sells strategic materials to the Soviet bloc. How-ever, the risk taken was not a great one : the Battle Act does permit exceptions to be made 'when unusual circumstances indicate that the cessation of aid would clearly be detrimental to the security of the U.S.,' and precedents had already been set for invoking this exclusion clause by Ceylon when it exported rubber to China in 1952–6, and by Morocco when it sold cobalt to China in 1960.[41] In any case there was no real like-lihood of the U.S.S.R. ever exercising its option to buy since its own deposits at Lovozero, near Arkangel, are thought to be some of the largest in the world, and in fact it has never purchased Nigerian columbite.

The net effect of this episode was to help establish Nigeria's credentials as a non-aligned state. In the hope of providing some leadership in Africa and with a genuine desire to patch up the split between the Casa-blanca and Monrovia groupings, Nigeria had invited the African states to meet at Lagos in January 1962. The abrogation of the defence pact in December 1961 can be seen as an attempt to remove any pretext that the 'radical' Casablanca states might have about attending. Four months earlier, in August 1961, Balewa had shrewdly given his domestic radicals a forum for their views when an All-Nigeria People's Conference was held in Lagos and discussed, *inter alia*, foreign affairs. The decision on columbite may best be viewed in the same light as the defence pact abrogation and the People's Conference : to those who doubted Nigeria's independence the retort could be made that the federal government had gone so far as to risk the loss of American aid rather than deviate from its independent commercial policy.

Such cheap but effective gestures were not, however, sufficient to stifle domestic opposition. The government claimed that as evidence of its non-alignment and in order to further Nigeria's economic interests it was keen to promote trade with the centrally planned economies. In a speech from the throne, President Azikiwe announced that bilateral trading agreements would be signed where appropriate and a week or so later the Minister for Commerce and Industries said that he was actively considering expanding sales to the Eastern European countries which offered a large market for cocoa and palm products.[42] Then in 1962–3 trade agreements were signed with the Eastern European countries and they were hailed by the Government as a great act of non-alignment.[43]

Despite these gestures the reality was rather different. M.P.s complained that there was discrimination against the importation of Russian cement, and restrictions on the import of other Russian goods.[44] The conclusion of trade agreements did little to alter the situation since they were in no way binding on either side. Trade remained at a low level and, in fact, Nigeria sold nothing directly to the U.S.S.R. until 1965. The critics of Government policy were not mollified by these gestures and demanded more concrete action. The Government began to concede ground. In April 1962 the Minister of Foreign Affairs announced that all passports issued to adults would henceforth be valid for all countries of the world, and the Government also repealed the ban on Communist literature.[45]

The Students Lend a Hand

The subversion trial of 1962 in which Chief Awolowo and twenty-four of his leading supporters were accused of planning to overthrow the government by force caused a flutter of subversion scares, and ominous references were made to the receipt of Communist money by the trade unions.[46] The restrictions on travel to the Soviet Union were not formally reimposed, but the government became increasingly disturbed at the number of young Nigerians studying in Soviet bloc countries. While there were restrictions on travel to the Soviet Union many aspiring students had travelled to Russia illegally via Ghana or the Sudan to take up scholarships administered in Nigeria by a host of unofficial organisations.[47] Even when travel restrictions were lifted for adults, they still applied to the younger students, and the clandestine travel continued. Having no control over the administration of awards and no idea of how many young people had drifted to Eastern Europe, the government was perturbed, especially when stories began to circulate about students undergoing military training in Bulgaria and attending courses on subversion in other Communist countries.

Shortly before the alleged Action Group plot was uncovered it was announced that all foreign scholarships would henceforth be awarded through the federal government, and in October 1962 the first sixteen students to go through the new official channel left for the U.S.S.R.[48] Nevertheless, the government was still unable to control the outflow of students, nor did it have any accurate idea of how many had gone before it took a direct interest in the matter : it estimated that there were 200, but what they were studying and where it did not know.[49] The sixteen students sent on official scholarships had been chosen from 700 applicants. The U.S.S.R. had actually offered forty-five scholarships, twenty-three of them at the post-graduate level, but in the view of the government there were not enough qualified applicants to fill them all.[50] In such circumstances, with a pool of frustrated applicants on the one hand, and on the other a number of political and industrial figures who were on better terms with the Soviet authorities than was their government and who wished to enlarge their personal following by the distribution of largesse, the illicit traffic in young Nigerians was bound to continue. The Nigerian government could not stem the flow unless it vigorously policed its own borders – a most difficult task considering the size of the country – or maintained more cordial relations with the Soviet authorities. Plans for the establishment of an embassy in Moscow were by then well under-way. In 1961–2 two foreign service officers had learned to speak Russian. One had returned to Lagos to work in the ministry of foreign affairs, while the other was posted to Moscow as chargé d'affaires. In 1964 an embassy of a similar size to that in Bonn was opened.[51] The Nigerian mission began to pay a £N10 monthly subsidy to those students who came to register and in this way some further information was obtained, but the scheme nevertheless missed many.

The weakening of the government's resolve to keep its distance from the Soviet Union was given further impetus by the economic situation of the country. After independence the government experienced great diffi-culty in fulfilling all the economic aspirations aroused by the nationalist movement. The cost of living increased faster than wages, giving rise to strikes and contributing to a constitutional crisis. Calls to austerity came ill from the lips of those whose wealth had clearly grown faster than their official incomes would permit. Yet the economy was unable to expand fast enough to absorb all those who passed through the educational system and poured into the cities. One report indicated that the creation of jobs in industry for 5 per cent of the working population would re-quire a capital expenditure of about £N2,400 million, i.e. over twice the total budget of the 1962–8 National Development Plan.[52] However, it was becoming clear that there would be difficulty in obtaining external finance even for the more limited objectives set out in the development plan. One of its basic assumptions had been that 50 per cent of all capital expenditure would be met from external sources, i.e. £N327·1 million.[53] In the event, during the first three years of its operation firm offers of loans worth only £N177·72 million were received, and between 1962 and 1964 only 12·3 per cent of capital expenditure was accounted for by foreign aid.[54] Consequently, recourse had to be made to suppliers' credits with all their attendant dangers of corruption and the misallocation of resources. The progress report of the plan therefore declared that 'the Federal Government is now making strenuous attempts to attract ex-ternal aid from all sources, including the Eastern bloc countries which have not financed Nigeria's Development Plan so far.'[55] The government had claimed to be seeking socialist aid even earlier. In 1961 a joint Regional and Federal Economic Mission to Europe had included the Soviet Union and Eastern Europe in its itinerary. While in the U.S.S.R. they had met Khrushchev, and according to some estimates the Soviet government had expressed its willingness to render economic and technical assistance to the extent of $44·5 million.[56] However, nothing more was heard of this offer. The opposition claimed, not without justification, that the exercise had been mere window dressing and recalled that the leader of the delegation, the minister of finance Chief Festus Okotie-Eboh, had told a group of businessmen in London that 'I am going behind the Iron Curtain, but I can assure you I am going to return to this country with my colour intact and untarnished.'[57] Despite the statements in the development plan progress report, and despite numerous requests from regional leaders and the Nigerian press, the government still seemed unwilling to take the plunge. The only tangible example of Soviet aid received under the civilian First Republic was a gift of 650 books for the National Library.

Military Government and Civil War

In 1966 the civilian government was overthrown by a series of *coups*. The new military government which finally emerged had not the same prejudices to the same degree as its predecessor, and it increased the tempo of the movement towards a fuller relationship with the Soviet Union. On 16 January 1967 the permanent secretary in the federal ministry of finance publicised the earlier aid offers from the Soviet Union and Eastern Europe and indicated that Nigeria was interested in utilising them. The former Eastern Region showed most interest in exploiting the new aid source, possibly because of its radical tradition or possibly with an eye to future secession. On the following 18 April agreement was reached for the construction of a 600-bed hospital in Enugu, and a loan of £N117,000 was offered for this purpose. £N35,000 of this had been disbursed for design work before the civil war disrupted work. This was the only project on which work had actually begun before the outbreak of war, but assistance to the University of Nigeria at Nsukka and the establishment of factories for soft drinks, blanket weaving, textile bags, textile printing, cement, paint, asbestos products and radio assembly were discussed.

The war accelerated still further the development of contacts between the two countries. However, the decision to request armaments from the U.S.S.R., after Britain and America had declined to supply the weapons that the federal military government felt it needed, was not taken lightly or quickly. Although the civilian regime had aroused criticisms because of its extreme hesitancy in the development of relations with the U.S.S.R., there were, nevertheless, deep seated suspicions of Soviet intentions in the minds of many men of affairs. Soviet economic aid, well controlled by the Nigerian government, was one thing: military aid with its corollaries of the presence of Soviet military instructors, and the potential power given to the supplier of spare parts, was quite another.

In June 1967 a Nigerian delegation visited Russia ostensibly to inspect the Nigerian embassy in Moscow, but, in fact, to talk to Russians about arms.[58] A month later another delegation went to the Soviet Union and was joined there by Chief Enahoro, the federal commissioner for information, who led the negotiations, which were ostensibly for a cultural co-operation agreement. Despite his closeness to Chief Awolowo, Enahoro has not been a strong advocate of closer ties with the Soviet Union, and on his return to Nigeria the best he could say of his hosts was that he had formed a 'quite warm' impression of the place and that its leaders had a 'fair understanding' of Nigeria's problems. During the negotiations, the Soviet Union offered unlimited credit for arms, but the Nigerians declined and insisted that they would pay either in cash or in cocoa. The Soviet Union diplomatically fell in with their sentiment, which also accorded with its own desire not to alarm the other great powers, and its embassy in Lagos announced that the deal was 'a purely commercial transaction' and in no way amounted to a Soviet involvement in the Nigerian crisis.[59] At first the federal military government preferred to purchase its arms from Czechoslovakia, which had been selling to both sides before the war began. The federal air force was soon flying Czech Delphin L-29 jet fighters, while the Soviet Union supplied a large number of jeeps and, after the Dubček government prohibited the export of arms, MIG jet fighters.* This was a source of embarrassment to some Nigerians, and even in October 1968 the chief of staff of the Nigerian army was reported as saying that 'we don't buy arms from Russia'.[60]

When the war was over there was a natural feeling of gratitude for the help that the Soviet Union had provided. Nigeria's ambassador in Moscow announced that 'the sky is the limit' for future economic and technical co-operation.[61] An Agreement on Economic and Technical Assistance was signed while the war was still in progress, in November 1968, and work continued on implementing this. Benefiting from the Ghanaian experience and from a healthy distrust of foreign governments, the agreement lays down stringent regulations concerning the payment of technical assistance personnel and omits the amount of Soviet credit offered.[62]

However, the euphoria that accompanied the end of the war was clearly only a passing phase, and Nigeria has now settled into the course, begun tentatively by the civilian government, of gradually developing closer ties with one of the world's two superpowers. There appears to be a division of opinion within the government on this matter, with some ministers and senior civil servants wanting fuller economic contacts with the socialist countries as part of a general strategy of economic diversification, while others sound a note of caution. This note has been present

* See Chapter 6 below.

since independence, and even at the height of the civil war was still being expressed. After the signing of the 1968 aid agreement, the federal commissioner for economic development was constrained to remind his audience that 'I cannot end my remarks without using this occasion to state publicly that the determination of the political and economic future of Nigeria is exclusively the prerogative of the people of this country.'[63] The actual signing had to be delayed for nine days to reach agreement on the document's detailed provisions.[64] At present the Soviet Union is conducting a feasibility survey for an iron and steel complex, and is giving assistance in the medical, veterinary and educational fields, but not on any great scale. It has also expressed an interest in assisting Nigeria's oil industry, and in April 1972 an agreement was signed with Technoexport for the construction of an oil production training centre, for which the federal government has earmarked £N1 million.[65] The Rumanians are also giving assistance in prospecting and exploration, and in the production and refining of oil.[66] Given the increasing militancy of the oil producers and their dislike of the dominant position of the major Western oil companies, this may be a growing field of co-operation with the socialist countries.

Whether co-operation in this particular field does occur or not, it is very likely that contacts between the two countries will continue to grow. Nigeria's economic potential and her dominant position in Africa, which General Gowon's government exploited, make the country an obvious centre of interest for the Soviet Union, which has recently been attempting to calm the doubts of the deeply religious north by encouraging meetings between Soviet and Nigerian Muslims.* On the other hand, the centrally planned economies may prove valuable to the Nigerian government as it attempts to assert its economic independence. Nigeria provides the largest contingent of Africans studying in the U.S.S.R., some 1000 of them in 1971. In 1968 the two countries signed an agreement on mutual recognition of academic qualifications, and there are now some graduates of Russian universities in the Nigerian civil service. These are not rabid revolutionaries: the old adage that you send a man to Paris to make him a Communist, and to Moscow to produce a capitalist, still has much truth. However, they will be used to dealing with the Russians and will find it perfectly normal in a way that their predecessors did not.

Nevertheless, contact is likely to remain on a very business-like footing for at least some time to come. Much of the Soviet Union's success in Nigeria has been attributed to the personality of their ambassador, A. I. Romanov, reputedly a scion of the old Tsarist family, who was created a

---

* For example, a ten-man delegation of Soviet Muslims toured Nigeria in 1970 reciprocating an earlier visit to the U.S.S.R. made by the Emir of Kano. *West Africa*, no. 2754, 21 Mar 1970, p. 322.

commander of the office of the Niger at the completion of his tour for 'outstanding services to Nigeria and his country'. General Gowon, when making the award, noted that Romanov was 'very objective, constructive and sympathetic in his appraisal of the situation in the country'.[67] His successor, Boris Vorolyev, has few of Romanov's outgoing qualities and appears not to be particularly well equipped to handle the post-euphoric situation. Certainly he appears to be making very little progress in the diplomatic field, where the government has refused a request that Soviet consular offices be established outside Lagos.* On other matters, too, the government has not hesitated to take measures displeasing to the Soviet Union. Their commentary on the invasion of Czechoslovakia was generally restrained, but this was largely due to their dislike of the Dubček regime which had stopped the supply of Czech arms. In 1969 a delegation of the left-wing Nigerian Trade Union Congress was deprived of its passports at Lagos airport as it was about to embark for an Afro-Asian Solidarity Conference at Khartoum. Then Dr Otegbeye and S. O. Martins, an official of the Nigeria–Soviet Cultural and Friendship Association, were arrested on their return from a World Communist meeting at Moscow; Otegbeye was not released for forty-three days.[68] The government is also doing all that it can to ensure that it controls the flow of students between the two countries, and in August 1972 fifty students, about to travel to Moscow on scholarships arranged through the Nigerian trade unions, had their passports seized and their qualifications investigated.[69]

KENYA

In Kenya the chain of events stands in complete contrast to that in Nigeria. The violence of Mau Mau put the Kenyan nationalist movement into a category that the Soviet Union thought it could understand, and some nationalist leaders reciprocated this interest. Before and for two years after independence, the U.S.S.R. appeared to have vocal and influential friends in the Kenyan government, most notably in the person of Oginga Odinga. Then this group lost power and Kenya began to sever its ties with the Communist countries. In so doing the government, largely under the influence of the master strategist Tom Mboya, exhibited far more finesse than did its Nigerian counterpart, and it was able to reduce the country's effective ties with the Communist world to a level which might well have been envied by the Balewa government.

Early Prospects

During the 1960s, African nationalism in Kenya developed under the cloud of Mau Mau. During and after the emergency, nation-wide

* The Soviet Union was reported to have asked for consulates in all eleven states outside Lagos. *West Africa*, no. 2706, 12 Apr 1969, p. 426. Currently, the U.K., the U.S.A., Sudan, Spain, Niger, France, W. Germany, Egypt, Italy and Lebanon all have consulates outside Lagos.

African political parties were banned and Jomo Kenyatta was detained, robbing the movement of its one acknowledged national leader and heightening his stature in the eyes of the people. The result was the formation of regional and tribal parties dominated by a handful of leaders of approximately equal status who vied with each other for power on the national stage. The most significant rivalry for the future was that between Tom Mboya, who was young, with a weak tribal but a strong trade union power base, and Oginga Odinga, who was older and appeared first as the conservative spokesman for the Luo tribe. The dispute between these two was essentially one of power, although they later disagreed on the right path of Kenya's development. However, they soon tarred each other with ideological brushes: Mboya was labelled pro-Western and Odinga pro-Eastern; an American stooge versus a Soviet agent. In the best tradition of English political parties, the factions accepted the names they were given and embroidered them, particularly when it was found that they could be turned to financial advantage. Mboya was the chairman of the I.C.F.T.U. area committee for Eastern, Central and Southern Africa and a member of its executive council in Brussels. His Kenya trade union, the Kenya Federation of Labour, both appealed for and used I.C.F.T.U. financial aid to defeat its opponents. When appealing for such funds it was found politic to make use of cold war terminology and to argue that they were needed to defeat Communists, when in fact the money was used to bolster the leadership against opposition of any political hue.[70] Odinga in his turn visited Moscow, and when Mboya organised an airlift of students to the U.S.A., Odinga did the same to the U.S.S.R. He was also widely reported to be receiving substantial sums of money from Communist sources, and £50,000 was mentioned in one reference.[71]

In contrast to his popularity with Africans, Kenyatta was loathed and feared by the colonial government in Nairobi as, in the words of one governor-general, 'a leader unto darkness and death'. The government would greatly have preferred someone else to have led the nationalist movement, and there were strong suspicions among his rivals that Mboya was being groomed for the job. Whether this is the case or not, he was certainly a major power to be reckoned with by Kenyatta on his return from detention and restriction in August 1961. Relations between the two reached a very low point in August 1962 when Mboya used the threat to form a party of his own based on trade union support to ward off his critics.[72] With Mboya as a major opponent, Kenyatta looked favourably on Odinga. Further, Kenyatta had not only to assert his authority within K.A.N.U., but he also had to defeat the Kenya African Democratic Union (K.A.D.U.), which had been formed by the smaller tribes who feared Kikuyu–Luo domination and which had accepted portfolios in the Colonial government. There was keen rivalry between the two parties, and the K.A.D.U. president, Ronald Ngala, accused his opponents of planning to take power by a *coup d'état* after independence if they did not win it in the 1963 elections and of sending students overseas for military training to this end.[73] It was later learned that the students had gone to Bulgaria, the Soviet Union, East Germany, the U.A.R. and Israel.[74]

In the circumstances, the future for co-operation between an independent Kenya and the socialist countries appeared bright. The colonial government had itself taken a lead in January 1962 when it announced the relaxation of restrictions on trade with the Soviet bloc.[75] The following year, Bruce McKenzie, the minister for land settlement and water development and a white man who was close to Kenyatta, told a press conference at the conclusion of a tour of Britain, Europe and Pakistan, 'It has become obvious that with our agricultural surplus which we are unable to sell we can only find an outlet in the Communist bloc. This must be one of the first steps of the new government, as far as agriculture is concerned.'[76] Two months later he informed the house of representatives that the government intended to send a delegation to the U.S.S.R. and Eastern Europe to find buyers for Kenya's pyrethrum, maize and coffee.[77] After the tour, it was announced that these countries would buy 10,000 tons of coffee annually.[78]

In accordance with the spirit of enquiry into what the Soviet Union had to offer, an embassy was established in Moscow less than a year after independence, making it one of the first six foreign missions to be opened. It was a similar size to that in Bonn, and was larger than the Kenyan embassy in Washington.[79] Kenya had received even less official preparation for the conduct of foreign affairs than had Nigeria. Politicians – African, Settler, Asian and British alike – were far too concerned with domestic politics, voting rights, federalism and the protection of minorities, to have time for the creation of a foreign service. The constitutional conferences of 1960 and 1962 made no reference at all to foreign affairs. All that was done was to send a few civil servants on training courses abroad. Nevertheless, the government rapidly expanded its diplomatic network after independence; when career diplomats were lacking, outsiders were brought in. The first two ambassadors accredited to the Soviet Union were non-career diplomats who left the service after their term of office. Neither spoke Russian but this was found to be a surmountable barrier as the Russians provided interpreters when necessary. The third ambassador was a career diplomat, and he learned Russian. In the domestic field, Achieng Oneko, a radical who became minister for information and broadcasting, soon gained full control over the Kenya Broadcasting Corporation, which under the name of the Voice of Kenya began to draw increasingly for its news on Tass, and relayed more and more material on the world revolution.

The Reaction

Despite this heartening start, events did not unfold in a way that was favourable to the U.S.S.R. The root of the trouble was that Odinga tended to act as if he, and not Kenyatta, was the real representative of Kenya in Soviet eyes. In November 1963 forty-six students sponsored by the ministry of education to study in Bulgaria were turned back at Nairobi airport and their places taken by fifty-five other students escorted by Odinga.[80] The forty-six were eventually found places to study in India but not before a heated debate in the house of representatives over what the minister of education termed the 'sabotage' of his ministry's plans, and the announcement by the government that it would establish a central selection board to administer overseas scholarships.[81] There was feeling against Odinga both because his action was high-handed and because he was strongly suspected of reserving Eastern European scholarships for his own tribe, and even his own family.[82] By contrast, the students sent to the U.S.S.R. through the central selection board when it was set up were fairly well balanced tribally.[83]

Odinga's high-handedness came to be seen against an increasingly uneasy background. Violence and talk of Communism are no strangers to Kenya, which had seen the emergency of the 1950s. In June 1964, just before leaving London after a Commonwealth conference, Kenyatta expressed certain misgivings that there were 'hidden forces' at work, bent on opposing or overthrowing the government. This was taken to be a reference to Odinga and his group, and a whispering campaign led by K.A.D.U. suggested that he had planned to seize power while the president was outside the country. Nevertheless, while suspicious of Odinga, Kenyatta continued to support him in an effort to separate Mboya from his trade union base. According to one account, money was channelled to Odinga through his main tactician Pio Pinto until as late as January 1965, and that a month later Kenyatta changed his tactics, fearing that his greatest threat now came from Odinga's faction.*

The threat from Odinga was seen as being closely related to the Soviet Union, where there were an unknown number of Kenya students who had been sent before independence for military training. April 1965 brought these fears into the open partly as a result of a number of unexplained incidents and partly because Odinga's opponents did their best to keep tensions high. On 1 April T. N. Malinda gave notice to the house of representatives of a motion which referred to 'evidence that arms and ammunition are continuously being smuggled from communist and other foreign countries' for the purpose of overthrowing the

---

* Richard Sandbrook, 'Patrons, Clients & Unions', *Journal of Commonwealth Political Studies*, vol. x: 1, Leicester (Mar 1972), p. 18. Pio Pinto was murdered in mysterious circumstances in February 1965 without his assassins being apprehended.

government and involving the country in external conflicts. The motion came up for discussion on 2 April, but Malinda, who had been in the chamber earlier in the day, was curiously absent. As the house was due to recess at the end of the day, and as the motion had aroused much interest and concern, the matter was discussed on a motion for the adjournment. Without Mr Malinda there was wild debate about the 'evidence' he claimed in his motion to have unearthed. The atmosphere was further electrified by one member who claimed that he also had definite evidence of plans to overthrow the government but declined to produce it in the absence of a full debate led by Malinda. The alleged source of the danger was graphically revealed by the minister for health and housing, J. D. Otiende, when he exclaimed, 'We did not fight the British Government, and we did not send away the Europeans, so that the yellow men could take over the country.' Not surprisingly, and presumably with intended effect, the debate was extremely heated and members left in a state of high tension. Yet when the house sat once more eighteen days later, and Mr Malinda had apologised for being absent because he had 'miscalculated the time', it was discovered that he had no new evidence to impart.[84]

By this time other events had occurred. At 3.00 a.m. on 8 April sixty troops and police arrived at Odinga's vice-presidential office and removed a number of boxes and took them to the armoury. While the boxes almost certainly contained arms, it is not clear whether they were in the vice-president's office by common consent or secretly. The previous night Tom Okelo-Odongo, one of Odinga's lieutenants, had told a meeting that 'Kenya must bend a little more to the Eastern bloc at this moment.'[85] On 12 April the president made his first public intervention in the subversion scare when, after a strong personal attack on Bildad Kaggia – a longstanding nationalist, fellow defendant with Kenyatta at the Kapenguria trial at which they were accused of directing Mau Mau, and a radical associate of Odinga – he warned those who planned subversion that they would not succeed.

No sooner had these incidents taken place than there was a flurry of activity around Mombasa. The Royal Navy commando carrier H.M.S. *Albion*, on her way to the Far East, picked up provisions and fuel at Mombasa on the 15 April, but the Kenya government requested that she stay a little longer 'to show the flag'. It was first announced that the carrier would stay for four days and that the public would be admitted. In fact, she stayed for over twice as long and there were no public tours. The day before the request the minister for internal security and defence, Dr Njoroge Mungai, had told a press conference of a 'small consignment of arms' which was a gift from the Soviet Union and was expected to arrive very soon at Mombasa. The arms would be used to modernise the Kenya army where modernisation was necessary, and a few Russian technicians would be coming to show how to assemble them. However, he added, 'the Russians are not going to train our army'.[86] Until this announcement it was not known that Kenya had an arms agreement with the Soviet Union. In all probability it was signed by Odinga, and Kenyatta may not have been informed until a later date. On 21 April it was learned that the ship conveying the arms, the *Fizik Lebedev*, had been seen in Kenyan territorial waters but had then disappeared, only to reappear in Dar es Salaam harbour. When questioned on this in the house, the assistant minister at the president's office replied cryptically that the ship might have 'run into a turbulent storm, maybe a political storm . . .'[87] The ship finally arrived on 24 April after *H.M.S. Albion* had departed, and Mombasa port was sealed off. On 25 April, Kenyatta told a rally that Kenya should be allowed to decide its own destiny. 'Outside influence will not be tolerated,' he said.[88] After a three-day wait in the roads, during which time the floating crane which can unload ships at anchorage was not used, the *Fizik Lebedev* docked at the quayside, and on 28 April she began to unload a quantity of arms including armoured troop carriers and T–34 tanks. It was the latter which caused difficulty. The development trend of the Kenya army was towards a reconnaisance squad equipped with Ferret armoured scout cars, to which the troop carriers might be a logical addition. The tanks, however, which were of Second World War vintage, would be useful only in the case of widespread disaffection and would require the presence over several months of Soviet training personnel. On 29 April the Soviet ambassador was summoned to an audience with the president, who may well have desired the troop carriers while being sceptical of the tanks. No compromise between the two was reached, for ten minutes after the ambassador left, Kenyatta announced that his Government had decided to reject the arms on the grounds that they were all 'old and secondhand and would be of no use to the modern army of Kenya'.[89] It was later added that the government was concerned at the possible activities of the Russian trainers if they were allowed into Kenya.[90] In March of the following year Dr Mungai announced that the U.S.S.R. and other Eastern European countries had been asked to transfer any students receiving military training to other courses.[91]

After May 1965 Odinga's star began to wane appreciably. In that month fears were given additional impetus by the discovery of a mysterious consignment of Chinese arms in the Nyanza region – Odinga's power base. The official explanation was that the weapons were in transit from Tanzania to Uganda and were taking a 'short-cut' through Kenya. Unfortunately, the Kenya government appears not to have been notified in advance. Odinga's opponents, masterminded by Mboya, sought first to restrict him on the ideological front. On 4 May Mboya, as minister for economic planning and development, introduced the now famous sessional paper number 10 on *African Socialism and its Application to Planning in Kenya*. This paper, which was to form the basis of the government's economic and social ideology, was essentially a formulation of capitalism with a human (African) face. Of Marx it said that his descriptions bore little similarity to Kenya in 1965, and it opposed 'indiscriminate nationalisation'. While the radicals were unhappy with the document, it was phrased in such a way and so obviously had the backing of the president that there was little they could do to oppose it. Their main tactic was to welcome it as a base from which to move onwards. However, when they tried to move onwards they were met with a sharp rebuff. The locus of the attempted great leap forward was the Lumumba Institute.

The institute was opened by the president on 12 December 1964. It was established with the help of the U.S.S.R., which was understood to have provided $84,000 for its construction and two members of the teaching staff. It was formed as a training centre for party, co-operative, trade union and government cadres from Kenya and ultimately from elsewhere in Africa. Its founders were Kenyatta and Odinga, and the chairman of the board of management was Bildad Kaggia; Mboya was noticeably not involved at all. The first and only course ran from March to June 1965. It was intended to study external relations, general principles of socialism, party organisation, the socialist state and constitution, a biography of Jomo Kenyatta, and African socialism. In the event, it concentrated on the last of these and became a platform for radical criticism of the government's philosophy. The students held a press conference at which they announced their rejection of sessional paper number 10, and that they intended to use their prerogative under the K.A.N.U. constitution to summon a national delegate conference.[92] In June 1965 they made an abortive attempt to takeover the K.A.N.U. headquarters in Nairobi and install their own nominees in national office.[93]

Long before this final incident, however, the conservatives had raised the institute's activities in parliament and a private members motion had urged the government to take it over. The government's reaction was extremely diplomatic: the minister for education, M. Koinange, tactfully amended the motion, while Mboya was at pains to point out that: 'we in the Government are very deeply appreciative of those who donated funds and material to make it possible for the Lumumba Institute to be built.'[94] Three months later some of the anti-radicals were still complaining that the government was holding back from control of the institute.[95] However, they need not have worried, for quietly but effectively the Lumumba Institute was put to silence.

In June Odinga made a public attack on Mboya and Ronald Ngala, accusing them of working for the British, and he went further and stated that American and British diplomats often tried to influence the president. This implied attack on Kenyatta was most unwise, and three days later it was announced that Odinga had been dropped as head of the Kenyan delegation to the forthcoming Commonwealth prime ministers meeting in London.[96] In July he was removed as vice-chairman of the K.A.N.U. Parliamentary Group, the party's only functioning organ. A number of other snubs indicating Odinga's fall from grace followed, culminating in the party conference at Limuru on 12 and 13 March 1966. The conference was called after the anti-radicals had persuaded Kenyatta that an open split would strengthen rather than weaken the government. It adopted a new constitution abolishing Odinga's post of national vice-president and creating eight provincial vice-presidents directly responsible to the president in its stead. Neither Odinga nor any of his associates won re-election, and all the new party officials were known to oppose him. At the closing session the president warned those whom he called 'puppets without brains' and exclaimed 'Let them go on and form a new party. They should be told that we know their paymasters and we are picking them up one by one.'[97] The radicals took his advice, and a month later Odinga resigned from both the government and K.A.N.U. and with a small band of followers crossed the floor to form the Kenya People's Union (K.P.U.).

Implications for Russia

The President's reference to his adversaries' 'paymasters' was his first major attack on foreign powers who supported factions within the Kenya government. It was not, however, the first indication that the Soviet Union's fortunes were closely linked to those of Odinga. The Limuru conference was widely seen as the showdown between Odinga and Mboya, and as in the past both sides sought financial assistance from wherever they might. The Soviet Union and other socialist countries continued to support Odinga, and for their pains four Communist diplomats and two journalists were expelled from the country at twenty-four hours' notice shortly before the conference; no reasons were given.* Then, after the conference had ended another five Communist officials were expelled.† These were the first acts taken against Soviet officials, apart from an incident in October 1964 when the Russian ambassador had indiscreetly addressed a public meeting at Machakos. They were

---

* *Daily Nation*, 11 Mar 1966, p. 1. They were Y. A. Youkalov and V. A. Kodakov, the two first secretaries of the U.S.S.R. embassy; Stanislaw Kozubik, second secretary at the Czechoslovak embassy; a clerk at the Chinese embassy; Yuri Kuritsin of Novosti, and Zdenek Kubes of the Czech News Agency.

† Ibid., 17 Mar 1966, p. 1. They were Yao Chun, third secretary at the Chinese embassy; Jan Carda, third secretary at the Czech embassy; Janos Novak, third secretary at the Hungarian embassy; L. Soliakov, a correspondent of Tass, and Y. A. Kovler, who worked for Sovexportfilm.

not, however, the last. Five more were expelled in the following years because their continued presence was 'against the national interest'. The last one, a *Pravda* correspondent, remarked in a rare burst of ironic humour that it had 'become traditional to expel Russians from the country during the months of March and April'.* The reciprocal of this policy was that the Kenyan embassy in Moscow was run down: by 1972 50 per cent of the established posts there were vacant, as compared with an average for all Kenya's missions of about 29 per cent.[98]

Despite this the Kenya government maintained a determined posture of diplomatic rectitude: in July 1966 it made it clear that the recent expulsions of Communists had not caused it to cease regarding Eastern countries as friendly; in November 1968 a Soviet naval squadron was welcomed to Mombasa on a courtesy visit; and the government maintained an embassy in Peking until 1970 even though there was very little trade between the two countries and there were no Kenyans in China apart from embassy personnel. The Russians also tried to avoid aggravating the situation and accepted the expulsions, save for the last, without reprisals. However, by 1969 their patience had obviously worn thin and they saw no further point in placating the Kenyan government: they expelled the second secretary at the Kenyan embassy in Moscow, and when some Luo students in Moscow invaded the offices of the embassy, Soviet policemen on duty outside did nothing to restrain them.[99]

The Soviet Union's set-backs were not only on the diplomatic front. After independence, Odinga and Joseph Murumbi had travelled to Moscow to negotiate an aid agreement with the U.S.S.R. On 17 May 1964 the fruits of their discussions were announced: the Soviet Union had agreed to build and equip a 200-bed hospital and polyclinic, and a technical college for 1000 students as a gift; and to help in the construction of four factories, a radio station, and certain agricultural projects; the Soviet Union was also interested in financing a paper mill at the Broderick Falls.† By the end of the year a high powered Soviet delegation had visited Nairobi, had signed an agreement providing for a Soviet loan of up to R40 million ($45 million), had added some extra projects, and had defined the 'certain agricultural projects' as a scheme to irrigate 35,000 acres of the Kano Plains, preceded by a 500-acre pilot scheme.[100]

In the new year as Odinga's influence began to wane so did support for the Soviet Union's aid proposals. During the debate on sessional paper

---

* A Mr Bekhterev, named by Yuri N. Loginov, a Soviet spy arrested in South Africa, as his contact in Kenya left in December 1967. In February 1968 Veniamin Zakharov of Novosti and Eduard Agadzhanov in charge of Sovexportfilm were given forty-eight hours to leave the country. In April 1969 Mikhail Domogatskih, a *Pravda* correspondent, and Victor Eliseev, first secretary at the Russian embassy, were expelled. *East African Standard*, Nairobi, 15 Feb 1968, p. 1, 14 Apr 1969, p. 7.

† The four factories were a textile mill, fish cannery, fruit processing factory and sugar factory. *Daily Nation*, Nairobi, 18 May 1964, pp. 1, 16.

number 10 in the house of representatives, Tom Mboya referred to the difficulties of financing the local costs of Soviet projects and he was supported by the minister for agriculture and animal husbandry, Bruce McKenzie.[101] In January 1966 Mboya, McKenzie and the minister for commerce, industry and co-operatives, Ngala Mwendwa, visited Moscow for further discussions. On their return they adopted the euphemistic Russian journalese of 'frank and friendly' to describe their talks, i.e. the two sides were at loggerheads. Their mission had gone to find an alternative to commodity credits for raising the estimated £6 million needed to cover the local costs of the Kano scheme. They sought to persuade the Soviet government either to provide the sum in convertible currency or to make arrangements with a third party which would provide Kenya with cash in return for deliveries of Soviet goods. They also requested that the repayment terms for the Kano Plains credit be renegotiated, as a twelve-year amortisation period was no longer acceptable. In addition, there seems to have been some argument over whether a project report by the Russian organisation Grypovodhoz could be accepted in lieu of the 500-acre pilot scheme; the Kenyans wisely insisted that it could not as it ignored many relevant factors. A number of other wide ranging alterations to the other projects were proposed. These included the substitution of two secondary schools for the technical college, the deletion of two of the seven agreed schemes, and the indefinite postponement of four others. The Russians asked for time to consider these far reaching proposals that would have reduced their immediate activities to three projects. They replied on 3 February in an *aide memoire* in which they agreed to start discussions on the pilot scheme for the Kano Plains but regretted that they could not alter the provisions of the 1964 agreement regarding local costs in either of the ways suggested. The Kenya government, therefore, decided not to proceed with Soviet assistance for the Kano Plains project and approached other countries and groups for help. This left the U.S.S.R. providing only the Kisumu hospital and the secondary schools, and of these only the hospital actually materialised.*

This was a considerable blow to the U.S.S.R. In only two cases did the Kenya government give its reasons for the deletions and postponements : the proposed sugar factory, which was deleted because Kenya was already engaged in a major expansion of existing factories, and the Kano Plains scheme. The latter was the most important of all the projects, and the government gave the reasons for its deletion in some detail. They hinged on the unsuitability of commodity credits. The deletion,

* *East African Standard*, Nairobi, 19 Feb 1966, and *Daily Nation*, Nairobi, 19 Feb 1966. The projects deleted were a bush clearing scheme in the inshore region of Lake Victoria, and a sugar factory. Those postponed indefinitely were the cotton textile factory, a fish cannery, fruit and vegetable processing factories, and a radio transmitter.

according to Tom Mboya, was prompted by a desire to speed the implementation of the Kano Plains scheme, and to disarm potential critics he offered the carrot of an even larger scheme than that planned by the Russians. The problem with Soviet assistance, in his opinion, was that

> Such arrangements . . . would take too long . . . The Government is convinced that it would be wrong to continue to ask the people in the Kano Plains to exercise patience. Each year is a year of misery for these people. They suffer from either drought or flood. The land in area has a very high potential and we can no longer afford to see it lie idle. The Government has, therefore, approached other countries and groups to help finance this scheme. In addition, it has now been decided to establish irrigation on a much wider scheme than initially was envisaged under the Kano Irrigation Plan. Instead, the Government now wishes to cover a total of 134,000 acres as against the previous 35,000 acres.[102]

If the government's sole aim in this instance was to speed the implementation of the scheme and to alleviate the suffering of the Kano inhabitants, they perhaps ought to have discussed the matter more fully with the 'other countries and groups' from which finance was now sought. In the event these proved not to be forthcoming. A small contribution has been received from the Netherlands, and U.N.D.P.–F.A.O. have established a research station, but despite Mboya's optimistic assurances nothing on the scale of the proposed Soviet assistance, let alone aid for a more ambitious scheme, has been obtained from external sources.

There need have been little difficulty in utilising the commodity credit. The amount involved was £6 million, to be raised over a four-year period. The Soviet Union has shown itself prepared to supply petroleum on credit, and Kenya annually imports £9 million of crude petroleum through East African Oil Refineries, a consortium in which the government is the major shareholder. To oil may be added a number of other goods which Kenya imports in large quantities and which she has in the past bought from the Soviet Union at competitive prices.* From the evidence in the chapter on aid it is clearly not wise for an African country to put the U.S.S.R. in a monopoly position to supply a particular good, but £6 million of competitive goods could have been imported without allowing the U.S.S.R. to supply more than a small proportion to total imports in any one commodity. In fact, Kenya's position appears to have marked a complete policy change from its earlier views. As the delegation of Mboya, McKenzie and Mwendwa must have

---

* In the four years after Mboya's speech, Kenya imported over £12 million of sugar (S.I.T.C. 061 20) and simply worked iron and steel (S.I.T.C. 673 10,20,90, and 674 49 and 422) in all of which the U.S.S.R. has been a major supplier.

known, the Soviet Union has never given large amounts of convertible currency for economic development projects in Africa, and the request that it do so, coupled with the action taken against other projects, bears a strong resemblance to a pretext for suspending aid. If a pretext, it was a very subtle one. Whereas the critics of Nigeria's policy could point to the aid that was being lost as a consequence, in Kenya such accusations, though they did occur, cut little ice; the government had its reply – Soviet aid had been tried and found wanting.

In their different ways the experiences of both Kenya and Nigeria reveal quite clearly the strengths and weaknesses of the Soviet Union's and Africa's position *vis-à-vis* each other. Despite its size, wealth and power the Soviet Union has not been able to demand the attention and respect of Africa simply by virtue of its position as a superpower. On the contrary, the success of its policies in Africa has depended very much on chance alliances and friendships with groups of Africans, and on the outcome of political conflicts that may have their roots completely elsewhere. In Kenya, as in the Congo, the Soviet Union was unlucky in the groups which sought out its patronage: it became involved in domestic battles which intimately affected its political fortunes but which it was quite unable to influence effectively. It seems clear that the K.P.U. was supplied with funds from Soviet sources, but these sources were unable to give it other forms of help. After the ill-fated consignment of the *Fizik Lebedev* there is no evidence of Russian armaments entering Kenya on any great scale, and any practical assistance in planning and implementing strategy and tactics was made impossible by the government's policy of expelling errant Soviet diplomats and journalists, and reducing the opportunities for help to enter the country in the guise of technical assistance personnel working on aid projects.[103] As in the Congo, the Soviet Union's allies did not win their battle. Odinga was not a very powerful figure in Kenyan politics despite his prominence : apart from his own Luo tribe, which rallied to him *en masse* after the formation of the K.P.U., his popular support was not high. An opinion poll gave him only 2 per cent support in 1960 and 7 per cent in 1961, as against 42 per cent and 28 per cent for Mboya.[104] To an extent his lack of popularity was a result of his association with Communism: in 1961 supporters of K.A.N.U. and K.A.D.U. were asked by an opinion poll which man in Kenya they most distrusted, and 68 per cent of those who named Odinga gave the reason that he was Communist influenced, and a further 20 per cent that he used money for his own ends.[105] This feeling was concentrated among the K.A.D.U. supporters, 24 per cent of whom named Odinga, although 3 per cent of the members of his own party also named him. When K.A.D.U. and K.A.N.U. united, Odinga's position within the party was correspondingly weakened. On the other hand, there is no evidence that fears of Communism were electorally significant. There was a widespread association of Odinga *et al.*, Communism, and land nationalisation in the minds of many M.P.s, but this does not appear to have been true of the electorate at large. In the 1965 Senate by-elections, which were an important contest between the radicals and conservatives, several candidates sought to arouse popular fears of their opponents and accused them of being Communist. One candidate declared in his manifesto: 'Reject he who brings Communism to Kenya, Communism means shambas and all possessions belong to the Government. Wives are communal, and the Government takes the children after birth.' He was not, however, successful.[106]

Odinga was not a Communist in any meaningful sense of that word. Since the U.S.S.R. has been known to cut off support even to genuine Communists when they threatened to jeopardise its more immediate interests, it may be wondered why it did not break its connections with the K.P.U. and make its peace with Kenyatta. Such a move might well have been successful, but the president is an old man and while 'normalized' relations with his government might have been beneficial for the Soviet Union, the prospects after his death, with Odinga and the other radicals withdrawn from the scene, were far less promising. In addition, the Soviet authorities may have overestimated the K.P.U.s following. The appeals of the opposition have a long history in Kenya, and their policy that the land formerly worked by white settlers should be redistributed to benefit the landless rather than those with money was particularly well established. However, it was no longer, if it ever had been, a policy that commended majority support among Africans. During the emergency the colonial government had promoted the development of smallholder agriculture and the registration of land titles, so that by the mid-1960s there was a substantial group who had a vested interest in opposing the radicals' demands. Radicals, such as Bildad Kaggia who was the foremost exponent of their land policy, were still popular and it took a major effort by the government to unseat Kaggia when he joined the K.P.U., but as one close observer of Kenyan politics has neatly observed:

Kaggia was arguing that social justice demanded the return of African lands to Africans, without any cost to them or to the country. This was the argument of the 1930s, the 1940s, and the 1950s. Kenyatta was arguing that social justice demanded the recognition of the individual's right to the enjoyment of certain things, including fair treatment and just compensation if his property had to be resumed. Nationalisation of property was therefore not possible. This was the argument of the 1960s.[107]

There is evidence that the U.S.S.R. tried to restrain Odinga after his breach with Kenyatta and gave him only limited financial assistance.[108] They did not, however, come out openly in support of the government, and in the event the Soviet Union and Kenya's authorities did not make their peace and the K.P.U. did not win a large number of parliamentary seats. As if to underline the link between Soviet and K.P.U. fortunes, the government chose the riots which followed a possibly deliberately provocative speech by Kenyatta while opening the Soviet built Kisumu hospital, as the occasion to ban the K.P.U. and intern its leaders.

In Kenya the Soviet Union's activities brought it only discredit : in Nigeria by contrast its fortunes rose while it displayed masterly inactivity. Far from assisting the Action Group, the Soviet Union appears to have had few connections with its most vocal supporters in the civilian parliament. The factors that brought about that party's *volte face* had nothing to do with the Soviet Union and were quite uninfluenced by it. However, the growth of contacts between the two countries does not only underline the chance nature of many of the Soviet Union's contacts in Africa, it also points to its major strength : the fact that it is a superpower. It is clear from Kenya that this status alone has not been sufficient to guarantee it a place in every African country, but it has proved a major obstacle to those governments that would exclude it. In Kenya the government successfully overcame this obstacle, but in Nigeria it did not. Many African leaders proclaimed on independence that they would choose as friends whomsoever they desired provided only that the countries approached reciprocated that friendship. In the world situation prevailing at that time this meant that their choice seemed virtually unlimited. The experience of Ghana, Guinea and Mali suggests, however, that some constraints do exist. Similarly with Nigeria, only in a different way. The three radical states attempted a rapid rapprochement with the East but found political and administrative obstacles in their path; Nigeria by contrast sought to limit its circle of acquaintances, but it too found this position untenable. African states have experienced difficulties both in having too many new friends and in having too few. Aloofness from the Communist world is possible for an African state if its government is very strong, as in Ivory Coast, or very skilful, as in Kenya. The Balewa government was neither, and even in Nigeria's unfertile soil, critics arose to lambast the government for its timidity.

6 Military and Strategic Considerations

Military and strategic factors form an important, although not a paramount part of the Afro–Soviet relationship, but their weight is not immediately apparent. Supplies of military equipment and the provision of military instructors are the most tangible features of military and strategic links between the two continents, but even these have not formed a vital part of the Afro-Soviet connection. The amounts of merchandise in question are not large. This is not because the Soviet Union is unwilling to export armaments to Africa, but because Africa has not been interested in purchasing on a grand scale from the U.S.S.R. The Soviet Union's willingness to sell arms to the Third World may be gauged from Table 6.1 and from the fact that the U.S.S.R. and the U.S.A. sell similar quantities of arms and a similar proportion of their total weapons exports to Third World countries. Since 1950 some 40 per cent of Russia's exports of arms of all types have gone to the Third World, as have 45 per cent of her exports of major weapons.[1] The explanation for Africa's lack of interest in Soviet weapons is twofold. Firstly, Black Africa has not spent large sums of money on weapons from any source: during the 1960s it took only about 3 per cent of total Third World imports of major weapons. Secondly, small-scale suppliers and the former colonial powers play an important role in such arms trade as does exist. During the second half of the 1960s the U.S.S.R. was a bigger supplier than the U.S.A., France or Britain, but it still only satisfied 21 per cent of sub-Saharan Africa's intake (see Table 6.2).* Most African countries have tried to avoid one supplier, other than the ex-metropole, obtaining a dominant position, and in only Somalia, Mali and Guinea is the Soviet Union the major supplier.[2]

Nevertheless, the trade in armaments does present a number of interesting features which justify its attention. The overall area figures conceal a high level of concentration so that transfers to some individual states have not been negligible. Ten Black African countries account for nearly 60 per cent of the major weapons imported by all thirty of the states south of the Sahara. Five of these, which took the lion's share of Soviet exports, are among the countries being given special attention in this work.†

* These figures do not take any account of military bases operated by France and the U.S.A.

† S.I.P.R.I., *Arms Trade with Third World*, p. 608. The ten are Ethiopia, Ghana, Guinea, Liberia, Mali, Nigeria, Somalia, Sudan, Uganda and Zaire.

TABLE 6.1 Major Soviet exports of weapons to the Third World, by region 1950–69 (million U.S.$ at constant (1968) prices)

Region	1950	51	52	53	54	55	56	57	58	59	60	61	62	63	64	65	66	67	68	69	Total	% of U.S.S.R. total
Far East, inc. Vietnam	16·9	30·0	18·9	121·3	0·7	30·5	11·1	4·6	15·3	7·4	20·6	51·4	132·0	61·0	73·8	53·8	341·2	499·5	467·2	—	1,957·3	37·3
Indian sub-continent	—	—	—	—	—	2·0	2·5	9·5	6·3	6·8	30·9	36·4	39·1	40·6	5·6	46·8	168·3	136·8	112·7	178·3	822·6	16·0
Middle East	—	—	—	—	—	15·8	67·1	146·8	96·6	63·1	44·5	111·6	182·5	84·0	95·6	52·6	84·0	522·7	266·0	138·4	1,971·3	37·5
North Africa	—	—	—	—	—	—	—	—	—	—	4·4	16·2	10·7	5·4	41·5	37·9	37·3	—	—	153·4	3·0
Sub-Saharan Africa	—	—	—	—	—	—	—	—	—	—	4·4	13·0	0·2	2·9	2·0	17·1	5·7	8·4	2·3	7·4	63·4	1·2
Cuba	—	—	—	—	—	—	—	—	—	3·7	17·5	79·6	148·8	12·8	11·6	5·3	3·9	2·2	—	—	285·4	5·4
TOTAL	16·9	30·0	18·9	121·3	0·7	48·3	80·7	161·0	118·2	81·0	117·9	296·4	518·8	212·1	194·0	217·1	641·0	1,206·9	848·2	324·1	5,254·0	100·0

Source—S.I.P.R.I., The Arms Trade with the Third World, Table 4.1.

TABLE 6.2   Black Africa's sources of major weapons, by suppliers 1950–69 (million US$ at constant (1968) prices)

Supplier	1950–4 $m. annual av. (%)		1955–9 $m. annual av. (%)		1960–4 $m. annual av. (%)		1965–9 $m. annual av. (%)		1950–69 $m. annual av. (%)	
U.S.A.	2	28·6	1	10·0	7	21·9	5	13·2	71	16·7
U.K.	5	71·4	8	80·0	7	21·9	6	15·8	128	30·2
France	—	—	—	—	4	12·5	6	15·8	47	11·1
U.S.S.R.	—	—	—	—	5	15·6	8	21·1	64	15·1
Other	0	2·9	1	10·0	9	28·1	13	34·7	114	26·9
TOTAL	7	100	10	100	32	100	38	100	424	100

Source: S.I.P.R.I., *The Arms Trade with the Third World.*

It is safe to assume that the Soviet Union exports weapons to the Third World largely for political purposes, since it receives few identifiable economic returns from its transactions. The numbers of weapons involved are insignificant in relation to those produced for the U.S.S.R. itself and its Warsaw Pact allies, and can thus have little effect on production costs. In the last twenty years, for example, the Soviet Union has supplied the developing countries with 1600 MIGs of various models – an insignificant number when set against the 8000 MIG aircraft it currently operates and the fact that about 30 per cent of those 1600 MIGs were of types being phased out by the Soviet military.[3] Moreover, the price at which they are offered is generally low, and they are often made available under aid agreements. Nigeria, for example, was offered unlimited credit for arms during the civil war, and it was only by her own choice that cash payments were agreed.

Until 1953 Soviet arms supplies to the Third World were exclusively directed to members of the socialist bloc and were not large. Since then there have been roughly three phases in the development of the U.S.S.R.'s selling policy, each phase reaching customers farther away from the Soviet heartland. In the first phase the Soviet Union tried to undermine the web of alliances around its borders which the Western powers were so carefully constructing. Support was given to the Egypt–Syria–Yemen axis opposed to the Baghdad Pact and then to Iraq after its revolution. This phase concerned Black Africa not at all. Although the territories south of the Sahara could be used as a second line of defence – attack by the West, as the debate over the Nigerian Defence Pact revealed, they were not of immediate concern to the U.S.S.R. and, being still under colonial rule, they were in no position to respond to any initiatives the Soviet Union might have made.

The second phase occurred during the late 1950s and early 1960s when the Soviet Union began to supply weapons to countries which, while not close to its borders, were in areas that were of strategic interest. The Red Sea area is a prime example. The U.S.S.R. began to supply the Yemen with arms from 1956. South Yemen has received Soviet arms almost since its independence in 1967, with the first shipment arriving in 1968. This Soviet interest has spread across the Red Sea to Somalia and down the African coastline to Kenya and as far as Zanzibar. It is this area that provides the most significant example of phase two in Black Africa, although the U.S.S.R. has been anxious to acquire refuelling and supply facilities in many places and these have on occasion burst into the headlines: the refusal of Guinea, for example, to permit Cuba-bound Soviet planes during the missile crisis to refuel at Conakry airport, specially lengthened by the Russians for this purpose, played an important part in the American triumph.[4]

Apart from these cases, the supply of Soviet weaponry to Black Africa largely falls within the third phase which developed during the 1960s and particularly during the latter half of the decade, when the Soviet Union showed itself willing to negotiate arms deals in many different parts of the world in an apparent attempt to compete for influence on a world-wide basis. The competition was initially directed against the Western powers but was later with China also. Not only is Black Africa largely concerned with this period; it probably gives the best illustration of the dynamics of the phase.[5] Since 1959 the U.S.S.R. has concluded military agreements with the Sudan, Guinea, Morocco, Ghana, Mali, Zaire, Tanzania, Kenya, Uganda, Nigeria and Mauretania. They have not led to the degree of influence or intimacy found in phases one or two. Most agreements were single deals, and even when regular supplies have occurred they have supplemented rather than replaced Western deliveries. The arms sent to the horn of Africa clearly have to be discussed within the context of overall Soviet strategy, particularly as it involves the Red Sea and Indian Ocean. The trade elsewhere, however, is more interesting for the insight it provides into the modalities of the very delicate political–military relationship that exists everywhere in Black Africa, even when the political organs are themselves controlled by men in uniform. Soviet expectations in phase three were apparently not very high. The least that was expected was the destruction of the Western monopoly; the most was a position of significant influence.[6] However, the degree of influence and the extent of arms supplies has generally depended on the strength of the radical forces within the recipient country, rather than *vice versa*.*

African motives for purchasing Soviet arms have been various, but four stand out as particularly important. In none of these four cases does

* See Chapters 4 and 5 above.

the U.S.S.R. benefit directly since there are a number of possible sources to which Africans may turn, but in all cases it clearly benefits indirectly. In a number of cases the West has been reluctant to supply the quantity or the type of weapons desired. Nigeria and Guinea are, of course, classic examples of this, as is Somalia. In the Somali and Nigerian examples an existing dispute made the desire for weapons urgent, while Guinea felt itself threatened by its isolation. Such disputes and fears seem to be an important, although not necessarily an essential catalyst. The advantages of the U.S.S.R. over the U.S.A. are that the former supplies more weapons to more states. When dealing with countries with which it became involved during phases one and two, the Soviet Union has tended to keep a good eye on its own strategic interests and to disburse only such weapons as do not adversely affect these interests. No such circumspection has been necessary in respect of phase three states, which have largely been free to choose for themselves which weapons they do or do not require. This open handed attitude has obvious advantages for a recipient, but it also places upon it the burden of deciding which weapons can be economically and militarily justified. This may indeed be a leaden cope : in a situation where the political authorities are attempting to restrain the military's demands for more equipment without provoking retaliation the refusal of foreign powers to supply the weapons in question may act as a *deus ex machina* to save the government from embarrassment. It also requires an efficient administrative system in the recipient country. Kenya's refusal of the T–34* tanks offered by the U.S.S.R. indicates the caution that must be exercised.†

A second category of African countries that have looked to socialist sources for military equipment includes those states whose relations with the West are good at first, but then deteriorate. Tanzania, Ghana and Mali are good examples from Black Africa, and one might also add the Sudan, Uganda and Morocco. The events which culminate in the arms agreement with the U.S.S.R. are interesting, but the agreement itself is less so, since it is normally followed by only isolated arms deals. A third group of developing countries are those whose ideological aspirations impel them to purchase arms from the Soviet Union as soon as independence is won. This group finds no representative in Black Africa. Even the Lumumba government, which requested Soviet arms sooner after independence than any other Black African country, asked the West and then the United Nations before turning East. The nearest examples geo-

* See Chapter 5 above.

† Ghana had a similar experience, although with civilian not military aircraft: eight Ilyushins were purchased by Ghana Airways, although it had originally been intended to obtain only four: when the remainder proved to be, indeed, surplus to requirements, the Soviet Union was persuaded to take them back. *Report and Financial Statements by the Accountant-General and Report of the Auditor-General for the year ended 30 September 1962* (Accra), para. 49.

graphically are to be found in Algeria and South Yemen. The fourth reason for soliciting Soviet supplies is that many African governments favour the diversification of their arms supplies and sources of military instruction: diversification, by preventing the formation of a unified officer corps, can reduce the likelihood of military action against the political regime.

THE HORN OF AFRICA AND THE INDIAN OCEAN

Peter the Great's remarks about Russia's need for 'warm water ports' notwithstanding, Russian interest in the Indian Ocean is of fairly recent origin. Indeed, standard Soviet texts on strategy make no specific mention of either the Indian Ocean or of naval tasks in any kind of a war short of a general nuclear holocaust.[7] However, since the mid-1960s there has been an increase in Soviet naval activity in the Indian Ocean.

The growing Soviet interest in this ocean may best be seen as a response to the development of the American Polaris A–3 missile. In June 1962 its predecessor the Polaris A–2 became operational with a range of 1600 nautical miles. Its introduction into the Mediterranean made the major industrial centre of the Ukraine, the Baku oilfields, and parts of Soviet Central Asia vulnerable to attack, while both it and the earlier A–1, if deployed in the Barents Sea, put Moscow and Leningrad at risk. This was not a situation which the U.S.S.R. could tolerate with equanimity, and when the U.S.A. negotiated a naval base at Rota with the Spanish government in 1963, the Soviet navy began to appear in the Mediterranean. At the same time the longer-range A–3 Polaris missile was being developed and was first deployed operationally in September 1964. Its 2500 nautical miles range for the first time made the Indian Ocean a feasible deployment area for an attack against the U.S.S.R. The northwest corner of that ocean acquired a fresh strategic significance as Polaris submarines equipped with A–3 missiles operating from there could threaten the whole area between the western Soviet border and eastern Siberia on an arc extending almost as far north as Leningrad and including all the major industrial areas from the Ukraine to the Kuzbas.

The threat was, however, a potential rather than an actual one. Although it stationed seven Polaris submarines in the Pacific, the American navy did not at that time maintain a regular force in the Indian Ocean. There were thus two options open to the U.S.S.R. to ward off the danger. It could build up its military presence in the offending area to make it less attractive to the U.S.A. But this in itself was not a complete solution. A naval presence would not contribute to an improved deterrence posture, since the Indian Ocean offered the U.S.S.R. no fresh targets that were comparable with those it promised the West. Soviet vessels could not deter an American attack by threatening retaliation against an area of vital interest to the West. All they could do would be to defend Soviet territory by hunting down the Polaris submarines. This is by no means an easy task, and the Kremlin could not expect complete protection from its force. The other alternative was to reach an agreement to make the Indian Ocean a nuclear free zone. The two palliatives were not mutually exclusive, and in the event the Soviet Union pursued both. On 7 December 1964 it presented to the United Nations a memorandum 'on measures for further easing international tension and restricting the arms race', which included a proposal that the Indian Ocean be taken out of the area of nuclear competition. There is no direct evidence of a link between the Polaris development and the memorandum, but there are a number of circumstantial points which suggest that a link there was.[8] This action was not immediately followed by the appearance of a Soviet naval presence. In the first place, the new Brezhnev–Kosygin team was busy increasing defence expenditure by a build-up of missiles at home and was unlikely to regard favourably proposals to open up simultaneously a new theatre for operations. In the second place, the British government was then debating whether to withdraw troops east of Suez, and it would have been clearly unpropitious for the U.S.S.R. to lend ammunition to those who favoured staying. By early 1968 this second constraint was removed, and the Soviet navy began to make small scale appearances in the Indian Ocean. Such a low profile had a number of advantages: it went some way to meeting the Navy's need for area familiarisation, it 'showed the flag' to the non-aligned coastal states, and it increased the stature of the navy, but it was not so large as to provoke the very American presence it was designed to deter or to create hostility from the non-aligned.*

This two-pronged policy could also be used to support other Soviet interests in the Indian Ocean which, while not so vital as nuclear defence, are none the less important. One such consideration is merchant shipping. In 1967 as many Soviet ships of over 1600 g.r.t. sailed in the Indian Ocean as in the Mediterranean or the Pacific. Some 350 ships of this size (or 20 per cent of the Soviet fleet) used the Indian Ocean that year. This figure represents three times the number of U.S. boats sailing in the Ocean and is almost the size of the British contingent.[9] The U.S.S.R. also operates more oceanographic and hydrographic research vessels than all the rest of the world put together, and some of these find their way into the Indian Ocean.[10]

The Soviet Union's two-pronged strategy entailed a number of corollaries for its relations with the coastal states. The pursuit of a nuclear free zone required a diplomatic offensive to enlist their support, while the

---

* The importance of area familiarisation should not be underestimated. When in July 1961 Britain sent troops to defend Kuwait against possible attack from Iraq, one-fourth to one-half of the men flown in from temperate climes were prostrated by the heat.

military, merchant and research naval presence was aided by the acquisition of bases or other support facilities on the shore. Soviet naval visits began in March 1968 and thereafter settled into a regular pattern, with a 'major force' leaving Vladivostok before the onset of winter, arriving in the Indian Ocean in December or January and departing for home between April and June, shortly after the arrival of a 'minor force' to maintain the presence for the remainder of the year.* The number of shore visits made by these vessels indicates that the east coast of Africa is their most important focus of activity, followed by the Red Sea. Between January 1968 and November 1971 fifty-four visits were made to East African ports (including Mauritius) as against forty-two to the Red Sea and only sixty-six to the rest of the ocean's coast (see Table 6.3). These figures may be somewhat distorted by incomplete observation of ships and disregard for the length of visits, but should be valid as a rough guide.

TABLE 6.3   The geographical distribution of Soviet visits to the Indian Ocean, by region

Area	1968	1969	1970	Jan–Nov 1971	Total
Red Sea (inc. Aden)	3	18	9	12	42
Persian Gulf	9	14	6	1	30
Indian sub-continent	14	5	7	1	27
E. African coast (Somalia to Mauritius)	13	15	16	10	54
Singapore	0	2	4	3	9
TOTAL	39	54	42	27	162

Source: Joint Committee on Foreign Affairs, Australian Federal Parliament, *Report on the Indian Ocean Region*, Appendix 1, cited by Geoffrey Jukes, *The Indian Ocean in Soviet Naval Policy* (London, 1972), p. 17.

The figures for East Africa may be broken down still further. Thirty-two of the fifty-four visits were to the three Somali ports of Berbera, Mogadishu, and Kisimayo, making Somalia the Indian Ocean country most frequently visited by Soviet warships. Indeed, so marked is this concentration on the horn of Africa that it has put into shade even the traditionally important area to the north: in 1970–1 the port of Berbera alone received twice as much attention as the entire Persian Gulf.[11] This, of course, does not mean that the U.S.S.R. attaches to Somalia a higher

---

* The major force usually consists of a cruiser, a couple of destroyers and support vessels; the minor force normally includes nothing larger than a destroyer. G. Jukes, *Indian Ocean in Soviet Naval Policy*, pp. 15–16.

priority than to the Persian Gulf. There are many reasons why naval visits to this oil rich area might be counter-productive. However, it is clear that Somalia and its position at the mouth of the Red Sea is an important adjunct to Soviet strategy. Its significance has been recognised for some time by the U.S.S.R., and Soviet military assistance to Somalia is of long-standing. Such assistance was first requested because the Soviet Union appeared to be sympathetic to the principal aim of Somali foreign policy : the reunification of all the Somali people into a Greater Somalia. The British were viewed with suspicion for incorporating the Northern Frontier District into Kenya; the French were distrusted because of their activities in the Djibouti enclave; and the Americans were seen to be giving large scale support to Ethiopia. To achieve its ambition, the Somali government required a well equipped army, and for three and one-half years it negotiated with the West for military aid.[12] By the end of 1963 the U.S.A., West Germany and Italy were prepared to offer military equipment worth about $18 million, but the Americans imposed the condition that their aid would only be forthcoming if other offers were rejected. By this time, however, the Russians were also offering military hardware worth approximately $30 million. Not surprisingly, in view of the difference in size and the affront to Somali dignity made by the American condition, it was the Western offer that was rejected.[13] In addition to providing military equipment, the U.S.S.R. has built a modern port on the northern coastline at Berbera and has provided military training for about 700 young Somalis in the U.S.S.R. and Somalia.[14]

The Soviet offer is notable for several reasons. First, it illustrates the speed with which the Soviet machinery of government can move if required. In contrast to the three and one-half years taken by the West, the Russian offer was arranged in three months: the skeleton agreement was apparently fixed during a lightning twenty-four-hour visit to Moscow by Prime Minister Abdirashid Ali Shermarke and Minister of Information Ali Mohammed Hirawe on 10 August; the details were then probably worked out with the commandant of the Somali army, General Abdulle Hersi Daud, when he visited the Soviet Union in September.[15]

Secondly, it illustrates Soviet willingness to accept the recipient's own estimation of its requirements. The Western offer would have provided for an army of 5000–6000 men, a fairly large increase over the 4000 strong existing force, but the Soviet offer was probably sufficient for an army of around 20,000 together with some air power.[16] This, of course, may not be a wholly good thing. Certainly, Somalia appears to have suffered from an *embarras de riches* : it was only possible for the army to grow to 10,000 men, and it was reported in 1966 that most of the twenty to thirty MIG–17s supplied remained in their crates because the expense of operating them could not be justified.[17] However, Somalia is a very tough little country and it is probable that there would have been a high level of military expenditure even without the Soviet supplies. The proportion of the total budget allocated to the ministry of defence was 14 per cent in 1961, and this figure slowly crept up to 26·5 per cent for 1971. In cash terms the 1971 figure was some So.Sh.81·2 million (£4·7 million).[18] In view of the Soviet Union's favourable attitude to the rescheduling of Somalia's other debts, it is likely that this figure includes only the servicing and not the purchase of Soviet equipment. In this instance the Soviet Union's readiness to accept a recipient's own estimation of its requirements has been tempered by the realisation that Somalia is situated in an area of strategic interest, and that as a result caution is sometimes necessary. In the mid-1960s it adopted a more circumspect attitude towards Somali requests and there is evidence that it reached a tacit agreement with the U.S.A. to prevent a mini arms race between Somalia and Ethiopia both of whom badgered their patrons for more sophisticated weapons to offset the requests of the other.[19]

A third significant feature is the advantage that accrued to the U.S.S.R. by being a newcomer. One reason for the small size of the American offer was its desire not to offend Ethiopia, which had every reason to fear that it might be on the receiving end of those weapons once in Somali hands. The Soviet Union was fettered by no such countervailing ties. Its freedom was, however, transitory; as it built up friendship with some countries, so it had to accept the possibility of animosity being shown by its friends' enemies. In the case of Somalia, this meant that relations with Ethiopia and Kenya were sometimes cool. On his arrival in Nairobi, the first Soviet ambassador to Kenya admitted that military aid to Somalia might well be one of the topics that the government would discuss with him, and he went on to blame the imperialist press for using the arms issue to damage relations between friendly states.[20] Although he quickly added that these attempts had had no effect, the Kenya government took the opportunity of the later deterioration of its relations with the U.S.S.R. to issue a document in which it attacked the U.S.S.R., and to a lesser extent China and the U.A.R., for providing Somalia with weapons which were passed on to the Shifta.[21]

It is extremely difficult to assess how much the U.S.S.R. benefits from its relationship with Somalia. The Soviet navy receives the facilities of Somali ports, particularly Berbera, but there is no evidence that it has bases there. The term 'base' is much misused : it refers to a sanctuary that provides guaranteed physical security, storage for ammunition, spares, stores and fuel, and often overhaul facilities, together with

---

* Such caution seems now to have been put to one side. In mid-1974 it was reported that the USSR had supplied Somalia with 7 MIG-21s. *Africa Research Bulletin*, vol. 11, no. 7 (Aug. 1974) p. 3315c.

political guarantees that this haven will not be withheld during a political crisis. As far as is known, the Soviet Union has no bases thus defined in Black Africa. What the Soviet navy has in Somalia are berthing stations of which it had, in 1969, a total of thirteen in the Indian Ocean area. A berthing station is little more than a fancy title for a mooring buoy. So far, the Soviet presence in the Ocean has not required it to develop bases. During its short cruises its main requirements have been stores, water and fuel, and these can either be purchased on commercial terms at most of the world's ports or, and this is what the Soviet navy has so far chosen, can be provided by accompanying supply ships. Port calls then become a matter of 'showing the flag' and giving the crews periodic entertainment. However, if the Soviet navy were to send into the field a large permanent force it might well be necessary to acquire bases as the Western powers have done. In these circumstances the modern, strategically placed port of Berbera with its oil storage facilities to hand would be attractive.*

Whether it would be made available is less certain. The present Somali military government is clearly on good terms with the U.S.S.R., and has proclaimed 'scientific socialism' as its goal. This amity probably owes much to past Soviet military assistance. It is also clear that the Somali authorities have taken a number of steps in the world arena that would seem to benefit the Russians. However, these acts are better seen as examples of an aggressive independence than as moves designed to affect one or other of the superpowers. The two most significant events both occurred in 1970. The United States began to question the legality of American aid to the Somali Democratic Republic 'because 6 of the 60 vessels that fly the Somali flag of convenience were trading with North Vietnam.' The Somali government was requested to choose between American aid and the continued registration of those six boats; it chose the latter, and on 2 June the U.S. government announced the cessation of its $2 million aid programme and the recall of over fifty aid officials. Five days later the Somali Democratic Republic agreed to establish diplomatic relations at an ambassadorial level with North Vietnam. At about the same time, the Somali government received a delegation from East Germany and on 11 April a communiqué was issued stating that Somalia would recognise the G.D.R. diplomatically and exchange ambassadors. The Supreme Revolutionary Council in Mogadishu may have hoped that West Germany, under the influence of Chancellor Brandt's *Ostpolitik*, would adopt a more flexible position than it had done hitherto on the question of East German recognition. However, the Federal German ambassador was recalled for consultations, and when it became clear that

---

* The alleged presence of a Soviet missile base in Somalia is a completely new departure. Too little information is currently available to assess its impact.

Bonn would not let the matter pass unnoticed, the S.R.C. hardened its position. There followed a faintly comic interlude during which the West Germans several times denied that they had severed aid, while the S.R.C. insisted that they had.[22] When the air cleared it transpired that Bonn had agreed to fulfil aid commitments already planned worth DM119 million but would not enter into any agreements to utilise the remainder of the DM130 million which had been promised.[23]

Whether the Somali government would be prepared to sacrifice its non-alignment by giving the Soviet navy a base at Berbera is an open question. It would not be a negligible sacrifice, since under the influence of Foreign Minister Omar Arteh Ghalib the S.D.R. has been playing an active role in African and world affairs : Somalia's membership of the U.N. security council, and Omar's mediation between Uganda and Tanzania, his chairmanship of the Apartheid Committee of the U.N. and the Ministerial Committee of the O.A.U. being the most outstanding examples. It is not clear how much pressure the U.S.S.R. could exert to provoke a favourable agreement. It is estimated that there are roughly 300 Soviet military advisers in Somalia, as well as 100 technical assistance personnel, not all of whom need have purely economic interests.[24] The Somali army cannot operate without the presence of Soviet instructors who, in this capacity, were present during the 1969 military *coup*. However, on this occasion they seem to have observed a strict impartiality. The dominant position of the Soviet Union could give it a short and medium-term influence, through the activities of its technicians and through its control over spare parts and repairs. However, in the longer term Somalia should have no difficulty in finding an alternative supplier should Soviet demands become too onerous. Soviet influence within the military might be used to put favourably minded people into power, but the Russians' experience in Egypt and Guinea can hardly have encouraged them to think along these lines.

Where the Soviet leaders can relish definite gains from their relations with Somalia is in the diplomatic realm. Somali authorities have for long been favourably disposed towards the U.S.S.R., with the first Russian ambassador being awarded Somalia's highest decoration (the Order of the Grand Star of Somalia) on his departure.[25] Moves by the U.S.S.R. to maintain the Indian Ocean as a nuclear free zone are likely to strike a responsive chord in Mogadishu.

They would also strike a response in Tanzania, which has also been on the wrong end of the Hallstein Doctrine. The Soviet Union's strategic interest in Tanzania has in the past centred on Zanzibar, not least because President Nyerere on the mainland has been most unresponsive to Soviet advances. On 12 January 1964 a military *coup* put to an end 500 years of Arab rule in the clove island of Zanzibar, only a month after, to use

Keith Kyle's telling phrase, 'the Arab Sultan Jamshid had graduated from being His Highness under British protection to being His Majesty without that protection.'[26] The *coup* should hardly have been unexpected: the Arab parties retained power only as a result of gerrymandering and then proceeded to indulge in suicidal acts such as the dismissal of a number of African policemen without repatriating them to the mainland. The only surprising aspect of the operation was the man who led it. A number of groups were plotting the Sultan's demise, but they were beaten to it by a freelance force organised by the swashbuckling, self-styled 'Field Marshall' John Okello, an adventurer who soon revealed himself as inept at manoeuvring within the new government as he had been skilled at overthrowing the old. After the Sultan's flight Okello brought the leaders of the main opposition groups into a coalition, and they in turn swiftly managed to despatch the homicidal 'Field Marshall'. The government so formed presented a highly unified façade to the outside world but included a number of disparate points of view regarding the virtues and vices of the great powers. The two main groups were the Afro-Shirazi Party (A.-S.P.) and Umma, which between them took the major ministerial posts. Abdul Rahman Mohammed (Babu), who was closely linked with China and had once been a correspondent of the New China News Agency, combined the posts of minister of the interior and minister for external affairs. The prime minister was Abdulla Kassim Hanga, who had been educated in the U.S.S.R., travelled widely in Communist countries, and had a Russian wife who had worked closely with Professor Potekhin; when the Tanzanian national assembly passed a resolution of condolence following the assassination of President Kennedy, he walked out in disgust. The highest ranking official known to be favourably disposed towards the West was Othman Sharif, the minister of education, but the president, Abedi Karume, appears initially to have also been anxious for a cordial relationship with Britain.

The situation, as far as relations with external powers was concerned, was thus extremely volatile. In the event, it was the views of those favouring connections with the East that prevailed, largely because of the reticence of the West.[27] Recognition for the new regime came within a week of the *coup* from most of the Communist countries, with East Germany being first off the mark. The West was less prompt. Duncan Sandys regretted that the situation was 'obscure', and two warships stood off the coast to evacuate British citizens if necessary. The Americans abandoned their satellite tracking station on the island and removed all but two of their citizens. These moves were taken as an expression of no confidence, and the close British military presence provoked fears that there would be intervention on the Sultan's behalf. Added to this, the Western press was strongly opposed to the new regime and saw Cuban and Chinese influences everywhere. In fact, the first Red Chinese to appear arrived after the *coup* and had been appointed ambassador to the Sultan's government![28] The Zanzibaris retaliated by detaining four American journalists on 15 January and expelling the U.S. chargé d'affaires when he tried to intervene on their behalf. This left Washington with only a third secretary on the spot, and as a result it tended to rely on London's assessment of the situation.[29]

The new government had been anxious for British recognition: Okello sent a telegram to London two days after the *coup* requesting it, and Karume sent a similar message later. But no recognition came for six weeks. The only Western country to see an opportunity was West Germany. After a period of discussion, the Federal Republic recognised the Karume government on 12 February, but the recognition soon fell foul of the Hallstein Doctrine. The West Germans apparently believed that Zanzibar would not recognise the G.D.R. Whether they were mistaken in thinking that they had received assurances on this point, or whether there was a realignment of forces inside Zanzibar is not clear. In any event, Bonn discovered on 20 February that the East German government had been recognised and an ambassador approved, and it withdrew its support for Zanzibar four days later.[30] Certainly, there was in this period a hardening of the Zanzibari attitude towards the West. Early in February British diplomats were warned that they would be expelled if recognition was not forthcoming, and this warning was repeated by Professor Franck, the Canadian legal adviser to the A.-S.P. when he visited London on 14–16 February.[31] On the 16th there were mass demonstrations against British and American non-recognition and on the 20th both missions were expelled. Recognition followed four days later and the missions returned, but by then the damage had been done. A month later all Britons in the government service apart from doctors, dentists and ships' officers were ordered to leave before the end of April. Before this time limit had expired, Otham Sharif had lost his cabinet post and the West had then lost their main sympathiser on the island. He was made ambassador to the U.K. and on his arrival in London he argued that Zanzibar was being 'forced to the East' by undiplomatic statements in the Western press.[32]

The departing Britons were replaced largely by East Germans, and the security of the new regime was assured by shipments of Soviet and Chinese arms. The Soviet Union also provided the island with military training instructors, numbering thirty to forty in 1969, while the East Germans gave assistance to the security services. According to some reports, the Zanzibaris found the Germans a little too efficient and ruthless.[33]

The island of Zanzibar has for centuries occupied a strategic position in relation to the East African mainland only twenty miles away. On 20

January (shortly after the Zanzibar *coup*) troops of the first battalion of the Tanganyika Rifles mutinied against their British officers and marched into the capital Dar es Salaam. This mutiny provoked similar uprisings in Tanganyika's East African partners, Kenya and Uganda. The example of Zanzibar was a contributory cause to these disturbances, but there is no evidence of direct involvement from the island, and the mutinies were soon quelled. However, the Tanganyika government was clearly shaken and could not face with equanimity the existence off its shores of what began to appear more and more like a Communist base; a jumping-off point for who knew what. By a deft exercise in diplomacy, plans for a union of the two countries were announced on 23 April 1964.

However, the union did not extricate mainland Tanzania from the disruptions of the Cold War. The Soviet Union was channelling much of its aid to Zanzibar through East Germany, possibly in order to moderate Western fears and possibly with the aim of securing recognition for the Ulbricht government. Whether it was a major Soviet objective or not, the Zanzibar and G.D.R. governments did establish diplomatic relations. The government in Dar es Salaam, however, did not recognise East Germany, not only because such recognition would forfeit West German aid, but also because President Nyerere did not accept the legitimacy of a divided Germany. The president had also shown himself to be by no means overweening in his support for the U.S.S.R. in Africa. Shortly before the union was announced he had issued his now-famous warning to a preparatory meeting for the second Afro-Asian conference (the ill-fated 'second Bandung') that the U.S.S.R. was one of the countries involved in a second 'Scramble for Africa' more dangerous than the first. The Soviet Union for its part had never ranked the Tanganyika government very highly, and its attitude had been a natural sequel to the West's high esteem for Nyerere.

After the union, the Tanzanian authorities had to sort out the problem of East German recognition. On the one hand, Zanzibar was reluctant to accept the demotion of the East German representation, but on the other, if this status was maintained the United Republic would lose West German aid. There followed a complicated piece of diplomatic negotiation and wrangling in which both the Dar es Salaam and Bonn Governments appear to have misunderstood each other's position. The solution finally adopted by Tanzania was for East Germany to be accorded consulate-general status, and for the announcement of this to be accompanied by a statement that such representation did not imply diplomatic recognition of the Ulbricht government. This was unacceptable to West Germany, which withdrew its military assistance. The Tanzanian government, fearing that the remaining West German aid would be used to influence its subsequent policy, ordered that all aid be withdrawn.[34]

Public Tanzanian irritation at this petty squabble was largely directed at West Germany, but there is evidence that it also provoked resentment at the role played by East Germany and the U.S.S.R. Nyerere's main concern was that a dispute between the two Germanies was being transformed into a conflict between Zanzibar and the mainland, which might destroy the fragile basis of the union. Karume was predisposed to favour East Germany, remembering the assistance it had given him after the *coup*. However, Berlin was anxious to make sure of its position. The announcement of the union was followed by a flurry of diplomatic activity. Five days after it, a high level G.D.R. delegation arrived, stayed for a week, and offered technical assistance. A week later another delegation arrived to settle the details of this aid. In June, the government in Dar es Salaam ordered that all embassies in Zanzibar be demoted to consular status, but Karume remained obdurate on the issue of East German recognition. According to T. C. Niblock, East German Ambassador Fritsch reminded him of past help and advised him that it would be better to leave the union than to accept the proposal.[35] At the end of June, Karume was again reminded of East German kindness by the arrival of a high-level trade delegation. The mainland reacted strongly and on 26 June published an attack on the G.D.R. which, it said, was trying to destroy the union.[36] At the Saba Saba Fair, Nyerere warned the people to use care with 'baskets full of presents; they have poison in them'.[37] As a result of Zanzibar's intransigence, the East Germans were accorded a consulate-general rather than the consulate originally intended, and Eastern Europe's position on the island remained unimpaired.

While the Soviet bloc showed itself able to outmanoeuvre the West, it was less successful in competition with the Chinese. Peking also had a position to lose in Zanzibar, but it played a much more discreet hand than the U.S.S.R., which openly backed East Germany. Ho Ying, their ambassador in Dar es Salaam, assured Nyerere of the P.R.C.'s support for the union, while the U.S.S.R. appeared to be actively against it. The Chinese always worked through Nyerere, and disbursed their aid through the union government; the U.S.S.R. and East Germany, in contrast, dealt directly with Zanzibar.* The subsequent rapprochement between China and Tanzania has been well recorded.[38] In June 1964 Vice-President Rashidi Kawawa returned from Peking with an interest-free loan of £5 million and a free grant of £1 million. In August 1964 the Chinese agreed to train Tanzania's army : it was stated that they would send an eleven-man mission for a maximum of six months; it is still there. In February 1965 Nyerere visited China and was much impressed by what

---

* A. C. A. A. Ogunsanwo, *China's Policy in Africa 1958–71* (London, 1974), Chapter 4. According to Ogunsanwo, the Soviet attitude towards the union was a major reason why the Soviet aid offer was hardly utilised.

he saw, particularly Chinese discipline and austerity. Then in 1967 came the announcement that China was to build the Tanzam Railway. Soviet aid activity, in contrast, is minimal.

In Zanzibar, however, the Chinese did not at first appear to be as well placed as their Communist rivals. Their main supporter, Babu, was weakened by being sent off to the mainland as a cabinet minister. But then Hanga was implicated in an attempt to overthrow the island's government and was executed in 1969. Some observers saw a three way division within the ruling group between those who were absolutely loyal towards Karume, those who favoured Eastern Europe, and those who were predisposed towards China.* During the year Karume showed himself irritated by attempts to import the Sino-Soviet dispute to the island, and at the end of the year he began to eliminate this possibility by removing one of the contestants. The Russians were asked to withdraw their military advisers, but the sixty to eighty Chinese instructors remained.[39] In June the following year, this policy was followed through to its conclusion when the East German consul was also asked to leave; by the end of the year all G.D.R. technical assistance had been terminated at Zanzibar's request. A suggested reason is that the East Germans charged interest on their loans while the Chinese did not.[40]

The political and military relationship between the Soviet Union and Kenya was considered in the last chapter. Taking Somalia, Kenya and Tanzania together, the U.S.S.R.'s success in Africa's independent eastern seaboard has been moderate, but the U.S.S.R.'s aims were also moderate. Somalia, Kenya and Tanzania, despite their differing relationships with the Soviet Union, are all likely to support its diplomatic aim of keeping the Indian Ocean a nuclear free zone. All are likely to provide Soviet ships with supply and berthing facilities on normal commercial terms. Even Kenya has welcomed Soviet warships to Mombassa. It is doubtful whether Soviet diplomatic and military activity on the seaboard has acquired for it more power than this. However, it is difficult to see what additional power could have been hoped for. Blockading the mouth of the Red Sea has not been a political possibility, although recent developments in Ethiopia and a new regime in Djibouti could change this. It would, no doubt, be possible for Soviet forces to seize an Indian Ocean port and even to control its hinterland, but the political cost of such an action would rule it out except in extreme emergencies (none of the extreme emergencies most frequently envisioned as smiting the

---

* *Africa Contemporary Record 1969/70* (Exeter, 1970), p. B197. In the first group were Aboud Jumbe and Brigadier Yussuf Amir, the military commander. In the second were Ibrahim Majunju, head of security, and Khamis Daresh, assistant commissioner of police. In the third group were Brigadier Yussuf Hamidi and the remaining three ex-members of Umma in the cabinet: Ali Sultana, Ahmed Kolikan and Khamissa Abdulla.

U.S.S.R. would be relieved by such an act of piracy). T. B. Millar suggests that just as the Soviet naval presence in the Mediterranean now makes it improbable that the West could again intervene as they did in Jordan and the Lebanon in 1958, so the Russian fleet in the Indian Ocean could deter intervention by, say, the Chinese on the African mainland.[41] No doubt it could, but such intervention is politically unlikely anyway, at least in the immediately foreseeable future.

LESS STRATEGIC AREAS

Other parts of independent Black Africa have not touched as closely on the Soviet Union's vital strategic interests. Their inclusion into the sphere of the U.S.S.R.'s active military interest largely coincides with the expansion of Soviet arms sales during the 1960s. Although this has been termed 'phase three' of the U.S.S.R.'s post-1955 policy on arms sales, it occurred concurrently with the development of Russian military interest in Africa's eastern seaboard. The first direct transfers of armaments from the Soviet government to governments in independent Black Africa took place in 1960. Soviet bloc arms had been supplied to Guinea shortly after its independence, but the U.S.S.R. had cautiously followed the precedent set with Egypt and used Czechoslovakia as an intermediary. Then in March 1960 these scruples were set aside when a direct Soviet–Guinean military aid agreement was signed, following which Guinea acquired eight MIG-17s, six transports, small arms, and many armoured vehicles, including T-34 tanks.[42]

In the summer that year Antoine Gizenga on behalf of Lumumba signed a military aid agreement with the Soviet Union which, while it was never fully implemented, was to have far more serious consequences for both the recipient and the donor than its Guinean predecessor.[43] The accord did not provide for the supply of any clearly offensive weapons but only for transport planes, radio sets and supplies.[44] However, in the situation in which he found himself, Lumumba's greatest military requirement was mobility, and this the Soviet supplies would have given him. The deal enraged the West, and in the event only about half the planes arrived; they were hamstrung at a critical moment by the U.N.'s closure of Leopoldville airport, and they left when the Russian embassy was expelled.*

In both these cases the Soviet Union was presented with an *entrée* by the West's refusal to provide the weapons and support that were requested from them. Towards the end of the decade it again found itself in this situation as civil war broke out in Nigeria. These crises reveal

* The exact number of Soviet planes in the Congo is unclear. Radio Moscow and Izvestiya both announced on 2 September that there were ten planes (*BBC Monitoring Service*, pt 1, no. 426, 2 Sep 1960, and *Izvestiya*, 2 Sep 1960), but Catherine Hoskyns (*The Congo Since Independence, January 1960 to December 1961* (London, 1965), p. 190), puts the number at seventeen (sixteen for transport and one for Lumumba's own use).

some of the modalities of Soviet arms supplies. They illustrate the way in which the U.S.S.R. finds it convenient on occasion to operate through a third party. The Czech role in arms sales has long been recognised. Czechoslovakia is a traditionally aggressive exporter of armaments in its own right, but in addition to activities in its own interest it has served to supply weapons in areas where the Soviet leaders feel it necessary to tread cautiously. It was for this reason that in 1955 it supplied weapons to Egypt, and it was probably to the same end that it was the first Soviet bloc country to grant military aid to Guinea.[45] Such a role is likely to be of diminishing utility as lines of communication between the Kremlin and the White House improve. Nevertheless, the first Soviet bloc planes to appear in Nigeria were twelve Czech Delphin L–29s, followed by ten Soviet MIG–17s which were channelled through Czechoslovakia and six of Poland's MIG–15s.[46] It was not until 1968, at the time when the Dubček government was considering suspending arms sales to Nigeria, that the Soviet Union began to supply direct or in conjunction with the U.A.R. Egypt has now joined Czechoslovakia as an *interlocuteur valable* of the Soviet arms trade. It does not, of course, manufacture its own weapons, but it is able to provide personnel to operate the more sophisticated equipment. When the U.S.S.R. is requested to fill a gap left by the West, it is not unlikely that it will be asked for sophisticated hardware that must be put into action almost immediately. Given the political considerations that normally preclude the Soviet Union from providing its own operators, it is clear that there will often be a problem of finding trained personnel. In Nigeria's case, the situation was exacerbated because the 100 or so trained pilots, who might have adapted to the Soviet planes fairly quickly, were Ibos. On the other hand, it would be unacceptable to the Soviet Union for Westerners to fly their planes. The solution, to provide Egyptian pilots, indicates one of the advantages that a long-term military training agreement with a non-aligned country has for the U.S.S.R.*

Whether because of the problem of trained personnel or because it feared to provoke a serious Western reaction, the Soviet bloc was at first reluctant to send Nigeria its most destructive weapons. The Delphin L–29s which the Federal Military Government first received and six of the MIGs that arrived later in the year were training aircraft.† How-

---

* The Egyptians are also being used as training teams. In Somalia they have provided the instructors for the country's *Poluchai* patrol vessels. *East African Standard*, 1 June 1967, p. 3.

† After this initial phase this reticence was discarded. By the end of the war the Federal Military Government had received twelve Delphin L–29s, six MIG–15UTIs, thirty-six MIG–17s, two MIG–19Ps, four to five Sukhoi Su–7s, and five IL–28s. S.I.P.R.I., *Arms Trade with the Third World*, p. 858. For glossary see Appendix B. The U.S.S.R. also supplied vehicles and 122 mm. Howitzers, the heaviest artillery used during the war. *West Africa*, no. 2746, 13 Jan 1970, p. 69, no. 2743, 27 Dec 1969, p. 1593; *New Nigerian*, 23 Oct 1968, p. 1.

ever, while it was reticent in the type of weapons it would supply, once it had decided to provide weapons the Soviet bloc was not slow to act. As was seen in the case of Somalia, the Soviet bloc can operate very quickly once it has decided to fill a gap left by the West. The first Czech arms shipment to Guinea was reported arriving at Conakry at the end of March 1959, and these reports were confirmed by Diallo Telli in early April.[47] In Nigeria, the decision to acquire aircraft was precipitated by the bombing of Lagos and some towns in the north by the Biafrans flying a few old DC–6s purchased in Rhodesia. Since they had no aircraft or anti-aircraft defences, the F.M.G. reacted with alarm. A mission was sent to Britain but returned empty handed, since the Wilson government did not wish to see an escalation of the conflict. The United States was not willing to rush in where Britain feared to tread, and Dean Rusk announced that 'We regard Nigeria as part of Britain's sphere of influence.'[48] Less than a fortnight after the Nigerians finally decided to request Soviet bloc assistance, two Czech jet fighter planes in Nigerian colours were seen refuelling at Accra *en route* to their new master.[49] They were soon followed by crates containing MIGs.[50]

The hesitation shown by the Soviet Union in supplying weapons directly to Lagos may have had roots not only in caution lest it provoke competition from the U.S.A., but also in uncertainty as to which side to support. Early Soviet comment on the developing conflict between the Ibos and the rest of Nigeria was indecisive and contrasted sharply with the U.S.S.R.'s clear-cut position regarding Guinea and the Congo. It is believed that even at the height of the war a Biafran delegation was received in Moscow.[51] In favour of the Biafrans was the fact that the Ibos were considerably more 'progressive' in Communist eyes than were the F.M.G.s 'feudal' supporters in the north. In the interlude between the 1966 *coups* and the outbreak of hostilities the former eastern region had shown the most interest in utilising Soviet aid. The exact reason why the Soviet Union decided to support the Federal Military Government is not clear, but the move did have much to recommend it. When the first arms shipments were made both the U.K. and U.S.A. had indicated that they did not consider the conflict to be one that was vital to their interests. Despite Soviet references to Biafra as being another Katanga, it was certainly not another Elizabethville–Léo situation as far as the great powers were concerned. Since at that stage no African state had come out in support of Biafra, the Soviet commitment did not immediately prejudice its prospects elsewhere on the continent. However, when Tanzania and Zambia declared for Biafra another blow was struck against the U.S.S.R. and for the Chinese in East Africa, since the latter were supporting the secessionists.

A decision by an African government, facing a severe crisis, to request from the U.S.S.R. weapons with which the West will not supply it, is a very newsworthy event. It is not, however, the only circumstance in which the Soviet Union has supplied military assistance to Black African governments. Bearing in mind the threat posed by their own armed forces, a number of governments have sought to ward off a *coup d'état* by dividing their military establishment against itself. One such was the government of President Nkrumah in Ghana. Save for an airfield at Tamale, Soviet military assistance to Ghana was almost entirely confined to training, organisation and equipment.* A Russian military mission arrived in Ghana in mid-1960 to make a report on the training of the armed forces. The report when completed recommended a rapid increase in the size of the military at a time when the chief of the defence staff, a Briton, Major-General H. T. Alexander, was advising caution.[52] No major step was taken to effect this expansion until the following year. Then in October 1961 it was announced that 400 officer cadets would be trained in the U.S.S.R. The decision was taken by Nkrumah while on his tour of Eastern Europe and conveyed directly to the Ghana army by radio. Alexander objected that there were no young men suitable. When he was told to send some rejected Air Force trainees, he refused, and his refusal was one of the reasons behind his subsequent dismissal.[53] In the event, only eighty trainees could be found, and those were sent without proper vetting of their educational background. They returned to Ghana in January 1963. In view of the proportion of their sojourn which must have been spent learning the Russian language, their training was not highly regarded by the officer corps, which recommended the immediate discharge of most of them on the grounds that they were not suitable officer material. This advice was rejected. All but a few of the cadets were absorbed into the armed forces after retraining.[54] A high proportion of these Soviet trained men were taken into the President's Own Guard Regiment. This was created in January 1961 and became increasingly independent of the rest of the army. It began to be supplied with Russian equipment and Russian instructors. It received priority treatment and by October 1963 it had been turned into a well equipped battalion.[55] This was Nkrumah's army defence against a *coup*.

However, he also sought Soviet bloc assistance in the field of security. Following the attempt on his life at Kulungugu in 1962, a Russian security expert was brought to Accra. This facility had first been offered to the Ghanaian president by Khrushchev when they met in the Crimea during the 1961 tour but had been declined.[56] After Kulungugu, how-

---

* There has been some speculation about the Tamale airfield suggesting that it was being built by the Russians as a remotely sited replacement for Conakry airport, for the purpose of refuelling Soviet military aircraft. Norman Uphoff, however, records that the Ghanaian army, when officered by Britons, had requested an airfield at Tamale as early as 1959, and that the Russian Government claimed to have favoured an extension to Accra airport. *Ghana's Experience*, Chapter 4, n. 118, 121.

ever, he was considerably shaken at the ineffectiveness of his existing security service. Following the Russian's report a presidential detail department was created. The President's Own Guard Regiment formed its military wing and in addition there was a Russian trained para-military civilian unit. A special intelligence unit was also created, supposedly with the task of conducting surveillance activities among Ghanaians. It received technical assistance from Russia and East Germany, but the specialists supplied made little progress: the head of the unit was Ambrose Yankey, a wily fellow tribesman of Nkrumah's who was not only illiterate but also incompetent and packed the service with his less able cronies.

Unfortunately for Nkrumah, Soviet assistance was sufficient to irritate the armed forces but not sufficient to weaken them. It did not prevent one of Nkrumah's own guards attempting to assassinate him in January 1964. According to one account a platoon of the President's Own Guard Regiment stood on hand for ceremonial purposes, but at the time of the attack their guns were not loaded, and no one ordered them to move until after Nkrumah had escaped.[57] At the time of the successful 1966 *coup* the President's Own Guards were being rapidly expanded to the size of two battalions. This expansion was not yet complete when the *coup* took place. However, even had it reached its full strength, it seems improbable that the outcome of the *coup* would have been any different. The first battalion of the P.O.G.R. defended Flagstaff House, the president's headquarters, and did so with great tenacity. Flagstaff House was a focal point of the *coup* and those inside probably felt that they had to fight for their lives. Unfortunately, they had no artillery. The heavy guns were with the second battalion, garrisoned thirty-two miles outside Accra in the Shai Hills, but the second battalion, in which Nkrumah had put his faith, offered no resistance whatsoever to the *coup*.

As with aid and trade, so with military assistance; the U.S.S.R. is still a marginal great power in relation to Black Africa, but its very marginality gives it a certain strength and endows it with some attraction for Africa. The U.S.S.R. can provide regimes with support, *but it cannot guarantee their safety*. It was far beyond the Ghanaian government's pocket to reorganise its forces so that a significant proportion of the military had received Soviet training and operated Soviet equipment. Little was heard of the Russian assisted Guinean army when the country was invaded in November 1971. Then, it was the People's Militia with its Chinese orientation on which Sékou Touré relied. Although the militia was none too successful either, there has been a tendency for some African states to prefer Chinese to Soviet military assistance, and some evidence that the former may be more successful. As with economic assistance, however, Chinese military aid is often very successful, but it is also highly concentrated, with appreciable assistance being currently received by only four governments in Black Africa.* If the Soviet Union has had little success in competition with the Chinese, it has received more joy when dealing with the West. The Congo revealed that the U.S.S.R. could not operate in Africa if the West were determined to prevent it. This situation has probably not changed, although it is likely that the West now considers it to be counter-productive to exhibit such determined opposition.

* S.I.P.R.I., *Arms Trade with the Third World*, Table 13.1. In addition, the Chinese assist a large number of liberation movements.

7 The Soviet Union and Black Africa

In the first chapter a commitment was made that this book would eschew grand theories in favour of an analysis of specific situations. In the course of this analysis a number of minor theories and proposals have arisen. In Chapter 2 it was suggested that bilateral trade with the U.S.S.R. may hold clear advantages to an African country provided that it exports a commodity for which there is a high elasticity of demand on to an unstructured world market in which it is a major trader, and provided that it can absorb as payment sufficient quantities of the raw materials that the Soviet Union is able to supply. If some of these conditions do not apply, then trade may still be advantageous but attention must be given to how the problems associated with bilateralism will be overcome. The evidence of Chapter 3 suggests that Soviet aid has many pitfalls, but that it is not unique in this. Provided that the recipient exercises due control over the selection of projects and the implementation of aid, these pitfalls may be overcome.

Chapters 4 and 5 examined the modalities of Afro-Soviet political intercourse within the context of domestic African politics. They suggest that there are definite constraints to Africa's freedom of manoeuvre which restrict the speed at which it can break out of old patterns of behaviour, and limit the extent to which it can ignore important parts of the world around it. Chapter 6 looked at the military aspect of the Afro-Soviet relationship both in the context of the superpowers' global strategy and within the more parochial but none the less important arena of African domestic politics. It suggests that some parts of Africa have clear strategic value for the Soviet Union, which in turn has a number of attractive features that could encourage African states to purchase its arms.

In addition to the conclusions reached in these topic oriented chapters, there are a number of more general points that may be made. There is always the danger of losing the wood for the trees. A number of advantages and disadvantages have been observed accruing to the Soviet Union from its relationship with Africa, and the advantages can be used to explain its continued interest in the continent. But they do not answer the more general question of why, from a global perspective, the

U.S.S.R. was attracted to Africa in the first place. What were its goals when it first made contact with the newly independent states? Have these goals been fulfilled, and if not have they been succeeded by fresh goals which are more likely to be achieved? In short, what was and is the perceived 'value' of Africa to the Soviet Union?

During the past twenty years the Soviet Union has had dealings on an increasing scale with the countries of the Third World. These contacts have been between on the one hand a superpower, one of the strongest nations that the world has ever known, and on the other hand states characterised by varying degrees of weakness. Yet it would be wrong to assume that the U.S.S.R. has been able to dominate the relationship. It would be wrong largely because of what David Vital has described as the 'Fortunate circumstance that the great powers operate today in a climate of thought which promotes caution and hesitation, particularly where the use of force is concerned'.[1] Although the circumstances have been fortunate, it would be misleading to suppose, as Vital appears to do, that they are necessarily transitory. This climate of thought has profoundly affected the Soviet Union's relations with Africa and shows no signs of dissipating in the near future.

The state of relations between the U.S.S.R. and Africa is the product of two factors : the enthusiasm of the Soviet Union and the receptiveness of the partner. Defined in this way the initiative for starting the relationship clearly lies with the U.S.S.R., as befits its superpower status. On occasion an African partner has attempted to reverse this situation and to take the initiative itself. Such appears to have been the case when Lumumba appealed for Soviet military assistance. Lumumba was partially successful, but success is rare. More typical than the Congo is the Guinean government's periodic announcements that the Soviet Union has 'agreed' to sponsor the $250 million Konkouré Dam; the world still waits for a concrete manifestation of this agreement. Although the U.S.S.R. holds most of the initiative for starting the relationship and for defining its upper limits, it lies with the African partner to define its lower limits, and in the international situation that has obtained during the period in question it is this power of limitation that has frequently been the more significant variable. There have been several instances of African states reducing the Soviet presence but no instance of the U.S.S.R. imposing a presence on an unwilling African partner. 'The Soviet Union proposes, Africa disposes' is not too far from the mark.

The Soviet Union proposed on two main fronts : the diplomatic and the economic. On the diplomatic side it must be borne in mind that the U.S.S.R. is a superpower and that it seems in the contemporary world to be incumbent upon a superpower to be represented and have interests in all corners of the globe; its activity in Africa has helped it to achieve this. With regard to more specific diplomatic goals its activity has been less successful. Recognition for East Germany has been a recurrent theme of Soviet activity. In March 1960 Guinea prepared to recognise the G.D.R. and sent Seydou Conté to Berlin where a film of him presenting his credentials as the new ambassador was shown on East German television. The West Germans reacted vigorously and Sékou Touré had first to argue that Conté was simply an emissary on a specific mission, and then after further representations from Bonn to issue a statement denying any intention of establishing diplomatic relations with East Germany.[2] Nkrumah may also have considered recognising the G.D.R.: during his 1961 tour of Eastern Europe he visited East Berlin to receive an honorary doctorate from Humboldt University, much to Bonn's dismay, and he was generally favourable to the idea of a divided Germany in his public statements on the subject. However, after considering the economic importance of West Germany to Ghana he became far more restrained in his outlook.[3] East Germany had more success in Zanzibar, but not in mainland Tanzania. In recent years it has achieved recognition from a number of African states, but this reflects the declining vigour with which the Hallstein Doctrine is enforced rather than any increase in the effectiveness of Soviet and East German pressure.

Soviet diplomatic interest is, therefore, fairly easily explained. Its economic strategy raises more problems for, as Raymond Aron has remarked, 'If the West is convinced that it is helping to maintain liberal institutions by the development of metallurgical industries why is the Soviet Union doing likewise when, according to all observers, its aim is entirely the opposite?' Aron's own preferred explanation is that by giving economic assistance the U.S.S.R. 'puts the homeland of socialism on the same level as the homelands of capitalism. The operation is profitable in terms of prestige, and it is not costly on other levels.'[4]

Soviet actions during the 1960s, particularly the early 1960s, lend plausibility to Aron's contention that one Russian goal was prestige. The sports stadium it built in Mali and the polytechnic in Guinea are obvious manifestations of this, but so is the iron and steel mill planned for Nigeria and the River Juba barrage being contemplated in Somalia. However, economic assistance only bolsters prestige if it is seen to result in projects that successfully raise the standard of living of the recipient whether this is measured in economic or in other terms. Soviet aid has not, in general, been seen in this way. Some of the criticisms levelled against it are invalid and unfair, but they are nevertheless widely expressed, and it is the popularity of these notions rather than their validity that affects prestige. The U.S.S.R. appears to have become more cautious in giving aid since the early days and now candidly admits that developing countries cannot rely on the socialist world for all their needs and must solicit aid from all possible sources.

If Soviet activities failed to win prestige, did they at least succeed in remaining cheap? The answer is probably no. There is evidence that Soviet aid givers fully expected the loans they gave to be repaid, but often this has not happened. Such losses have not generally been offset by 'exploitative' profits from trade gained by the Soviet Union receiving more for its exports or paying less for its imports than the world market price. While trade has, as the trade agreements put it, been 'mutually beneficial' there have been few opportunities for the Soviet Union to reap the kind of harvest that it has garnered from its socialist trade partners. Whether the Soviet leaders ever intended to 'exploit' their African trade partners is a matter for pure speculation. To do so would, however, have been self-defeating in the medium or long term so long as the Soviet Union lacked effective political control over its partners. Exploitation in trade is a function not only of the price charged but also of the quantities exchanged: if no goods are traded then there can be no exploitation. Black African countries have in general retained the power to limit their trade with the U.S.S.R. without incurring major political or economic obstacles. It has sometimes been the case that 'exploitation' has occurred by default: poor bargains have been struck by African partners presumably as a result of ignorance and inexperience, but in such cases Soviet economic policy has been in danger of contradicting its political objective of winning support.

Nevertheless, the politico-economic account is not entirely negative. The Soviet Union and its allies have helped to prevent a colonial political appendage of Western Europe from becoming an 'independent' economic appendage of North America and Western Europe. It has also gained from its trade, even if it has not been able to displace the West as Africa's dominant economic partner. There appears to be some correlation but not a close link between the U.S.S.R.'s economic and foreign policies. If one considers the size of Soviet aid *commitments* to various countries in Black Africa there does appear to be a relationship between Soviet pronouncements and the amount of aid offered. In the period 1959–66, for example, Ghana, Guinea and Mali were offered more than were, for example, Senegal, Uganda or Tanzania* (see Table 7.1). However, Somalia did equally as well as Ghana, Guinea and Mali if *per capita* commitments are considered, yet it was not viewed as an especially progressive state until after 1969. Kenya, too, had been offered considerably more than Senegal, Uganda or Tanzania. Indeed, the Soviet promise to Kenya of $45 million was greater than any single offer made to the other countries in Table 7.1, and it may reasonably be argued that more would have been forthcoming had the relationship between the two countries not deteriorated as drastically as it did. Yet Kenya was not a

---

* Senegal and Uganda flirted with the U.S.S.R. but were not normally included in the lists of most progressive states, while Tanzania was not included in the lists during the period in question.

TABLE 7.1   Soviet aid commitments to selected African countries 1959–68

State	Commitments ($m.)	Total commitment ($m.)	Estimated population (million)	Per capita commitment ($)
Ghana	40,42	82	8·6	9·6
Guinea	35,21,13	69	3·9	17·4
Kenya	45	45	10·9	4·1
Mali	44,11	55	4·9	11·2
Somalia	44,5·6	49·6	2·7	18·4
Tanzania	20	20	12·9	1·6
Senegal	6·7	6·7	3·8	1·8
Uganda	15·4	15·4	9·8	1·6

Sources: Commitments: Robert Legvold, *Soviet Policy in West Africa* (Cambridge, Massachusetts, 1970), W. A. Nielsen, *The Great Powers and Africa* (London, 1969), B. R. Stokke, *Soviet and Eastern European Trade and Aid in Africa* (New York, 1967), and Chapter 3 above; Population: *Whitakers Almanack 1973*.

member of the most progressive group even though the U.S.S.R. showed strong partiality to one of its factions. There are also incongruities within the most progressive group: of the three Guinea was promised by far and away the largest amount *per capita* although during the period when the greatest ideological innovations were underway it was dropped from the list of most progressive states.[5]

If any pattern in aid commitments can be discerned, it is that in the late 1950s and early 1960s the U.S.S.R. tended to make initial offers of about $40 million to Black African countries in which it took a particular interest, whether by virtue of their anti-'imperialist' foreign policy, their strategically important position, their domestic policy, or even the signs they gave of potential future 'progressiveness'. If the relationship matured, then further sums were promised. Elsewhere, in so far as the countries given in Table 7.1 are indicative of any general tendency, the U.S.S.R. offered smaller amounts which, while varying widely in total, are very similar if considered on a *per capita* basis.

Aid commitments are not, however, a very satisfactory means for measuring operational policy: promises are made at discrete intervals and so reveal Soviet intentions only at fixed points in time; comparison between offers made to different countries at different times is complicated because variations may partly be due to a rising or falling trend in Soviet aid commitments to Black Africa or the Third World as a whole. Data on actual aid flows would overcome these difficulties, but they are not available, and even if they were their value would be limited since they involve a number of imponderables such as the efficiency with which the recipient utilises the aid offered.* Information on trade provides a continuous measure of tangible benefits passing between the U.S.S.R. and Africa. However, in the case of trade there is even less positive statistical correlation between operational and declaratory policy than in the case of aid. The Soviet Union has clearly tended to conduct more trade with the 'progressive' African countries, but this is not surprising since one of the criteria for assessing whether a country is 'progressive' or not is its determination to break away from 'imperialist economic domination'. When it comes to the prices at which commodities are exchanged there is, if anything, a negative correlation between the two levels of policy.[6] Comparisons are difficult because different commodities are involved in different countries and even at different times within the same country. However, it can be seen from Table 2.10 above that Kenya did not make less favourable bargains with the U.S.S.R. after 1966 than it did before, and Ghana did just as well under the N.L.C. as under Nkrumah. When it comes to exports, Nigeria received better prices for the cocoa it sold to the U.S.S.R. than did Ghana, while of the four countries considered in Table 2.11 above Mali did the least well when the price paid by the U.S.S.R. is compared to the price paid by other purchasers. There are, no doubt, perfectly legitimate reasons for these disparities – the difference between the Soviet prices for Nigerian and Ghanaian cocoa, for example, stems largely from differences in the quantity involved. However, it is clear that the U.S.S.R. has not maintained any consistent policy of helping those countries it favours by departing very far from free market prices.

These then are some of the broad goals of the U.S.S.R. – diplomatic and economic recognition in all parts of the world. In addition, of course, there have been other more specific objectives in individual states. A statement that diplomatic and economic recognition are the motives behind the U.S.S.R.'s general interest in Africa is a far cry from the talk of Communist subversion which was very prevalent in the early 1960s and is still heard in some quarters.[7] It is quite possible that an element in Soviet thinking, particularly during and before the Congo crisis, was that Africa might be drawn into the socialist commonwealth. Undoubtedly, judging from Soviet writing, this is still the transcendental goal of Soviet African policy. But such transcendental goals have a tendency not to be taken too literally when day-to-day policy is decided. This is particularly likely in a bureaucratised administration, and one recent observer of great power activities in Africa has concluded :

* There is the further problem that some commitments may be secret, as in the case of the current Soviet–Nigerian aid agreement. However, judging from the figures that are available on debt repayments, it does not appear that clandestine commitments are very important.

'. . . in the substance of its policies the Soviet Union has behaved conservatively as the kind of nation-state it is – a great power with its own vested interests, heavily bureaucratised, and constrained constantly by the necessity to reconcile conflicting objectives, establish priorities and calculate costs.'[8]

The evidence presented in this book would certainly support this assessment. There is no evidence of the single minded pursuit of well considered objectives that form the backbone of the 'Communist subversion' arguments. No doubt when each major Soviet decision was made those making it had a clear set of objectives in mind. However, to argue that Soviet policy makers 'knew what they wanted' implies that their objectives were rational in the sense that they accurately considered and evaluated all the relevant factors affecting the situation, and that the objectives were consistently held or at least modified in a consistent fashion throughout the period in question. This does not appear to have been the case. It was not the case because to a large extent the Soviet Union's position in Africa has only been as strong as that of its local ally, and the strengths of the various factions within an African state have been variables that the U.S.S.R. has had considerable difficulty in calculating. This is hardly surprising since none of the great powers nor even many African leaders have shown infallibility in this realm. The Soviet Union has suffered setbacks, as when Nkrumah was overthrown, but so has Britain, as when Nkrumah's successor Dr Busia was himself toppled; even France, more successful than most, has seen hard times in Guinea and in Madagascar.

In some countries the Soviet Union was fortunate in the groups with which it made friends; in others it was less so. Its fortune stemmed partly from its own characteristics and its own policy, and partly from factors quite outside its control. When it first came into active contact with Black Africa, the U.S.S.R. was possessed of two important features that were both strengths and weaknesses at the same time. The first was that it was a newcomer to Africa; the second was that it was a superpower. Russia, like America, has never held an African empire, and so both were able to propound what the colonial powers scornfully and bitterly dubbed 'the salt water theory of imperialism', which posited that a body of salt water must lie between two territories before there could be an imperial relationship between them. They were thus able to champion African independence without having their own more dubious activities called into question. Without any direct experience of the Soviet system of rule many Africans were attracted by the U.S.S.R.'s support for the Afro-Asian movement and by its appealing ideology of equality and fraternity for the oppressed of the world to complement the formal political liberty gained on independence day. Because it was working from a base level of almost zero contact with Africa, any increase in the number of ties between the two areas would appear to be a significant gain for the Soviet bloc. Thus, the number of Russians arriving in Ghana increased by over 1500 per cent between 1959 and 1965.[9] This was the positive side of being a newcomer; there was, however, another side. Because it had to work from a low base, the Soviet Union had a long way to go before it could become a major rival to the West. Taking migration statistics once again as an illustration, even in 1965 the Russian contingent of visitors to Ghana was barely one-tenth of the size of the British contingent. At the same time, lack of contact also meant lack of knowledge. Richard Pipes has asserted that:

> It is simply unthinkable that the Soviet Union would ever plunge into a major foreign intervention without acquiring beforehand a solid store of historical, economic, political, social and cultural information on the country in question ... The Russians are not likely to undertake any action on the basis of highly generalised assumptions; they usually arrive at decisions on the basis of concrete factual data in which everything bearing on the 'correlation of forces' is given the most careful scrutiny.[10]

Of course, it all depends on how 'major foreign intervention' is defined, but in the Congo, Guinea and elsewhere in Africa the U.S.S.R. has given every appearance of plunging in with only scanty knowledge and on the basis of 'highly generalised assumptions'. This has affected its success in elaborating a consistent set of objectives and in achieving the various goals that it has from time to time set itself.

The Soviet Union's other major characteristic – its status as a super-power – has been similarly double-edged. When factions within an African country have sought an external patron the U.S.S.R. has been well placed for consideration. Sometimes it has been the faction which controls the government that has sought Soviet assistance, perhaps to enable it to bargain more effectively with the West, or perhaps to help it strengthen its position *vis-à-vis* rival groupings at home. Such was the case with Ghana, Guinea and Mali, but as was seen in Chapter 4 governments wishing to multiply contacts with the Soviet Union must have not only the desire but also the capability. Since the states concerned are, in varying degrees, underdeveloped politically and administratively as well as economically they are liable to experience severe constraints limiting the ability of their governments to reorient their outlook.

The experience of those countries where minority factions having no control or only a partial control over the machinery of government seek out the patronage of the U.S.S.R. may profitably be considered as part of a more general study of polarisation within political communities. The lack of internal integration in many new states has been considered an important determinant of their external policies for a number of years.[11] One early concept was that an 'outside threat' from a foreign country might be fabricated to encourage domestic unity; in such cases the threat would be purely imaginary. In other cases an external power might actually intervene in a domestic conflict to support one side, as Somalia did to give support to the Shifta in Kenya. In between these two extremes are cases where factions seek an external patron as an 'insurance' against attack by their domestic rivals. Patron seeking by one side can be expected to provoke reciprocal action by the other; for example, the most satisfactory explanation for Chief Awolowo's sudden and unexpected espousal of the cause of good relations with the Soviet Union is that his opponents were associated with the West. As this Nigerian example makes clear, the 'patron' need not give its consent (nor even be asked) before it becomes a patron, and its tangible patronage may be minimal. Such a situation may bring the patron windfall gains but it may also prove embarrassing. Richard Sandbrook has expressed surprise at the gullibility of the great powers who seemed to be prepared to give generously to any Kenyan who mouthed appropriate slogans even though he did nothing to implement the beliefs so expressed.[12] It is not, however, so inexplicable. Once the great powers had become associated with a Kenyan faction, even though their initial contribution to it may have been small, they found that their interests and those of their allies were linked: a victory for Odinga might not have heralded a socialist Kenya but victory for his rivals certainly meant that the Soviet Union lost prestige and influence.

Although it might be drawn into a situation not of its own choosing, the Soviet Union's position as an obvious patron gave it a potential *entrée* into many countries from which it had previously been excluded. However, its status as a superpower has not always created openings: sometimes it has resulted in locked doors. Because the Soviet Union is strong it is also feared. Just as its slogans attracted many, so its alien practices and its apparent power to impose those practices elsewhere repelled others. The northerners in Nigeria feared Communism as does President Houphouet-Boigny of Ivory Coast, who may be influenced by his own experiences with the French Communist Party.

The first of these two important characteristics of the Soviet Union – that of being a newcomer to Africa – has been modified by time. The Soviet Union now knows more about Africa and has an acknowledged place in many African states. The second characteristic – its position as a superpower – has lost a number of its more prickly features. Although the Soviet Union may still be drawn into domestic conflicts, as may the U.S.A., improved communications between Washington and Moscow have reduced the risks formerly associated by nuclear strategists with these 'shadowy third areas' where either superpower could miscalculate the intentions of the other and provoke a major conflict. On the other hand, its superpower status remains the major key to African interest in the U.S.S.R. It was shown in Chapters 2 and 3 that there are solid benefits to be obtained by many African states from aid and trade with the U.S.S.R., and while Chapter 4 indicated that caution must be shown, the countries that jumped at the opportunity of strengthening ties with the socialist world have made available to others a wealth of experience from which the appropriate lessons may be drawn. It is not the case, as some have asserted,[13] that these flirtations with the Soviet Union achieved nothing, although it may prove to be the case that they benefited onlookers more than they benefited participants.

African states have played a major role in determining the nature of the relationship that has developed between their continent and the Soviet Union since independence. It nevertheless remains the case that the initiative for setting the upper limit to this relationship lies with the U.S.S.R. Recent years seem to have witnessed a declining Soviet interest in Black Africa, although the recent upsurge of Chinese activity may reverse this trend. In the future the Soviet Union's attitude may well be influenced by the way in which Africa develops. Despite African claims to be able to avoid class stratification, evidence is growing that classes are beginning to emerge in the more industrialised states of the continent. It seems quite possible that in the years to come three types of state will emerge in Africa : those like Nigeria, Zaire and perhaps Kenya, Ivory Coast and Zambia which possesses the wealth to achieve self-sustained growth; those like the Saharan states and Somalia where the prospects for development are extremely slim; and those like Ghana, Dahomey and Uganda which displayed an early promise that has since gone sour. If this is indeed the way in which matters develop, then the first group may well find themselves with a class situation that the Soviet Union recognises, while the third group will very probably be characterised by frequent changes of government and anomic violence as frustrated members of the elite seek more power. In such circumstances both ideology and self-interest would concentrate Soviet attention on the first group of states and discourage interest in the third group. The U.S.S.R. is clearly anxious to remain on good terms with Nigeria, has begun to mend fences with Zaire, and would probably like to improve relations with Kenya. By contrast, the Ghana government has been making a determined effort to re-establish bilateral trade links with Eastern Europe and to secure largesse from the Soviet Union, but at the time of writing it has had little success. As for the second category of states, they offer few attractions as a group. As individual countries they have more to recommend them. Some have value as a result, for example, of their strategic position, and they would appear to be more easy to dominate than richer states. For as long as France retains its active and expensive interest in

Africa, the opportunities for Soviet influence in the Saharan states will probably be slim.

The period 1953–73 has thus seen Afro-Soviet relations mature. They have matured both in the sense that they have developed from a few, simple links to a more complex and fruitful network of relations, and in the sense that both sides have replaced many of their early, naïve assumptions about the benefits and perils associated with contact by a deeper understanding of those areas in which Afro-Soviet intercourse offers clear advantages and those in which it does not. It is not possible to predict how relations between the U.S.S.R. and individual African states will develop, but it seems very probable that the Soviet Union will continue to exhibit considerable interest in a number of African states and that some will reciprocate this interest.

Appendix A: A Note on Currency Equivalents

The cause of a single world currency has no more ardent supporter than the writer on trade. This book embraces eleven currencies many of which are inconvertible and all of which have changed their parity during the period in question. When it has been necessary to compare values expressed to different currencies they have been converted to the most convenient common unit (normally dollars, roubles or pounds). Where possible, however, they have been left in their original form since currencies that are inconvertible may have official rates of exchange that do not reflect their true value. Where conversion has been made some readers may wish to reconvert back to the original and may do so after reference to Table A.1 below.

A special word is perhaps due with regard to Ghana, whose currency changes have been more complex than most. Until July 1965 the Ghanaian pound (£G) was the unit of currency and was valued at par with the pound sterling. On 19 July Ghana changed to a decimal cur-

TABLE A.1   Currency equivalents: national currencies per U.S.$ (only major changes in exchange rates given)

Ghana	Guinea	Mali	Nigeria
1957 – 0·3571	1957 – 175·00	1957 – 175·00	1957 – 0·3571
1965 – 0·8571	1959 – 246·85[b]	1959 – 246·85[b]	1972 – 0·3289[a]
1967 – 1·0204	1971 – 227·36	1967 – 493·71	
1972 – 1·2821[a]	1972 – 22·736[c]	1969 – 555·42	
		1971 – 511·57	

Somalia	Kenya and Tanzania	U.S.S.R.	U.K.	France
1957 – 7·143	1957 – 7·143	1957 – 4·00	1957 – 0·36	1957 – 420
1971 – 6·579		1961 – 0·90	1967 – 0·42	1959 – 491[b]
1972 – 6·925		1972 – 0·746	1971 – 0·40	1960 – 4·9
			1972 – 0·43[a]	1969 – 5·6
				1971 – 5.2
				1972 – 5.1

Notes: a=changed December 1971; b=changed December 1958; c= new unit, the Sily, introduced 2 October 1972; FG10=1 sily.

Sources: *U.N. Statistical Yearbook 1966* (New York, 1967), Table 187; ibid., *1971* (New York, 1972), Table 184; *U.N. Monthly Bulletin of Statistics*, vol. XXVII: 6, Table 66.

rency, the Cedi (C), based on 100 pennies. The Cedi thus equalled £Go.417, i.e. 8/4 sterling. This was considered to be impractical for calculation, and on 23 February 1967 the New Cedi (NC) was introduced, valued at 10/- sterling. On 8 July 1967 the New Cedi was devalued so that U.S. $1=NC 1.02.

Appendix B: A Glossary of Soviet Weaponry

	Type	Purpose	Year production begun
a Aircraft	MIG-15 UTI	fighter/trainer	about 1950
	MIG-17	interceptor/fighter	1953
	MIG-19	interceptor/fighter	about 1955
	MIG-21	fighter	about 1956
	IL-14	transport	about 1950
	IL-28	bomber	1950
	AN-2	light transport	1947
	AN-12	heavy transport	1958
	*L-29 Delphin	trainer	1963
	SU-7	fighter/ground attack	about 1956
b Tanks	T-34	32 ton main battle tank	World War 2

Note: * = Czechoslovak.
Source: S.I.P.R.I., *The Arms Trade with the Third World*, Appendix 5.

References

CHAPTER I

1   See, for example, David L. Morison, *The U.S.S.R. and Africa* (Oxford, 1964); Z. Brzezinski (ed.), *Africa and the Communist World* (Stanford, California, 1963); W. A. Nielsen, *The Great Powers and Africa* (London, 1969); Sven Hamrell and Carl Gosta Widstrand (eds). *The Soviet Bloc, China and Africa* (Uppsala, 1964); Robert Legvold, *Soviet Policy in West Africa* (Cambridge, Massachusetts, 1970); Bruce D. Larkin, *China and Africa, 1949–1970: The Foreign Policy of the People's Republic of China* (Berkeley, California, and London, 1971). A. C. A. A. Ogunsanwo, *China's Policy in Africa 1958–1971* (London, 1974).

2   Ruth Schachter-Morgenthau, *Political Parties in French-Speaking West Africa* (Oxford, 1964), p. 24.

3   R. Barbé, *Circulars 41 and 55 to GECs*, cited in Ruth Schachter-Morgenthau, *Political Parties in French-Speaking West Africa*, p. 24.

4   E. H. Hammonds, Ph.D. thesis (London, 1969), p. 304.

5   Ibid., p. 306, and Edward Mortimer, *France and the Africans 1944–1960: A Political History* (London, 1969), pp. 72–4.

6   Ibid., p. 118.

7   Ibid., pp. 128–9, 142–3.

8   Ibid., pp. 152–8.

9   Ibid., p. 180.

10   Ibid., p. 247.

11   Jean Lacouture, *Cinq Hommes et la France* (Paris, 1961), p. 329.

12   Harish Kapur, *The Soviet Union and the Emerging Nations* (Geneva, 1972), p. 42.

13   *Pravda*, 9 Aug 1953, cited ibid., p. 43.

14   D. Melinkov, 'Neutralism and the Current Situation', *International Affairs*, Moscow, no. 2 (Feb 1956).

15   *Large Soviet Encyclopaedia*, vol. 15, p. 460, cited by Aryeh Yodfat, *Arab Politics in the Soviet Mirror* (Jerusalem, 1973), p. 36.

16   Ibid., pp. 45–6.

17   Uri Ra'anan, *The U.S.S.R. Arms the Third World: Case Studies in Soviet Foreign Policy* (Cambridge, Massachusetts, and London, 1969).

18   *Pravda*, 23 July 1958, cited in Yodfat, *Arab Politics in the Soviet Mirror*, p. 147.

19   Larkin, *China and Africa*, p. 38.

20   *L'Humanité*, 6 Nov 1958.

21   Jean-Bosco Mamba, 'Les Relations entre le Congo et les Pays de l'Est', *Etudes Congolaises*, vol. XI, no. 3 (July–Sep 1968), pp. 104–11.

22   Herbert Weiss and Benoît Verhaegen (eds), *Le Parti Solidaire Africain (P.S.A.) – Documents: Les Dossiers du C.R.I.S.P.* (Brussels, 1963), pp. 263–4.

23   Thomas Kanza, *Conflict in the Congo: The Rise and Fall of Lumumba* (Harmondsworth, Middlesex, 1972), p. 141.

24   Ibid.

25   Ibid., pp. 189–90.

26   Cited in J. Gérard-Libois and Benoît Verhaegen, *Congo 1960 – Les Dossiers du C.R.I.S.P.*, vol. II (Brussels, 1961–2), p. 542.

27 *Pravda*, 13 July 1960, p. 2, cited by Arthur Wauters (ed.), *Le Monde Communiste et la Crise du Congo belge* (Brussels, 1961), pp. 64–5.
28 Catherine Hoskyns, *The Congo Since Independence, January 1960–December 1961* (London, 1965), p. 114.
29 Ibid.
30 Ibid., pp. 117–18.
31 Text cited in full in W. J. Ganshoff van der Meersch, *Fin de la Souveraineté Belge au Congo: Documents et Reflexions* (Brussels, 1963), pp. 478–81.
32 U.N. Security Council, doc. S/4383, 13 July 1960, cited in *Congo 1960*, vol. II, p. 553.
33 Hoskyns, *The Congo Since Independence*, p. 118.
34 *Congo 1960*, vol. II.
35 Telegram cited in full in ibid., p. 555.
36 Text in *Congo 1960*, vol. II, pp. 555–6, and *Soviet News*, 18 July 1960.
37 *Pravda*, 17 July 1960, p. 5, cited in Wauters, *Le Monde Communiste et le Crise du Congo belge*, p. 68.
38 Hoskyns, *The Congo Since Independence*, p. 132.
39 *Courrier d'Afrique*, 21 July 1960, cited *Congo 1960*, vol. II, pp. 610–11, emphasis added.
40 Wauters, *Le Monde Communiste et le Crise du Congo belge*, p. 69.
41 *Congo 1960*, vol. II, p. 614.
42 Kanza, *Conflict in the Congo*, p. 237.
43 Hoskyns, *The Congo Since Independence*, pp. 157–8.
44 Kanza, *Conflict in the Congo*, p. 273.
45 *Congo 1960*, vol. III, p. 56.
46 Ibid.
47 Full text cited in *Congo 1960*, vol. III, pp. 57–8.
48 Wauters, *Le Monde Communiste et le Crise du Congo belge*, p. 82.
49 Hoskyns, *The Congo Since Independence*, p. 195.
50 Ibid., pp. 201–2.
51 Ibid., p. 208.
52 Ibid., p. 213.
53 Tran-Minh Tiet, *Congo ex-belge entre l'Est et l'Ouest* (Paris, 1962), p. 76.
54 Verhaegen, *Congo 1961 – Les Dossiers du C.R.I.S.P.* (Brussels 1962), p. 187.
55 Jorge Beys, Paul-Henri Gende-Bien and Verhaegen, *Congo 1963 – Les Dossiers du C.R.I.S.P.* (Brussels and Leopoldville, 1964), pp. 106–7.
56 J. Gérard-Libois, *Congo 1966 – Les Dossiers du C.R.I.S.P.* (Brussels and Kinshasa, 1967), pp. 516–17.
57 See the limited nature of Soviet–rebel contacts in Gérard-Libois and J. van Lierde, *Congo 1965 – Les Dossiers du C.R.I.S.P.* (Brussels and Kinshasa, 1966), pp. 93, 283–4; also Verhaegen, *Rébellions au Congo – Les Dossiers du C.R.I.S.P.* (Brussels and Leopoldville, 1966–9), pp. 77, 131, 173–9.
58 Alvin Z. Rubinstein, *The Soviets in International Organisation: Changing Policy Towards Developing Countries 1953–1962* (Princeton, New Jersey), pp. 349–50.
59 *New York Times*, 15 Oct 1960.
60 David A. Kay, *New Nations in the United Nations 1960–1968* (New York and London, 1970) Appendixes G–J.
61 Legvold, *Soviet Policy in West Africa* deals with the U.S.S.R.'s relations with 'reactionary', 'moderate' and 'radical' states in West Africa.
62 A. I. Lekovsky, *Sovetskoe Vostokovedenie*, no. 1 (1957) pp. 174–84; A. M. Rumyantsev (ed.), *Sovremennoe Osvoboditelnoe Dvizhenie i Natsionalnaya Burzhuazia* (Prague, 1961), pp. 332–5, 345, cited in Yodfat, *Arab Politics in the Soviet Mirror*, p. 13.
63 E. M. Zhukov, 'The October Revolution and the Rise of the National-Liberation Movement', *International Affairs*, no. 9 (Sept 1957), pp. 40–1.

64 'Statement of the Meeting of Representatives of the Communist and Workers Parties', *New Times*, no. 50 (1960) Supplement, p. 11.

65 Boris Ponomarev, 'O gosudarstve natsionalnoy demokratii', *Kommunist*, no. 8 (May 1961) pp. 33–48.

66 R. Avakov and G. Mirskiy, 'O klassovoy strukture v slaborazvitykh stranakh', *Mirovaya Ekonomika i Mezhdunarodnye Otnoshenie (MeiMo)*, no. 4 (Apr 1962) pp. 68–82, trans. in Thomas Perry Thornton (ed.), *The Third World in Soviet Perspective* (Princeton, New Jersey, 1964) pp. 276–304.

67 R. Andreasyan, *Afrika i Azia Segodnya*, no. 10 (1966) pp. 2–5, cited in Yodfat, *Arab Politics in the Soviet Mirror*, pp. 23–4; 'N. Khrushchev replies to questions put by the Ghanaian Times, Alger Républicain, Le Peuple and Botatung', *New Times*, no. 52 (1963) p. 42; Mirskiy, 'Tvorcheskiy marksizm i problemy natsionalno-covobeditelnykh revolutsiy', *MeiMo*, no. 2 (Feb 1963) pp. 63–8; *Pravda*, 26 Nov 1963.

68 Mirskiy, *Afrika i Azia Segodnya*, no. 2 (1966), p. 7, cited in *Mizan*, vol. 6:6 (June 1964).

69 'The USSR and the Developing Countries', special issue of the *Mizan Newsletter*, vol 6:10 (Nov 1964).

70 Stephen Clissold (ed.), *Soviet Relations with Latin America 1918–1968: A Documentary Survey* (London, 1970), p. 43.

71 Ibid., p. 46.

72 For the importance of this action to the U.S.A. see Robert Kennedy, *13 Days* (London, 1968) p. 120.

73 See, for example, B. Ameillon, *La Guinee, bilan d'une independence* (Paris, 1964).

74 Legvold, *Soviet Policy in West Africa*, pp. 151–2.

75 Ibid., p. 152.

76 Larkin, *China and Africa*, p. 54.

77 Nicolas Lang, 'La Première Conférence de solidarité des Peuples d'Asie, d'Afrique et d'Amerique latine à la Havane', *Est et Ouest*, no. 352 (1965), p. 5.

78 Legvold, *Soviet Policy in West Africa*, pp. 215–16.

79 T. B. Millar and J. D. B. Miller, 'Afro-Asian Disunity: Algiers 1965', *Australian Outlook*, vol. 19, no. 3 (1965) pp. 306–21.

80 R. Ulyanovsky, 'The Third World Problems of Socialist Orientation', *International Affairs*, no. 9 (Sep 1971).

CHAPTER 2

1 See, for example, Glen Alden Smith, *Soviet Foreign Trade: Organisation, Operation and Policy 1918–1971* (New York and London, 1973) pp. 250–3. Joseph S. Berliner, *Soviet Foreign Aid* (New York, 1958) pp. 120–7 sees this as one reason for Soviet aid.

2 U.N.C.T.A.D., 'Review of trade relations among countries having different economic and social systems: Report by the U.N.C.T.A.D. Secretariat' (mimeo.) doc. no. TD/B/128, 21 July 1967, paras 19–21, doc. no. TD/B/359, 19 July 1971, Table 7.

3 Ibid., doc. no. TD/B/128, 21 July 1967, para. 22.

4 *Daily Times*, Lagos, 30 July 1971.

5 *Interview*, Robert Ocran, and 'Joint Recommendations of the Ghana and U.S.S.R. Government', *Ghana Treaty Series 1963*, pp. 12–14.

6 *Daily Nation*, Nairobi, 30 Sep 1964, pp. 1, 6.

7 Ghana, *Economic Survey* (Accra, 1971), para. 337. Another reason was corruption.

8 *Daily Nation*, Nairobi, 5 Nov 1963, p. 1. Ghana, *Parliamentary Debates*, vol. 43, 22 Feb 1966, cols 6487–8.

9 Smith, *Soviet Foreign Trade*, p. 229.

10 Much of the following section on Ghana's cocoa appeared in an early form in

'In Search of the Economic Kingdom: The Development of Economic Relations between Ghana and the U.S.S.R.', *The Journal of Developing Areas*, vol. 9, no. 1 (Oct 1974) pp. 3–26.

11　Ghana, *Statistical Yearbook 1967–1968* (Accra, 1970) Table 128.

12　Gill & Duffus Ltd, *Cocoa Market Report*, no. 246.

13　T. Killick, 'The Economics of Cocoa', in W. Birmingham *et al.* (eds.), *A Study of Contemporary Ghana*, vol. 1 (London, 1966).

14　J. H. Mensah, *The State of the Economy and the External Debts Problem* (Accra, 1970).

15　K. Amoaka-Atta, Ghana, *Parliamentary Debates*, vol. 38, 21 Jan 1965, col. 180.

16　*West Africa*, no. 2491, 1965, p. 240.

17　Ibid., 2497 p. 407.

18　G. A. Smith, *Soviet Foreign Trade*, pp. 228, 235. *West Africa*, no. 2191, 11 Apr 1959, p. 355

19　*Ghana Treaty Series*, Accra, Ministry of Foreign Affairs, no. 56 (1961) protocol articles 1, 2; interview, Ghanaian civil servant.

20　Gill & Duffus, *Cocoa Market Report*, no. 180, p. 3.

21　Ibid.

22　No. 184, p. 2.

23　K. Amoaka-Atta, Ghana, *Parliamentary Debates*, vol. 43, 22 Feb 1966, cols 6487–8, and information from the ministry of finance and economic planning, Accra.

24　Gill & Duffus, *Cocoa Market Report*, no. 191, p. 8.

25　E. Neuberger, 'Is the U.S.S.R. Superior to the West as a Market for Primary Products?', *Review of Economics and Statistics*, vol. XLVI:3 (Aug 1964) pp. 287–93; S. H. Goodman, 'Eastern & Western Markets for the Primary Products of Ghana', *Economic Bulletin of Ghana*, vol. X:4 (1966) pp. 23–8; Philip Hanson, 'Soviet Imports of Primary Products: a Case Study of Cocoa', *Soviet Studies*, vol. XXIII, 1 July 1971, pp. 59–77.

26　K. Amoaka-Atta, Ghana, *Parliamentary Debates*, vol. 43, 22 Feb 1966, cols 6487–8.

27　*Ghanaian Times*, 26 July 1965.

28　See, for example, the preamble to the Ghana–U.S.S.R. Trade Agreement of 1961.

29　Ghana, *Statistical Yearbook 1965/66*, Table 119.

30　Ibid., Tables 117, 119, 120.

31　Gill & Duffus, *Cocoa Market Report*, no. 242.

32　Ibid., no. 246.

33　See K. Amoaka-Atta, Ghana, *Parliamentary Debates*, vol. 43, 22 Feb. 1966, cols. 6487–8, and Home Service Broadcasts in English, Lagos, 18.00 G.M.T., 6 July 1965 (*Summary of World Broadcasts*, London, B.B.C.).

34　Oleg Hoeffding, 'Recent Structural Changes & Balance of Payments Adjustments in Soviet Foreign Trade', in Alan A. Brown and Egon Neuberger (eds), *International Trade & Central Planning* (Berkeley, California, 1968) pp. 312–37.

35　Article 14, para. h.

36　P. A. Cherviakov, *Organizatsia i Tekhnika Vneshnei Torgovli SSSR* (Moscow, 1962) Chapter 2, cited by B. R. Stokke, *Soviet & Eastern European Trade & Aid in Africa* (New York, 1967).

37　'Trade & Payments Agreement between the U.S.S.R. and Somali Republic, 2 June 1961', *U.N. Treaty Series* vol. 493:184.

38　'Protocol on the exchange of goods between the Republic of Ghana and the U.S.S.R. in 1963', Ghana, *Treaty Series* (1963).

39　*West Africa*, no. 2793, 19–25 Dec 1970, p. 1488; and *Somali National Bank Bulletin*, Mogadishu, no. 23–4 (July–Dec 1970).

40　See, for example, T. S. Khachaturov, 'The Development of External Economic Relations of the Soviet Union', paper presented to the International Congress of the International Economic Association, Montreal, 2–7 Sep 1968, and V. A. Martynov 'Soviet Economic Aid to the newly liberated countries', *Problems of Foreign Aid* (Dar es Salaam, 1965).

41 *Approaches to Multilateral Settlements in trade between socialist and developing countries*, a Study Prepared by the Institute for Economic and Market Research, Budapest, for the U.N.C.T.A.D. Secretariat, doc. no. TD/B/AC, p. 8 and Annex II Tables.

42 See, for example, Carole A. Sawyer, *Communist Trade with Developing Countries 1955–1965* (New York, 1966) pp. 52–63.

43 Bank of Ghana, *Report of the Bank for the year ended 30 June 1964*, p. 8; information from the Ghanaian ministry of finance and economic planning.

44 Ghana, *Treaty Series 1963*, p. 12.

45 *West Africa*, no. 2500, 1 May 1965, p. 493.

46 James Richard Carter, *The Net Cost of Soviet Foreign Aid* (Washington and London, 1969) pp. 36–9, Appendix Table 8.

47 'Economic Growth & Foreign Trade of the Socialist Countries', *Review of trade relations among countries having different economic and social systems: report of the U.N.C.T.A.D. Secretariat Pt. 1*, doc. no. TD/B/128/Add.1, 21 July 1967, paras 114, 115.

48 German Planning and Economic Advisory Group, Dr Hendrikson, *Report on the Improvement of the Accounting System of the State-owned Enterprises, pt II: Las Koreh Fish Canning Factory*, vol. 1: *Basic Data* (Mogadishu n.d.) para. 190.

49 Ibid., pt I: *The Kisimayo Meat Canning Factory*, p. 61, paras 176, 177.

50 Ghana, *Economic Survey 1961*, para. 337.

51 Ghana, *Economic Survey 1963*, para. 108.

52 W. E. Abraham, *Report of the Commission of Enquiry into Trade Malpractices in Ghana* (Accra, 1965) para. 47.

53 'Protocol on the Exchange of Goods between the Republic of Ghana and the U.S.S.R. for 1963', Ghana, *Treaty Series 1963*.

54 Ghana, *Economic Survey 1964*, para. 112; Ghana, *Parliamentary Debates* vol. 38, 28 Jan 1964, col. 453–4.

55 *West Africa*, no. 2499 1965, pp. 445, 462.

56 Ghana, *Parliamentary Debates*, vol. 43, col. 657.

57 Ghana, *Economic Survey 1966*, para. 116.

58 Ghana, *Economic Survey 1970*, para. 93.

59 *N.R.C. Budget Statement for 1972–73 by Colonel I. K. Acheampong, Chairman of the N.R.C.*, Ministry of Finance, Accra, 13 Sep 1972, para. 65.

60 See M. J. H. Yaffey, 'Special Bilateral Payments Agreements (Clearing Agreements) between Socialist and Non-Socialist Countries', Economic Research Bureau Paper 660, University of Dar es Salaam, mimeo, 5 Aug 1966.

61 Institute for Economic and Market Research for U.N.C.T.A.D. Secretariat, *Approach to Multilateral Settlements*.

62 *East–West Trade News*, 13 Feb 1969.

63 See K. Nazarkin, chairman of I.B.E.C., cited in *International Affairs* (Aug 1966) p. 66.

64 Cited in *Review of Trade Relations among countries having different economic and social systems*, U.N.C.T.A.D. TD/B/359, 19 July 1971, para. 30 and para. 30, n. 1.

CHAPTER 3

1 See Carter, *Net Cost of Soviet Aid*, Chapter 2.

2 Compare B. Rounov and G. Rubinstein, 'Rélations économiques soviéto-africaines', *Revue francaise d'études politiques africaines* (Le Mois en Afrique) no. 15 (Mar 1967) pp. 64–79, and Youri Tcherkassov, 'Problèmes d'accumulation en Afrique', ibid., no. 32 (Aug 1968), pp. 79–82.

3   N. Uphoff, *Ghana's Experience in Using External Aid for Development 1957–1966: Implications for Development Theory and Policy* (Institute of International Studies, Berkeley, California, 1970) pp. 559–60. See also U.N., *Export Credits & Development Finance: National Export Credit System* (New York, 1969) pp. 81–5.

4   République du Mali, *Annuaire Statistique* (1966). 'Agreement for Economic and Technical Co-operation between Kenya and the U.S.S.R. on the establishment of industrial and agricultural enterprises and projects 20 November 1964, laid Before the House of Representatives by the Minister for Home Affairs on Behalf of the Minister for Economic Planning and Development, 4 Mar 1965'. German Planning and Economic Advisory Group, Dr Hendrickson, *Report on the Progress of Development Projects in the Somali Democratic Republic* (Mogadishu and Frankfurt, 31 Dec 1969) Table 4.3.

5   Lester B. Pearson *et al.*, *Partners in Development: Report of the Commission on International Development* (London, 1969) Table 21.

6   'Agreement on Economic and Technical Co-operation between the U.S.S.R. and the Somali Republic, 2 June 1961', *U.N. Treaty Series*, vol. 457:263, Article 8; 'Agreement for economic and technical co-operation between Kenya and the U.S.S.R. on the establishment of industrial and agricultural enterprises and projects', *House of Representatives*, Nairobi, Article 8; 'Agreement between the Government of the United Republic of Tanzania and the Government of the U.S.S.R. on economic and technical co-operation', *Tanzania Treaty Series*, vol. II' pt 1 (1967) Article 8.

7   Sawyer, *Communist Trade with the Developing Countries*.

8   I. M. D. Little, *Aid to Africa* (Oxford, 1964) p. 21.

9   An early account of the development of aid links between Ghana and the U.S.S.R. appeared in C. Stevens, 'In Search of the Economic Kingdom', *Journal of the Developing Areas*, vol. 9, no. 1 (Oct 1974) pp. 3–26.

10 Andrzej Krassowski, *Development & the Debt Trap* (London, 1974) Chapters 3, 4.

11 Ibid., p. 75.

12 *U.N. Treaty Series*, vol. 399, p. 61, and *Ghana Treaty Series*, no. 58 (1961).

13 *Federal Government Development Programme 1962–1968: First Progress Report*, sessional paper no. 3 (Lagos, 1964) pp. 5–19.

14 E. N. Omaboe, 'The Process of Planning', in Birmingham, *et al.* (eds), *A Study of Contemporary Ghana*, vol. 1 (London, 1966) p. 457.

15 'Statement of Public Debt – Foreign Credits as at 30 September, 1962', *Report and Financial Statements of the Accountant-General and Report of the Auditor-General for the year ended 30 September 1962*.

16 Krassowski, *Development and the Debt Trap*, pp. 57, 82–3.

17 Ibid., Chapter 6.

18 W. Scott Thompson, *Ghana's Foreign Policy 1957–1966: Diplomacy, Ideology and the New State* (Princeton, New Jersey, 1969) p. 274.

19 B. Fitch and M. Oppenheimer, *Ghana: the End of an Illusion* (New York, 1966).

20 *Morning Post*, Lagos, 12 Nov 1968, and information from the federal ministry of economic development.

21 See O. Aboyade, 'Industrial Location and Development Policy: The Nigerian Case', *Nigerian Journal of Economic and Social Studies*, vol. x:3 (Nov 1968).

22 German Planning and Economic Advisory Group, Dr Hendrickson, *Report on the Progress of Development Projects in the Somali Democratic Republic* (Mogadishu and Frankfurt, 31 Dec 1969) Table 1.2.

23 German Planning and Economic Advisory Group, Dr Hendrickson, *Economic Conditions and Possible Future Development of the Port of Berbera* (Moagdishu and Frankfurt, Dec 1968).

24 'Protocol to the Agreement for Economic and Technical Co-operation between

the U.S.S.R. and the Republic of Ghana of the 4 August 1960', *U.N. Treaty Series*, vol. 421, p. 351, Annex.

25 'Protocol to the Ghana–Soviet Agreements on Economic and Technical Co-operation of 4 August 1960 and 4 November 1961', *Ghana Treaty Series 1963*.

26 *Parliamentary Debates*, vol. 40, 24 Aug 1965, col. 31.

27 Information from Ghanaian civil servant.

28 Information from the Bank of Ghana.

29 Uphoff, *Ghana's Experience*, pp. 559–60.

30 Ibid., Chapter 8.

31 Information from federal ministry of economic development, Lagos.

32 The German Planning and Economic Advisory Group, Dr Hendrickson, *Report on the Progress of Development Projects in the Somali Democratic Republic* (Mogadishu and Frankfurt, 31 Dec 1969) Tables 1.2, 4.3.

33 State Projecting Institute (Ghipromyaso), *Project Report for Kisimayo Meat Factory* (Moscow, 1962).

34 German Planning and Economic Advisory Group, Dr Hendrickson, *Report on the Kisimayo Meat Canning Factory* (Mogadishu and Frankfurt, n.d.).

35 *West Africa*, no. 2733, 18 Oct 1969, p. 1260.

36 A. M. El-Barbary, *Report on Industrial Development in the Somali Democratic Republic* (Mogadishu, Aug 1971).

37 United Republic of Tanzania, 'Statement of Public Debt Outstanding', in *The Appropriation Accounts, Revenue Statements, Accounts of the Fund, and Other Public Accounts for the year – 1966/67 – 1970/71*.

38 *U.N. Treaty Series*, vol. 399:61 (1960) Article 1.

39 Ibid., vol. 421, p. 351.

40 B. R. Stokke, *Soviet and Eastern European Trade and Aid in Africa* (New York, 1967) p. 73.

41 Cement, nails and timber. *House of Representatives Debates*, 1 Mar 1966, col. 1541.

42 Ibid., paras 1537–8.

43 Uphoff, *Ghana's Experience*, Chapter 6, n. 90.

44 Joint Economic Committee, Congress of the United States, *Economic Performance and the Military Burden in the Soviet Union* (Washington, 1970) p. 222, cited in H. H. Ticktin, 'Towards a Political Economy of the U.S.S.R.', *Critique*, vol. 1:1 (Spring 1973), p. 25.

45 Uphoff, *Ghana's Experience*, Chapter 6, n. 82.

46 Ibid., Chapter 5, n. 86.

47 Ibid., Chapter 5, n. 90.

48 German Planning and Economic Advisory Group, Dr Hendrickson, *Report on the Improvement of the Accounting System of the State-Owned Enterprises*, pt II: *Las Koreh Fish Canning Factory*, vol. 1: *Basic Data* (Mogadishu and Frankfurt, n.d.).

49 'Protocol to the Agreement for Economic and Technical Co-operation between the U.S.S.R. and the Republic of Ghana', *U.N. Treaty Series*, vol. 421, p. 351.

50 *West Africa*, no. 2311, 16 Sep 1961, p. 1035.

51 Krobo Edusei, *Parliamentary Debates*, vol. 29, 12 Nov 1962, col. 325.

52 *Report of the Auditor-General on the Accounts of Ghana for the period 1 January 1965–30 June 1966*, para. 27.

53 Calculated from *Balance Sheet and Operating Statements for the year ended 31 December 1966; Balance Sheet and Operating Statements for the year ended 31 December 1967*, State Farms Corporation (Accra).

54 *New Era*, no. 3 (Mar 1971) pp. 38–40.

55 See, for example, Richard Symonds, *The British and their Successors* (London, 1966) p. 184.

56 Information from Ghana scholarships secretariat.

57 Information from manpower division, Ghana ministry of economic planning.

58 Ministry of Education, *Annual Summary* (Nairobi, 1970).
59 Information from the bureau for external aid to education, Lagos.
60 *House of Representatives Debates*, 3 July 1970, col. 2134.
61 *West Africa*, no. 2892, 13 Nov 1972, p. 1544.
62 *New York Times*, 16 Dec 1962.
63 *First Five Year Plan 1963–1967*, Planning and Co-ordinating Committee for Economic and Social Development (Mogadishu, July 1963) pp. 5, 148.
64 German Planning and Economic Advisory Group, Dr Hendrickson, *Report on the Progress of Development Projects in the Somali Democratic Republic* (Mogadishu and Frankfurt, 31 Dec 1969) Tables 4.3, 4.4.
65 *First Five Year Plan*, p. 141.
66 Ibid., p. 147.
67 Ozay Mehmet, 'Effectiveness of Foreign Aid – the Case of Somalia', *Journal of Modern African Studies*, vol. 9:1 (1971) p. 32.
68 *First Five Year Plan*, pp. 143–4.
69 James O'Connell, 'The Political Class and Economic Growth', *Nigerian Journal of Economic and Social Studies*, vol. 8:1 (Mar 1966) p. 129.

CHAPTER 4

1   Claude Meillassoux, 'A Class Analysis of the Bureaucratic Process in Mali' *Journal of Development Studies*, vol. 6:2 (Jan 1970) pp. 106–7.
2   *West Africa*, no. 2546, 19 Mar 1966, p. 330.
3   *West Africa*, no. 2271, 10 Dec 1960, p. 1389.
4   R. Avakov and G. Mirskiy, *MeiMO*, no. 4 (1962) pp. 76–9.
5   Kwame Nkrumah, *I Speak of Freedom* (London, 1961) p. 36.
6   Cited in Bankole Timothy, *Kwame Nkrumah* (London, 1955) p. 164.
7   For a fuller account of this see Jitendra Mohan, 'Ghana Parliament and Foreign Policy 1957–1960', *Economic Bulletin of Ghana*, vol. x:4 (1966).
8   Ghana, *Parliamentary Debates*, vol. 7, 29 Aug 1957, col. 309–10, emphasis added.
9   *Pravda*, 13 Feb 1957, pp. 3–5.
10 *Pravda*, 25 Feb 1957, p. 3; *Izvestiya*, 25 Feb, 1957. p. 3.
11 *Pravda*, 22 Feb 1957, p. 5.
12 Cited in W. Scott Thompson, *Ghana's Foreign Policy 1957–1966: Diplomacy, Ideology and the New State* (Princeton, New Jersey, 1969) p. 103.
13 Michael Dei-Anang, *The Administration of Ghana's Foreign Relations 1957–1965. A Personal Memoir* (London, 1975) p. 14.
14 Ibid., p. 1.
15 Thompson, *Ghana's Foreign Policy*, p. 250.
16 Ghana, *Annual Estimates*, for *1957/58, 1958/59, 1959/60* and *1961/62*.
17 Dei-Anang, *Administration of Ghana's Foreign Relations*, Chapter 1.
18 Ibid., Chapter 2.
19 Ghana, *Parliamentary Debates*, 3 Sep 1958, col. 2094.
20 Ibid., col. 2108.
21 Ibid., cols 2100–1. See also R. R. Amponsah, ibid., col. 2109. Emphasis added.
22 See, for example, ibid., 1 Aug 1958, cols 1096–1148.
23 See Mohan, *Ghana Parliament and Foreign Policy*.
24 Ghana, *Parliamentasy Debates*, 29 Aug 1957.
25 B. Fitch and M. Oppenheimer, *Ghana: End of an Illusion* (New York and London, 1968), p. 93; Jones Ofori-Atta, 'Some Aspects of Economic Policy in Ghana 1952–1956', *Economic Bulletin of Ghana*, vol. xi:3 (1967), and Krassowski, *Development and the Debt Trap*, p. 54.
26 Dudley Seers, 'The Stages of Economic Development of a Primary Producer in the Middle of the Twentieth Century', *Economic Bulletin of Ghana*, vol. viii:4

(1963) pp. 57–69; Roger Genoud, *Nationalism and Economic Development in Ghana* (New York, 1969) pp. 100–10.

27   E. H. Carr, *The Soviet Impact on the Western World* (London, 1947).

28   See R. Genoud *Nationalism and Economic Development*, pp. 17–58, and Samir Amin, *Trois Expériences africaines de développement: le Mali, la Guinée et le Ghana* (Paris, 1965) pp. 167–206.

29   E. N. Omaboe, 'The Process of Planning', in Birmingham *et al.* (eds), *A Study of Contemporary Ghana*, vol. 1 (London, 1966), p. 448.

30   See Chapter 2 above.

31   For further details see Stevens, 'Administrative Developments in Ghana – some effects of post-independence broadening of international contacts', *Journal of Administration Overseas* vol. XII, no. 3, pp. 206–14.

32   J. M. Lee, *Colonial Development and Good Government* (Oxford, 1967) p. 73.

33   *The Development Plan 1951* (Accra, 1951) para. 2.

34   E. N. Omaboe, in Birmingham *et al.* (eds), *A Study of Contemporary Ghana*, p. 446.

35   Ibid., pp. 450–1.

36   See, for example, *Programme of the Convention People's Party for Work and Happiness*, para. 33; cited in D. Apter, *Ghana in Transition* (New York, 1963) Appendix B; Amin, *Trois expériences*, p. 100; Seydou Badian Kouyaté, 'Planification économique: le plan quinquennial du Mali, *Afrique* (Feb 1962) p. 17.

37   *Seven Year Plan for National Reconstruction and Development 1963/64–1969/70* (Accra) Foreword. For comment on selection of projects see Omaboe, *Process of Planning*, p. 460.

38   Krassowski, *Development and the Debt Trap*, pp. 61–2.

39   Jon Kraus, 'Political Change, Conflict and Development', in P. Foster and A. R. Zolberg (eds), *Ghana and the Ivory Coast: Perspectives on Modernisation*; Krassowski, ibid., Chapters 3, 4.

40   Jean Suret-Canale, *La Republique de Guinée* (Paris, 1970) pp. 187–8.

41   Amin, *Trois expériences*, pp. 120, 124.

42   *Programme Triennial de Redressement Economique et Financier 1970–1972*, Direction Générale du Plan et de la Statistique (Bamako, June 1970).

43   Amin, *Trois expériences*, pp. 125–9.

44   Interview, Bank of Ghana.

45   Guy de Lusignan, *French-Speaking Africa since Independence* (London, 1969) pp. 184–5.

46   Yuri Bochkaryev, 'The Guinean Experiment', *New Times*, no. 25 (June 1960) p. 2.

47   Ministère d'état chargé des finances et du Plan – Direction de la Statistique Générale et de la Mecanographie. *Bulletin Special de Statistique (Statistique et Economie)* (Conakry, n.d.) Of course, these figures do not include clandestine trade.

48   Michael O'Connor, 'Guinea and the Ivory Coast: Contrasts in Economic Development', *Journal of Modern African Studies*, vol. 10:3 (Oct 1972) p. 422.

49   N. I. Gavrilov, 'Respublika Mali – Molodoe nezavisimoe gosudarstvo Afriki', *Narody Azii i Afriki*, 4 (1961) p. 35.

50   *Report of the Commission to Enquire into the Kwame Nkrumah Properties* (Accra, 1966) p. 34, para. 207.

51   *Ghana Economic Survey 1961*, para. 337. See also Ghana, *Parliamentary Debates*, vol. 40, 16 Sep 1965, col. 882, where the government's socialist commercial policy is outlined.

52   Gilbert Comte, 'Mali-quinze mois après la chute du President Keita', *Le Mois en Afrique*, no. 50 (Feb 1970) p. 17.

53   Suret-Canale, *La République de Guinée*, p. 360, and Claude Rivière, 'Les Con-

séquences de la reorganisation des circuits commerciaux en Guinée', *Le Mois en Afrique*, no. 66 (June 1971) pp. 74–96.

54 Suret-Canale, *La République de Guinée*, p. 176.

55 Ibid., p. 177.

56 *Plan triennal de développement économique et social de la République du Guinée: Conférence Nationale des Cadres des 2 au 5 Avril 1960 à Kankan* (Conakry) pp. 216–17; Suret-Canale, *La République de Guinée*, p. 211.

57 The words are Rivière's (*Les consequences*, p. 80).

58 Ibid., p. 83.

59 See, for example, B. Ameillon, *La Guinée bilan d'une indépendence* (Paris, 1964), and *Le Monde*, 20 Nov 1966.

60 Suret-Canale, *La République de Guinée*, pp. 210–11.

61 Ibid., p. 213, n.1.

62 Diaguissa Diallo, 'Un art guinéen: le complot', *France Eurafrique* (Jan 1970).

63 *Horoya*, no. 1511, 13 July 1968, cited by Suret-Canale, *La République de Guinée*, p. 214, n. 2.

64 *West Africa*, no. 2906, 19 Feb 1973, p. 252.

65 M. O'Connor, *Guinea and the Ivory Coast*, Table 3, pp. 416, 425.

66 *Comptes Economiques du Mali – 1969*, Direction Nationale du Plan et de la Statistique (Bamako, June 1971).

67 R. Avakov and R. Andreasian, 'Progressivnaya Rol Gosudarstvennogo Sektora', *Kommunist*, 13 (Sep 1962) pp. 92–6.

68 A. N. Hakam, 'Industrial Entrepreneurship in Ghana', mimeo. (University of Ghana Department of Economics, 1968). Cited by Uphoff, *Ghana's Experience*, p. 666.

69 Elliot J. Berg, 'Structural Transformation versus Gradualism: Recent Economic Development in Ghana and Ivory Coast', in P. Foster and A. R. Zolberg, *Ghana & the Ivory Coast: Perspectives on Modernisation* (Chicago and London, 1971).

70 Krassowski, *Development and the Debt Trap*, p. 22. See also p. 46.

71 Ghana, *Parliamentary Debates*, vol. 25, 25 Oct 1961, col. 206.

72 Ibid., vol. 35, 11 Mar 1964, cols 23–4.

73 For example, Dei-Anang, *Administration of Ghana's Foreign Relations*, p. 2.

74 See A. L. Adu in ibid., p. 13 n.

75 Cited by Thompson, *Ghana's Foreign Policy*, pp. 276–7.

76 J. H. Mensah, 'The Relevance of Marxian Economics to Development Planning in Ghana'; *Economic Bulletin of Ghana*, vol. IX:1 (1965).

77 Jon Kraus, in Foster and Zolberg, *Ghana and the Ivory Coast*, p. 63.

78 Gold Coast, *The Development Plan 1951*, paras 22–8.

79 Uphoff, *Ghana's Experience*, Chapter 6, n. 86.

80 See Chapter 3. Cited in Uphoff, *Ghana's Experience*, Chapter 6, n. 9.

81 See Lionel S. Tiger, 'Bureaucracy in Ghana', Ph.D. thesis (London, 1963), especially p. 149.

82 K. B. Asante, in Dei-Anang, *Administration of Ghana's Foreign Relations*, p. 31 n.

83 *Report by the Auditor-General on the Accounts of Ghana for the period 1 January 1965 to 30 June 1966*, paras 149, 158.

84 Ghana, *Economic Survey 1963*, para. 378.

85 Ghana, *Seven Year Plan*, p. 806.

86 Isaac Bissue, 'Ghana's Seven Year Development Plan in Retrospect', *Economic Bulletin of Ghana*, vol. XI:1 (1967).

87 Ghana, *Parliamentary Debates*, vol. 33, 12 Mar 1964, col. 182; W. E. Abraham, *Commission of Enquiry into Trade Malpractices in Ghana* (Accra, 1965) para. 63.

88 Uphoff, *Ghana's Experience*, pp. 510–11.

89 Ghana, *Parliamentary Debates*, vol. 29, 12 Oct 1962, col. 325.

90 *Report and Financial Statements by the Accountant-General and Report of the Auditor-General for the year ended 30 September 1962* (Accra) para. 134.
91 Interview with G.N.T.C. official; Maxwell Owusu, *Uses and Abuses of Political Power* (Chicago, 1970) pp. 272–3.
92 Interview with Robert Ocran; Rowena M. Lawson, 'The Growth of the Fishing Industry in Ghana 1954–1966', *Economic Bulletin of Ghana*, vol. xi:4 (1967).
93 K. D. Fordwor, 'An Evaluation of Ghanaian State-Owned Industrial Projects: a study in cost-benefit analysis', Ph.D. thesis (University of Pennsylvania, 1971) p. 32.
94 Alain Cournamel, 'Situation de la classe ouvrière en République de Guinée', *Partisans*, no. 61 (Sep–Nov 1971) pp. 119–36.
95 A. R. Zolberg, *Creating Political order: the Party-States of West Africa* (Chicago 1966), p. 159.
96 Ayi Kwei Armah, *The Beautiful Ones Are Not Yet Born* (London, 1968).

CHAPTER 5

1 O. Ojedokun, 'The Anglo-Nigerian Entente and its Demise', *Journal of Commonwealth Political Studies*, vol. ix:3 (Nov 1971).
2 *The Training of Nigerians for the Representation of their Country Overseas: a Statement of Policy by the Government of the Federation of Nigeria*, House of Representatives, sessional paper no. 11 (Lagos, 1956) para. 6. See also House of Representatives, *Debates*, session 1956, 13 Aug 1956, cols 2724–58.
3 Ibid., para 11.
4 See, for example, *Development Plan for Tanganyika 1961/62–1965/66* (Dar es Salaam, 1962) p. 15.
5 House of Representatives, *Debates*, 13 Aug 1956, cols 2733, 2750–1.
6 Ibid., 8 Mar 1957, col. 456.
7 Ibid., 6 Aug 1959, col. 1491.
8 Ibid., 20 Nov 1961, col. 3122.
9 K. W. Post, 'The National Council of Nigeria and the Camerouns', in John P. Mackintosh, *Nigerian Government and Politics* (London, 1966), p. 419.
10 Richard L. Sklar, *Nigerian Political Parties: Power in an Emergent African Nation* (Princeton, New Jersey, 1963) p. 263.
11 House of Representatives, *Debates*, 13 Aug 1956, col. 2745.
12 O. Awolowo, *Awo: The Autobiography of Chief Obafemi Awolowo* (London, 1960) p. 310.
13 *West Africa*, no. 2207, 19 Sep 1959.
14 Walter Schwarz, *Nigeria* (London, 1968) pp. 117–18.
15 See Abubakar Tafawa Balewa, *Nigeria Speaks: Speeches of Alhaji Sir Abubakar Tafawa Balewa* (London, 1964) p. 8 for an illustration of anti-Communism.
16 Post, *The Nigerian Federal Election of 1959: Politics and Administration in a Developing Political System* (Lagos, 1963) p. 314.
17 Ibid.
18 Sklar, *Nigerian Political Parties*, p. 271; see also ibid., pp. 263–8.
19 Cited ibid., p. 269.
20 Schwarz, *Nigeria*, Chapter 6.
21 House of Representatives, *Debates*, 4 Sep 1961, cols 2822, 2850.
22 See, for example, House of Representatives, *Debates*, 17 Mar 1964, cols 280–1.
23 See, for example, ibid., 26 Aug 1961, cols 2286–7, 29 Aug 1961, col. 2468, 30 Aug 1961, cols 2513–14, 6 Apr 1964, cols 1803–4, 1815–16, 1820.
24 Ibid., 20 Aug 1960, col. 2670.
25 Ibid., 25 Nov 1960, col. 478, 4 Sep 1961, col. 2793.
26 Ibid., 16 Jan 1960, col. 1834.
27 *New York Times*, 2 Nov 1960.

28 House of Representatives, *Debates*, 14 Apr 1962, col. 1680.
29 *Nigeria Speaks: Speeches Made by Alhaji Sir Abubakar Tafawa Balewa between 1957 and 1964* (London, 1964) p. 19.
30 House of Representatives, *Debates*, 25 Nov 1960, cols 11–12.
31 Ibid., 29 Nov 1960, cols 558–69.
32 Ibid., 21 Nov 1960, col. 142.
33 O. Awolowo, *Awo*, pp. 310–11.
34 House of Representatives, *Debates*, 24 Nov 1960, col. 379.
35 Ibid., col. 446.
36 Ibid., 17 Apr 1960, col. 1781.
37 *Nigerian Observer*, 12 Nov 1968, p. 1.
38 House of Representatives, *Debates*, 26 Apr 1965, col. 1493.
39 Ibid., 17 Apr 1962, cols 1971–88.
40 House of Representatives, *Debates*, 17 Mar 1964, cols 270–84.
41 For further details see D. G. Anglin, 'Nigeria: Political non-alignment and economic alignment', *Journal of Modern African Studies* (1964).
42 House of Representatives, *Debates*, 29 Mar 1961, col. 605, and 8 Apr 1961, cols 1034–5.
43 Ibid., 2–11 Apr 1963, cols. 334–1267.
44 Ibid., 16 Nov 1961, col. 2898, 23 Nov 1961, col. 256, 27 Nov 1961, col. 3473, 1 Apr 1963, col. 279–80.
45 Ibid., 14 Apr 1962, vol. 1711, 22 Nov 1961, col. 3232.
46 Ibid., 24 Apr 1963, cols 2007, 2012; *West Africa*, no. 2330, 27 Jan 1962, p. 103.
47 See letter from J. K. Tettegah to G. Rodionov, 16 July 1965, cited in B. A. Bentum, *Trade Unions in Chains* (Accra, 1966).
48 House of Representatives, *Debates*, 24 Apr 1963, cols 2007, 2012.
49 Ibid., 21 Aug. 1962, cols. 2546–52; *West Africa*, no. 2369, 27 Oct 1962, p. 1196.
50 House of Representatives, *Debates*, 8 Aug 1963, cols 2802–3; *West Africa*, no. 2424, 16 Nov 1963, p. 1304.
51 House of Representatives, *Debates*, 26 Mar 1964, col. 1006; *Estimates of the Government of the Federal Republic of Nigeria 1964/65* (Lagos).
52 *Report of the Comparative Technical Education Seminar Abroad, and Recommendations for a National Plan of Vocational and Training Education in the Republic of Nigeria* (Lagos, 1966) para. 8.7.
53 *National Development Plan: Progress Report 1964*, Federal Ministry of Economic Development (Lagos, Mar 1965), p. 30.
54 Ibid., Tables 2.5 and 2.8.
55 Ibid., p. 34.
56 Kurt Müller, 'Soviet and Chinese Programmes of Technical Aid to African Countries', in S. Hamrell and C. G. Widstrand (eds), *The Soviet bloc, China and Africa* (Uppsala, 1964) p. 117.
57 House of Representatives, *Debates*, 18 Nov 1961, col. 3024.
58 John de St Jorre, *The Nigerian Civil War* (London, 1972) p. 181.
59 *Daily Times*, Lagos, 25 Aug 1967.
60 *New Nigerian*, Kaduna, 23 Oct 1968, p. 1.
61 *Daily Times*, Lagos, 21 Jan 1970, p.3.
62 'Agreement on Economic and Technical Co-operation between the Government of the U.S.S.R. and the Government of the Federal Republic of Nigeria', in *Nigeria's Treaties in Force*, vol. 1: *for the period of 1 October 1960 to 30 June 1970*, Federal Ministry of Information (Lagos, 1971).
63 *Novosti Press Agency*, Lagos, 21 Nov 1968.
64 *Morning Post*, Lagos, 14 Nov 1968, p. 12.
65 *Daily Times*, 21 Apr 1972.

66 Nigerian Institute of International Affairs, *Nigeria: Bulletin of Foreign Affairs*, vol. 1:1 (July 1971) p. 21.
67 *Daily Times*, Lagos, 9 Oct 1970, p. 1.
68 *West Africa*, no. 2722, 9 Aug 1969, p. 942; *Daily Times*, Lagos, 14 Aug 1969, p. 5.
69 *West Africa*, no. 2879, 25 Aug 1972.
70 See a letter from James Karebe to I.C.F.T.U., cited in Richard Sandbrook, 'Patrons, Clients and Unions: The Labour Movement and Political Conflict in Kenya', *The Journal of Commonwealth Political Studies*, vol. x:1 (March 1972) p. 14.
71 *Daily Nation*, Nairobi, 27 June 1962, pp. 1, 16.
72 See Sandbrook, *Patrons, Clients and Unions*, p. 10.
73 *Daily Nation*, Nairobi, 8 Apr 1963, p. 16.
74 House of Representatives, *Debates*, Nairobi, 10 Mar 1966, cols 1917–20.
75 *Daily Nation*, Nairobi, 19 Jan 1962, p. 4.
76 Ibid., 18 Apr 1963, p. 1.
77 Ibid., 22 June 1963.
78 Ibid., 5 Nov 1963, pp. 1, 16.
79 *Estimates of Recurrent Expenditure* (Nairobi, 1965–6).
80 *Daily Nation*, Nairobi, 7 Nov 1963.
81 Ibid., 8 Nov 1963, p. 1; House of Representatives, *Debates*, 13 Nov 1963, cols 2118–19, 13 Mar 1964, cols 827–9.
82 *Debates*, 30 July 1964, cols 1176–93.
83 Ibid., 3 Nov 1965, cols 36–7.
84 House of Representatives, *Debates*, 1, 2, 20, 21 Apr 1965, cols 1083, 1176, 1178–88, 1287–9, 1239–41.
85 *Daily Nation*, Nairobi, 9 Apr 1965, p. 20.
86 *Daily Nation*, Nairobi, 15 Apr 1965, pp. 1, 24.
87 House of Representatives, *Debates*, Nairobi, 23 Apr 1965, cols 1443–5.
88 *Daily Nation*, Nairobi, 26 Apr 1965, p. 1.
89 Ibid., 30 Apr 1965, p. 1.
90 House of Representatives, *Debates*, Nairobi, 3 Mar 1967, cols 741–2.
91 Ibid., 10 Mar 1966, col. 1917.
92 *East African Standard*, Nairobi, 22 June 1965; *Daily Nation*, Nairobi, 30 June 1966.
93 *East African Standard*, Nairobi, 8 July 1965.
94 House of Representatives, *Debates*, 30 Apr 1965, col. 1741.
95 Ibid., 20 July 1965, col. 1193, 22 July 1965, col. 1334.
96 *Daily Nation*, Nairobi, 1 June 1965, pp. 1, 20, 4 June 1965, p. 1.
97 Ibid., 14 Mar 1966.
98 A. Kirk-Greene, 'The formation of foreign service cadres in Nigeria, Kenya and Uganda', paper presented to the Colston Society Symposium on Foreign Relations of African States at the University of Bristol (Apr 1973).
99 *East African Standard*, Nairobi, 5 May 1969, p. 1; House of Representatives, *Debates*, 5 Nov 1969, cols 1500–3.
100 'Agreement for economic and technical co-operation between Kenya and the U.S.S.R. on the establishment of industrial and agricultural enterprises and projects, 20 November 1964', Laid before the House of Representatives, 4 Mar 1965.
101 House of Representatives, *Debates*, 4 May 1965, cols 1801–3, 5 May 1965, cols 1864–5.
102 Ibid., 1 Mar 1966, cols 1538–9.
103 Ibid., 11 Oct 1966, cols 620–6, 22 June 1966, cols 959–68; *Daily Nation*, Nairobi, 24 Mar 1966, p. 1, 26 Mar 1966, pp. 1, 24.
104 Market Research Company of East Africa, *Spotlight on the Kenyan Election*, Marco Surveys, public opinion poll no. 3 (Nairobi, Jan 1961), p. 7.

105 Market Research Company of East Africa, *Public Opinion Poll on Politics in Kenya*, no. 9, pt. 1 (Jan 1962) question 25.
106 C. Gertzel, *The Politics of Independent Kenya 1963–1968* (Nairobi and London, 1970) p. 69.
107 Ibid., p. 46.
108 *East African Standard*, Nairobi, 3 Apr 1970, p. 1, 4 Apr 1970, p. 1.

CHAPTER 6

1 Stockholm International Peace Research Institute, *The Arms Trade with the Third World* (Stockholm, 1971) Table 1.1.
2 See S.I.P.I.R.I., *Arms Trade with Third World*, Table 19.1.
3 Ibid., p. 182.
4 Robert F. Kennedy, *13 Days* (London, 1969) p. 120.
5 S.I.P.R.I., *Arms Trade with Third World*, p. 206.
6 Ibid., pp. 206–7.
7 Geoffrey Jukes, *The Indian Ocean in Soviet Naval Policy*, Adelphi paper no. 87 (London, May 1972) p. 1. In the following references to Soviet naval strategy in the Indian Ocean, I am heavily indebted to this work.
8 Ibid., p. 8.
9 Cited by Keith Trace, 'International Trade and Commercial Relations', in A. J. Cottrell and R. M. Burrell (eds), *The Indian Ocean: Its Political, Economic and Military Importance* (New York and London, 1972) Table 6.
10 T. B. Millar, *The Indian and Pacific Oceans: Some strategic considerations*, Adelphi paper no. 57 (London, 1969).
11 Jukes, *Indian Ocean in Soviet Naval Policy*, pp. 16–18.
12 *Keesings Contemporary Archives 1963*, col. 19773D.
13 *New York Times*, 11 Nov 1963; *Guardian*, 12 Nov 1963.
14 The figure for the number of Somalis given military training is the estimate of A. A. Castagno, 'The Horn of Africa and the Competition for Power', in Cottrell and Burrel, *The Indian Ocean*, p. 161.
15 *New York Times*, 11 Nov 1963.
16 Ibid.
17 Colin Legum, *Observer*, 24 July 1966. The observation about the number deployed, although not the reason for their non-deployment, is confirmed by Richard Booth, *The Armed Forces of African States 1970*, Adelphi paper no. 67 (London, May 1970).
18 Calculated from *Budget for the 1962 Financial Year*, Table 3, and *Budget for the 1971 Financial Year*, Table 5 (Mogadishu).
19 Colin Legum, *Observer*, 24 July 1966.
20 *Kenya Broadcasting Corporation*, 16.00 G.M.T., 10 Mar 1964.
21 *East African Standard*, Nairobi, 3 May 1967, p. 9.
22 See, for example, the Broadcast on Somali Radio by President Mohammed Siyard Barre, and a West German Broadcast, both 2 June 1970: B.B.C., *Summary of World Broadcasts*, ME/3395/B 1–2.
23 *Keesings Contemporary Archives* (1970) col. 23983A.
24 *African Contemporary Record 1970–1971* (London, 1971) p. B159.
25 *East African Standard*, Nairobi, 3 Aug 1964, p. 1.
26 Keith Kyle, 'Coup in Zanzibar', *Africa Report* (Feb 1964) p. 18.
27 A very good account of the diplomatic developments in this period is given by T. C. Niblock, 'Aid and Foreign Policy in Tanzania 1961–1968', D.Phil. thesis (University of Sussex, 1971) pp. 195–215.
28 Ibid. The mystery of whether or not there were Cubans involved in the *coup* has been considered by Michael F. Lofchie, *Zanzibar: Background to Revolution* (London, 1965) p. 276. He concludes that there were not.

29 Niblock, *Aid and Foreign Policy in Tanzania.*
30 Ibid.
31 *Tanganyika Standard*, Dar es Salaam, 15 Feb 1964, p. 1, cited by Niblock, *Aid and Foreign Policy in Tanzania.*
32 *Tanganyika Standard*, Dar es Salaam, 15 Apr 1964, cited by Niblock, *Aid and Foreign Policy in Tanzania.*
33 *African Contemporary Record 1969–1970* (London, 1970) p. B199.
34 Niblock, *Aid and Foreign Policy in Tanzania*, pp. 215–63, gives a detailed account of these negotiations.
35 Ibid., p. 226.
36 Cited ibid., p. 227.
37 *Tanganyika Standard*, Dar es Salaam, 2 July 1964, p. 1, cited Niblock, *Aid and Foreign Policy in Tanzania.*
38 A. C. A. A. Ogunsanwo, *China's Policy in Africa*; also Bruce D. Larkin, *China and Africa 1949–1970. The Foreign Policy of the People's Republic of China* (London, 1971).
39 *Africa Contemporary Record 1969–1970* (London, 1970) p. B199.
40 *Africa Contemporary Record 1970–1971* (London, 1971) pp. B174–5.
41 T. B. Millar, 'Geopolitics and Military/Strategic Potential', in Cottrell and Burrel, *The Indian Ocean*, p. 66.
42 S.I.P.R.I., *Arms Trade with the Third World*, p. 621.
43 See Chapter 1 above.
44 See Chapter 1 above for details of the accord, and Appendix B below for a glossary of Soviet armaments.
45 For a detailed account of the Egyptian arms deal see Uri Ra'anan, *The U.S.S.R. Arms the Third World: Case Studies in Soviet Foreign Policy* (London, 1969).
46 S.I.P.R.I., *Arms Trade with the Third World*, p. 858.
47 *West Africa*, no. 2191, 11 Apr 1959, p. 357.
48 Ibid., no. 2616, 22 July 1967, p. 970.
49 John de St Jorre, *The Nigerian Civil War* (London, 1972) p. 181.
50 *West Africa*, no. 2621, 26 Aug 1967, p. 1099.
51 Suzanne Cronjé, *The World and Nigeria* (London, 1972) pp. 273–80, considers wartime relations between Biafra and the U.S.S.R.
52 H. T. Alexander, *African Tightrope* (London, 1965) pp. 99, 106.
53 *West Africa*, no. 2317, 28 Oct 1961, p. 1199; Alexander, *African Tightrope*, pp. 91–3.
54 Major-General A. K. Ocran, *A Myth is Broken* (Accra, 1968) pp. 11–13.
55 Ibid., pp. 29–39.
56 Thompson, *Ghana's Foreign Policy*, p. 184.
57 Peter Barker, *Operation Cold Chop* (Accra, 1968) p. 5.

CHAPTER 7
1 David Vital, *The Inequality of States: A Study of the Small Powers in International Relations* (Oxford 1967), p. 190.
2 Ameillon, *La Guinée bilan d'une independence.*
3 Thompson, *Ghana's Foreign Policy.*
4 Raymond Aron, *Peace and War* (London, 1966), p. 515.
5 See R. Legvold, *Soviet Policy in West Africa*, pp. 197–8.
6 William Moskoff assisted by J. William Benz, 'The U.S.S.R. and Developing Countries: Politics and Export Prices 1955–69', *Soviet Studies*, vol. xxiv, no. 3 (Jan 1973) pp. 348–63.
7 W. A. C. Adie, *The Communist Powers in Africa*, Conflict Studies, no. 10 (London, Dec 1970–Jan 1971).

8 W. A. Nielsen, *The Great Powers and Africa* (London, 1969) p. 219.

9 Ghana, *Statistical Yearbook 1965–1966*, Central Bureau of Statistics (Accra, 1969) Table 34.

10 Richard Pipes, 'Some Operational Principles of Soviet Foreign Policy', in Michael Confino and Shimon Shamir (eds), *The U.S.S.R. and the Middle East* (Jerusalem, 1973) p. 16.

11 See, for example, Robert Good, 'State Building as a Determinant of Foreign Policy in New States', in L. W. Martin (ed.), *Neutralism and Nonalignment* (New York, 1962).

12 Sandbrook, *Patrons, Clients and Unions*.

13 See, for example, J. D. B. Miller, 'The Intrusion of Afro-Asia', *International Affairs* (Nov 1970) special issue, pp. 46–55.

Bibliography

No attempt has been made to include in this bibliography all the works cited in the text. To do so would be to defeat one of the primary objectives of a bibliography, namely to direct the attention of the reader to those works that most fully develop the subject treated. Since this book has touched on several areas and functional specialisations, there are many references in the footnotes to works which, while relevant to the context in which they are cited, have little bearing on Soviet–African relations *per se*. The bibliography is, therefore, selective, and the method of selection is highly pragmatic. All government publications referred to in the text have been included. All books which are referred to twice or more plus some others have been included. Since the relevant life of periodical articles is transitory, they have been subjected to the most rigorous selection procedure, and only those of lasting importance or recent publication are included.

A. OFFICIAL DOCUMENTS
(i) Ghana
    Annual Estimates (Accra, 1957–8, 1958–9, 1959–60, 1961–2, 1966).
    Bank of Ghana, *Report of the Bank for the Year Ended . . .* (Accra, various).
    Ghana Economic Survey (Accra, 1961, 1962, 1963, 1964, 1966, 1968, 1969, 1970).
    Annual Report on External Trade Statistics of Ghana, vol. 1 (Accra, 1959–60, 1961–3, 1964–5).
    External Trade Statistics of Ghana, December . . . (Accra, 1967–70).
    The Development Plan 1951 (Accra, 1951).
    Second Development Plan 1959–1964 (Accra, 1959).
    Seven Year Plan for National Reconstruction and Development 1963/64–1969/70 (Accra, 1964).
    J. H. Mensah, *The State of the Economy and the External Debts Problem* (Accra, 1970).
    National Redemption Council Budget Statement for 1972–1973 (Accra, 1972).
    Parliamentary/National Assembly Debates (Accra, 1957–1966).
    Report and Financial Statements by the Accountant-General and

Report of the Auditor-General for the year ended 30 September 1962 (Accra).

Report by the Auditor-General on the Accounts of Ghana for the period 1 January 1965 to 30 June 1966 (Accra).

Report of the Commission of Enquiry into the Properties of Kwame Nkrumah (Accra).

Report of the Commission of Enquiry into Trade Malpractices in Ghana (Accra, 1965).

State Farms Corporation, *Balance Sheet and Operating Statements for the year ended* . . ., Accra, 31 Dec 1966, 31 Dec 1967.

Ghana Statistical Yearbook (Accra, 1967–8).

Ghana Treaty Series (Accra, 1961, 1963).

(ii) Guinea

Bulletin Special de la Statistique (Statistique et Economie), Ministère d'Etat chargé des Finances et du Plan, Direction de la Statistique Générale et de la Mecanographie (Conakry, n.d.).

Plan triennal de développement économique et social de la République du Guinée: Conférence Nationale des Cadres des 2 au 5 Avril 1960 ā Kankan (Conakry, n.d.).

(iii) Kenya

'Agreement for Economic and Technical Co-operation between Kenya and the U.S.S.R. on the establishment of industrial and agricultural enterprises and projects 20 November 1964', Laid before the Kenya House of Representatives, 4 Mar 1965.

Estimates of Recurrent Expenditure 1965–66 (Nairobi).

House of Representative Debates, various.

Ministry of Education, *Annual Summary* (Nairobi, 1970).

(iv) Mali

Mali Annuaire Statistique (Bamako, 1966).

Comptes Economiques du Mali (Bamako).

Elements du Bilan Economique 1964, Chambre de Commerce d'Agriculture et d'Industry de Bamako (Mar 1965).

Ministère de l'Education Nationale, *Statistiques Scolaires 1963–64* (Bamako, 1964).

Programme Triennal de Redressement Economique et Financier 1970–1972, Direction Générale du Plan et de la Statistique (Bamako, 1970).

(v) Nigeria

Estimates of the Government of the Federal Republic of Nigeria 1965/66 (Lagos).

Federal Government Development Programme 1962–1968: First Progress Report (Lagos, 1964).

House of Representatives Debates (Lagos, various).

National Development Plan, Progress Report 1964 (Lagos, 1965).

Nigeria: Treaties in Force, vol. 1: *for the period 1 October 1960 to 30 June 1970* (Lagos, 1971).

Nigerian Trade Summary (Lagos, Dec 1969–Dec 1970).

The Training of Nigerians for the Representation of their Country Overseas: a Statement of Policy by the Government of the Federation of Nigeria, House of Representatives, sessional paper no. 11 (Lagos, 1956).

(vi) Somalia

First Five Year Plan 1963–1967 (Mogadishu, 1963).

Somali Foreign Trade Statistics (Mogadishu, 1961–70). Between 1961 and 1965 the figures for the northern and southern regions of Somalia were published separately.)

German Planning and Economic Advisory Group, Dr Hendrickson, *Economic Conditions and Possible Future Development of the Port of Berbera* (Mogadishu, 1968).

German Planning and Economic Advisory Group, Dr Hendrickson, *Report on the Improvement of the Accounting System of the State-Owned Enterprises Pts. I and II* (Mogadishu, n.d.).

German Planning and Economic Advisory Group, Dr Hendrickson, *Report on the Progress of Development Projects in the Somali Democratic Republic* (Mogadishu, 1969).

Ministry of Information and National Guidance, *New Era*, no. 3 (Mar 1971).

Somali National Bank Bulletin, no. 23–4 (July–Dec 1970), 27–8 (July–Dec 1971).

(vii) Tanzania

The Appropriation Accounts, Revenue Statements, Accounts of the Fund, and other Public Accounts for the year . . . (Dar es Salaam, 1966–7 to 1970–1).

Development Plan for Tanganyika 1961/62–1965/66 (Dar es Salaam, 1962).

Tanzania Treaty Series, vol. 11 (Dar es Salaam, 1967).

(viii) U.S.S.R.

Vneshnyaya Torgovlia SSSR: Statistichesky Sbornik 1918–1966 (Moscow, 1967).

Vneshnyaya Torgovlia SSSR: Statistichesky Obzor (Moscow, various years).

(ix) United Nations

U.N.C.T.A.D., *Approaches to Multilateral Settlements in trade between socialist and developing countries* (New York), doc. no. TD/B/AC.

U.N.C.T.A.D., *Case Study Prepared by the UNCTAD Secretariat on trade and economic relations between the U.A.R. and the Socialist countries* (New York, 1967), doc. no. TD/B/130.

U.N.C.T.A.D., *Review of Trade Relations among countries having different economic and social systems: Report by the UNCTAD Secretariat* (New York, 1967), doc. no. TD/B/128 and (New York, 1971), doc. no. TD/B/359.

United Nations, *Export Credits and Development Finance: National Export Credit Systems* (New York, 1969).

United Nations, *The External Financing of Economic Development* (New York, 1963–7, 1964–8), UN E/4632, UN E/4815.

United Nations Treaty Series (New York, various issues).

United Nations Department of Economic and Social Affairs, *Yearbook of International Trade Statistics, 1969* (New York, 1971).

United Nations Economic Commission for Africa, *Foreign Trade Statistics of Africa Series A. and B.* (Addis Ababa, various).

United Nations F.A.O., *World Cocoa Statistics*, vol. 9, no. 3, vol. 14, no. 3.

United Nations Statistical Office, *Monthly Bulletin of Statistics*, vol. xxv, no. 7 (July 1971), vol. xxvi, no. 6 (June 1972).

(x) Other Multinational Organisations

East African Customs and Excise, *Annual Trade Report of Kenya, Uganda and Tanganyika* (Nairobi, 1964–71).

European Community Statistical Office, *Foreign Trade,* no. 5 (1968).

European Community Statistical Office, *République du Mali, Yearbook 1959–1966* (Brussels, 1969).

B. BOOKS

Abubakar Tafawa Balewa, *Nigeria Speaks: Speeches of Alhaji Sir Abubakar Tafawa Balewa* (London, 1964).

Africa Contemporary Record (London, 1968–9 to 1972–3).

E. A. Ajayi, 'Foreign Aid in Nigeria 1960–1968', Ph.D. thesis (London, 1970).

Major-General H. T. Alexander C.B., C.B.E., D.S.O., *African Tightrope: My Two Years as Nkrumah's Chief of Staff* (London, 1965).

I. O. Aluko, 'The Influence of Foreign Aid on Ghana's External Relations 1957–66', Ph.D. thesis (London, 1969).

B. Ameillon, *La Guinée, bilan d'une independence* (Paris, 1964).

Samir Amin, *Trois Expériences africaines de développement: le Mali, la Guinée et la Ghana* (Paris, 1965).

O. Awolowo, *Awo: The Autobiography of Chief Obafemi Awolowo* (London, 1960).

V. S. Baskin, G. I. Rubinstein and B. B. Runov, *Ekonomicheskoe Sotrudnichestvo SSSR so Stranami Afriki* (Moscow, 1968).

W. Birmingham, I. Neustadt and E. N. Omaboe (eds), *A Study of Contemporary Ghana*, vol. 1 (London, 1966).

Z. Brzezinski (ed.), *Africa and the Communist World* (Stanford, California, 1963).

James Richard Carter, *The Net Cost of Soviet Foreign Aid* (New York and London, 1969).

Helen D. Cohn, *Soviet Policy Toward Black Africa: The Focus on National Integration* (New York and London, 1972).

A. J. Cottrell and R. M. Burrell (eds), *The Indian Ocean: Its Political, Economic and Military Importance* (New York and London, 1972).

Suzanne Cronjé, *The World and Nigeria* (London, 1972).

Michael Dei-Anang, *The Administration of Ghana's Foreign Relations 1957–1965: A Personal Memoir* (London, 1975).

W. Raymond Duncan (ed.), *Soviet Policy in Developing Countries* (Waltham, Massachusetts, and London, 1970).

B. Fitch and M. Oppenheimer, *Ghana: the End of an Illusion* (New York, 1966).

P. Foster and A. R. Zolberg (eds), *Ghana and the Ivory Coast: Perspectives on Modernisation* (Chicago and London, 1971).

William H. Friedland and Carl G. Rosberg Jr (eds), *African Socialism* (Stanford, California, 1970).

Roger Genoud, *Nationalism and Economic Development in Ghana* (New York and London, 1969).

Cherry Gertzel, *The Politics of Independent Kenya 1963–1968* (Nairobi and London, 1970).

Marshall I. Goldman, *Soviet Foreign Aid* (New York and London, 1967).

David M. Gray, 'The Foreign Policy Process in the Emerging African Nation: Nigeria', Ph.D. thesis (University of Pennsylvania, 1965), University Microfilms no. 65–13,333.

E. H. Hammonds, 'A Study of Soviet and Chinese Communist Strategy in sub-Saharan Africa', Ph.D. thesis (London, 1965).

Sven Hamrell and Carl Gösta Widstrand (eds), *The Soviet Bloc, China and Africa* (Uppsala, 1964).

Catherine Hoskyns, *The Congo Since Independence: January 1960 to December 1961* (London, 1965).

A. Iskenderov, *Africa: Politics, Economy, Ideology* (Moscow, 1972).

W. Joshua and S. P. Gibert, *Arms for the Third World: Soviet Military Aid Diplomacy* (Baltimore, 1969).

Geoffrey Jukes, *The Indian Ocean in Soviet Naval Policy*, Adelphi paper no. 87 (London, May 1972).

Arthur Jay Klinghoffer, *Soviet Perspectives on African Socialism* (Madison, Wisconsin, 1969).

Andrzej Krassowski, *Development and the Debt Trap* (London, 1974).

Robert Legvold, *Soviet Policy in West Africa* (Cambridge, Massachusetts, 1970).

Bruce D. Larkin, *China and Africa 1949–1970: The Foreign Policy of the People's Republic of China* (Berkeley, California, 1971).

I. M. D. Little, *Aid to Africa* (Oxford, 1964).

Kurt London (ed.), *New Nations in a Divided World* (New York and London, 1963).

T. B. Millar, *The Indian and Pacific Oceans: Some Strategic Considerations*, Adelphi paper no. 57 (London, 1969).

David L. Morison, *The U.S.S.R. and Africa* (Oxford, 1964).

Edward Mortimer, *France and the Africans 1944–1960: A Political History* (London, 1969).

T. C. Niblock, 'Aid and Foreign Policy in Tanzania 1961–1968, Ph.D. thesis (University of Sussex, 1971).

W. A. Nielsen, *The Great Powers and Africa* (London, 1969).

Major-General A. K. Ocran, *A Myth is Broken* (Accra, 1968).

A. C. A. A. Ogunsanwo, *China's Policy in Africa 1958–1971* (London, 1974).

K. W. J. Post, *The Nigerian Federal Election of 1959: Politics and Administration in a Developing Political System* (Lagos, 1963).

Uri Ra'anan, *The U.S.S.R. Arms The Third World: Case Studies in Soviet Foreign Policy* (London, 1969).

John de St Jorre, *The Nigerian Civil War* (London, 1972).

Carole A. Sawyer, *Communist Trade with Developing Countries 1955–1965* (New York and London, 1966).

Ruth Schachter-Morgenthau, *Political Parties in French-Speaking West Africa* (Oxford, 1964).

Walter Schwarz, *Nigeria* (London, 1968).

Richard L. Sklar, *Nigerian Political Parties: Power in an Emergent African Nation* (Princeton, New Jersey, 1963).

Glen Alden Smith, *Soviet Foreign Trade: Organisation, Operations, and Policy 1918–1971* (New York and London, 1973).

Stockholm International Peace Research Institute, *The Arms Trade with the Third World* (Stockholm, 1971).

Jean Suret-Canale, *La République de Guinée* (Paris, 1970).

W. Scott Thompson, *Ghana's Foreign Policy 1957–1966: Diplomacy, Ideology, and the New State* (Princeton, New Jersey, 1969).

T. P. Thornton, *The Third World in Soviet Perspective* (Princeton, New Jersey, 1964).

N. Uphoff, *Ghana's Experience in Using External Aid for Development 1957–1966: Implications for Development Theory and Policy* (Institute of International Studies, Berkeley, California, 1970).

V. Ya. Vasileva, I. M. Lemin and V. A. Maslennikov (eds), *Imperialisticheskaya Borba za Afriku i Osvoboditelnoe Dvizhenie Narodov*, Akademiya Nauk SSSR, Institut Ekonomiki (Moscow, 1953).

David Vital, *The Inequality of States: A Study of the Small Powers in International Relations* (Oxford, 1967).

Arthur Wauters (ed.), *Le Monde Communiste et la Crise du Congo Belge* (Brussels, 1961).

Aryeh Yodfat, *Arab Politics in the Soviet Mirror* (Jerusalem, 1973).

C. PERIODICAL ARTICLES

R. Cornevin, 'La Russie et l'Afrique', *Afrique Contemporaine* (Jan–Feb 1970).

G. J. Idang, 'The Politics of Nigerian Foreign Policy: the ratification and renunciation of the Anglo-Nigerian Defence Pact', *African Studies Bulletin* (Sep 1970).

Arthur Jay Klinghoffer, 'Nigeria: Soviet Attitudes to the Secession', *Africa Report* (Feb 1968).

Jitendra Mohan, 'Ghana Parliament and Foreign Policy 1957–1960'. *Economic Bulletin of Ghana*, vol. x:4 (1966).

David Morison, 'U.S.S.R. and Third World', *Mizan* (Oct 1970, Nov 1970).

Milton D. Morris, 'The Development of Soviet African Studies', *Journal of Modern African Studies*, vol. 11:2 (June 1973).

Nigerian Institute of International Affairs, *Nigeria: Bulletin of Foreign Affairs*, vol. 1:1 (Lagos, July 1971).

Benjamin Nimer, 'The Congo in Soviet Policy', *Survey*, vol. 19:1 (86) (Winter 1973).

M. O'Connor, 'Guinea and the Ivory Coast: Contrasts in Economic Development', *Journal of Modern African Studies*, vol. 10:3 (Oct 1972).

Claude Rivière, 'Les Conséquences de la réorganisation des circuits commerciaux en Guinée', *Revue francaise d'études politiques africaines (Le Mois en Afrique)*, no. 66 (June 1971).

B. Rounov and G. Rubinstein, 'Rélations économique soviéto-africaines', *Revue francaise d'études politiques africaines (Le Mois en Afrique)*, no. 15 (Mar 1967).

Richard Sandbrook, 'Patrons, Clients and Unions: The Labour

Movement and Political Conflict in Kenya', *Journal of Commonwealth Political Studies*, vol. x : 1 (Mar 1972).

Dudley Seers, 'The Stages of Economic Development of a Primary Producer in the Middle of the Twentieth Century', *Economic Bulletin of Ghana*, vol. VIII : 4 (1963).

R. Ulyanovsky, 'The Third World – Problems of Socialist Orientation', *International Affairs*, Moscow, no. 9 (Sep 1971).

Elizabeth K. Valkenier, 'Recent Trends in Soviet Research on the Developing Countries', *World Politics* (July 1968).

Elizabeth K. Valkenier, 'New Trends in Soviet Economic Relations with the Third World', *World Politics*, vol. XXII : 8 (Apr 1970).

D. JOURNALS THAT FREQUENTLY CARRY
   ARTICLES ON AFRO-SOVIET RELATIONS

Afrika i Azia Segodnia (Moscow).
Bulletin of the Institute for the Study of the U.S.S.R. (Munich).
Est et Ouest (Paris).
International Affairs (Moscow).
Mirovaya Ekonomika i Mezhdunarodnie Otnosheniya (Moscow).
Mizan (London).
Narody Azii Afriki (Moscow).
New Times (Moscow).
World Marxist Review (Prague).

E. NEWSPAPERS, ETC.

B.B.C., *Summary of World Broadcasts* (London).
Daily Nation (Nairobi).
Daily Times (Lagos).
East-West Trade News.
Ghanaian Times (Accra).
Gill & Duffus, *Cocoa Market Report* (London).
Guardian (London).
Izvestiya (Moscow).
Keesing's Contemporary Archives (Bristol).
Le Monde (Paris).
L'Humanité (Paris).
Morning Post (Lagos).
New Nigerian (Kaduna).
New York Times.
News from the U.S.S.R. (Nairobi).
Nigerian Observer (Lagos).

Observer (London).
Pravda (Moscow).
The Times (London).
Tanganyika Standard (Dar es Salaam).
West Africa (London).

Index

Index